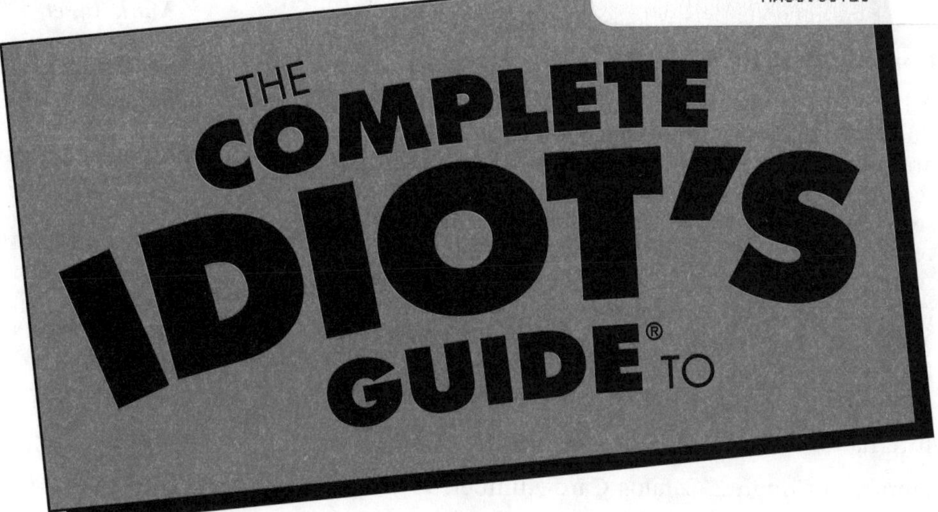

Microsoft® Outlook® 2000

Bob Temple

A Division of Macmillan Computer Publishing
201 W. 103rd Street, Indianapolis, IN 46290

The Complete Idiot's Guide to Microsoft Outlook 2000

International Standard Book Number: 0-7897-1981-9

Library of Congress Catalog Card Number: 99-61021

Printed in the United States of America

First Printing: May 1999

01 00 99 4 3 2 1

Trademarks

Warning and Disclaimer

Executive Editor
Mark Taber

Acquisitions Editor
Randi Roger

Development Editor
Rick Darnell

Project Editor
Carol Bowers

Copy Editors
Sean Medlock
Gene Redding

Indexer
William Meyers

Proofreader
Grechen Throop, BooksCraft, Inc.

Technical Editor
Kathy Edens

Illustrator
Judd Winick

Interior Design
Nathan Clement

Cover Design
Mike Freeland

Layout Technicians
Ayanna Lacey
Heather Hiatt Miller
Amy Parker

Contents at a Glance

Contents

About the Author

Bob Temple is the General Manager and Director of Web Services of a group of weekly newspapers in the suburbs of Minneapolis-St. Paul. He is also owner of Red Line Editorial, Inc., an editorial services company. This is his third book. His first book, *Sports on the Net*, was published by Que in 1995. His second, *Sams Teach Yourself AOL 4.0 in 24 Hours*, was published by Sams in 1998. He has served as a freelance sportswriter for the Associated Press for 11 years, covering all major professional sports at one time or another. He has written numerous articles for magazines and newspapers across the country. He can be reached at his email address: `btemple@summitpoint.com`.

Dedication

For Emily, Robby, and Sam, and for everything that makes each of them special.

Acknowledgements

There are so many people to thank that I hesitate to name them, lest I leave someone out. It's a little like winning an Oscar: There's no way to gracefully cite all those who have contributed. So the heck with all of 'em.

Just kidding.

Seriously, there are many people who worked their tails off to help get this book into print. Randi Roger, my acquisitions editor at Macmillan, puts up with my innumerable questions and even takes the time to answer them. Nice working with you again, Randi.

On the home front, there's Teri, my wife of 12-plus years. She holds down the fort when I'm gone (and when I'm there). Most importantly, she's maintaining sanity in the face of an 8-year-old daughter and twin 5-year-old boys.

My Dad, Robert E. Temple, contributes in myriad ways. This year, though, he believed in my business and, more importantly, in me.

To Emily Temple, age 8, thanks for staying my little girl, and don't be in such a big hurry to give up American Girls for Spice Girls.

To Robby Temple, age 5, thanks for the smiles that start every day, and please try not to drive your sister crazy.

To Sam Temple, age 5, thanks for always ordering what I do, and try to remember that kindergarten won't kill you.

Tell Us What You Think!

As the reader of this book, *you* are our most important critic and commentator. We value your opinion and want to know what we're doing right, what we could do better, what areas you'd like to see us publish in, and any other words of wisdom you're willing to pass our way.

You can fax, email, or write me directly to let me know what you did or didn't like about this book—as well as what we can do to make our books stronger.

Please note that I cannot help you with technical problems related to the topic of this book, and that due to the high volume of mail I receive, I might not be able to reply to every message.

When you write, please be sure to include this book's title and author as well as your name and phone or fax number. I will carefully review your comments and share them with the author and editors who worked on the book.

Fax: 317-581-4666

Email: `office_que@mcp.com`

Mail: John Pierce
Publisher
Que
201 West 103rd Street
Indianapolis, IN 46290 USA

Introduction

Microsoft Outlook has arrived.

After being kind of thrown into the Microsoft Office suite for a while, Outlook's last few upgrades have brought it up to par with the rest of Office.

Today, Outlook can help you with virtually all of your computing, if you let it. It can also help keep the rest of your life organized—the part away from your computer, that is.

Outlook is more than just a personal organizer, although it is an outstanding one. And anyone who believes that you have to have your computer turned on all the time in order to use a computerized information manager is just plain wrong.

Outlook brings all of your information together. Consider the following:

- A Calendar to help you keep track of both your personal and business appointments.
- A Task function that allows you to manage your long-term projects and to-do lists.
- A Contacts database that allows you to organize all of your addresses and telephone numbers into lists.
- A Notes module that allows you to post notes on your computer screen for important reminders.
- A Journal module that keeps track of your communications with contacts and other important information.

But Outlook offers more than this. You can communicate with people through Outlook's email and faxing capabilities. You can even surf the Internet without ever leaving Outlook.

The best part is that you can sort, group, and otherwise organize all of this information in a variety of ways. Outlook is the right program for just about everyone because it's customizable to individual tastes. And with Outlook Today, you can have at-a-glance access to all of this information on your screen.

Even better, you can access files from other programs within Outlook, and you can organize your disk drives within Outlook as well. That makes Outlook a valuable part of any computer system, even if there are parts of it you don't want to use.

What This Book Is

This book is an entry-level discussion of Outlook's features. It covers the basic reasons for the existence of each area of Outlook, its basic features, and how these features apply to everyday life.

It also goes beyond the basics to look at some of the fancier stuff that Outlook offers. It looks at how Outlook works with its Office buddies and other programs. And it covers how to use Outlook to organize your calendar, your contacts, your email, your tasks, and even the files on your computer.

The goal here is to give you a foundation of knowledge about Outlook. From here, you should be able to advance on your own to more complicated areas of Outlook. And this book will be a valuable reference for you in the future.

What This Book Isn't

This book is not a Tom Clancy suspense novel, a psychological thriller, a screenplay for a major motion picture, a Barbara Cartland romance, or a Marvel comic. Nor is it intended to be a complete manual for Outlook 2000 users.

There's no way to cover all of Outlook's features in a book of this length. And since this book is intended for beginning users, there's no reason to get too advanced.

So relax, lean back, turn on that computer, and let's get going!

Part 1

In the Beginning: Getting Started with Outlook 2000

Microsoft Outlook is full of fantastic features to help you simplify your life. But if you don't know the basics, Outlook will only frustrate you by making your life more complicated. Who needs that? So we'll begin with Outlook 101, the basics of the program. We'll briefly cover the many features of Outlook and discuss how to install and set up the software. We'll take a quick tour of the program and show how and where to get help. Then, we'll talk a little about file management and some of Outlook's tools. Giddyup!

Chapter 1

Where to Begin?

In This Chapter

- What Outlook's all about
- The many things Outlook can do for you
- Some things Outlook can't do for you
- The system requirements for running Outlook

I remember my first day of work at my first job out of college. There I was, a college graduate, an aspiring journalist, ready to embark on a career that would take me all the way to… well, to writing this book.

One of the first things presented to me was a "planner." I remember looking through this looseleaf paper organizer, amazed at all the different things I could keep track of with it. I was also amazed that it came with an instruction booklet. How hard could it be to write down my appointments, my addresses, and so on? After all, I was a college graduate. However, I soon found out how conscientious use of a good organizer could help manage my time.

In the roughly 400 years since that day, a lot has changed in the world of organizers. First of all, they're now called personal information managers (PIMs), they're often electronic, and they handle a lot more types of information.

What's All the Fuss About Outlook 2000?

Techno Talk

A *Personal Information Manager* is an electronic device (such as a PalmPilot) or a software program (such as Outlook) that helps you organize your life, both business and personal. Among other things, it may help you keep track of your calendar, your addresses, and your messages.

Outlook is Microsoft's personal information manager for your computer, and Outlook 2000 is the latest incarnation of the product. It's more than just an organizer for your appointments and addresses, however. It can help you organize your email and faxes as well, and can even help you organize the computer itself.

But I'm getting a little ahead of myself here. Let's stop and take a quick look at the many features of Outlook 2000:

- Email and fax tools to help you handle your messages
- A contact list to help you handle your addresses for business or personal use
- A calendar to help you keep track of appointments, meetings, and so on
- Tools to help you organize the files and folders on your computer
- Journals and notes for personal use
- Task lists to help you prioritize and track projects

Don't Panic!

If you're worried about having to learn all of these wonderful features, settle down. This chapter is an overview of what Outlook 2000 has to offer. You can learn about these features at your own pace because they're all covered in detail later in this book.

Here's the question of the day: What's more impressive, that Outlook 2000 has all these features or that they're all covered in this one little book?

The preceding list provides the basics of Outlook 2000's offerings, but believe it or not, there's more. When combined with the other programs in Microsoft Office 2000, Outlook becomes an even more powerful tool. For example, by using Outlook and Microsoft NetMeeting, you can schedule and carry out a live online meeting with both audio and video and with any number of participants. Or you can use Outlook to schedule an important business presentation, design it with PowerPoint, and then use Outlook to send emails and faxes to the contacts with whom you'll be meeting.

Outlook 2000 is also closely integrated with Internet Explorer 5, the latest version of Microsoft's Web browser.

What Outlook Can Do for You

All of these wonderful features are important to the product, but at its heart, Outlook 2000 is about organizing your daily activities. Let's take a brief look at the more basic features that Outlook 2000 has to offer.

Managing Email

Email was once limited to just business uses. Busy professionals found that sending off quick notes to their contacts was an inexpensive way to carry out business communications. But it was only a matter of time before email became a part of the daily lives of many nonprofessionals as well. Today, it helps us keep up our long-distance relationships without having to pay for phone charges, and it generally helps us keep in touch with friends, relatives, and so on.

Although some people worry that short little emails are taking the place of longer, "more meaningful" handwritten letters, that's for the philosophers and social scientists to sort out. Email is here, and it can be of great benefit to you.

Even if you're already an email veteran, Outlook can help you improve your emails through better organization. It can also help you spiff them up a little bit in terms of layout and design.

Outlook offers a full-featured email client that makes communication easier and more effective. You can use Outlook to do the following:

- Send and receive email
- Manage multiple email accounts
- Compose email and format text
- Send and receive attached files

Using Outlook's email feature is easy, too. You can compose an email message by opening the New drop-down menu and choosing Mail Message. A window appears like the one in the following figure.

Beyond the basics of email, however, you can also use Outlook to organize your emails into different folders. It also lets you handle junk emails quickly and effectively. In fact, there are so many email features in Outlook that we've devoted an entire section of this book to it—Part 2, "Get a Life: Talking to the Outside World."

Faxing

Here's another modern convenience that we can't possibly live without. With Outlook in your corner, faxing is extremely easy. Even better, faxing with your computer and Outlook saves you the trouble and expense of buying a traditional fax machine.

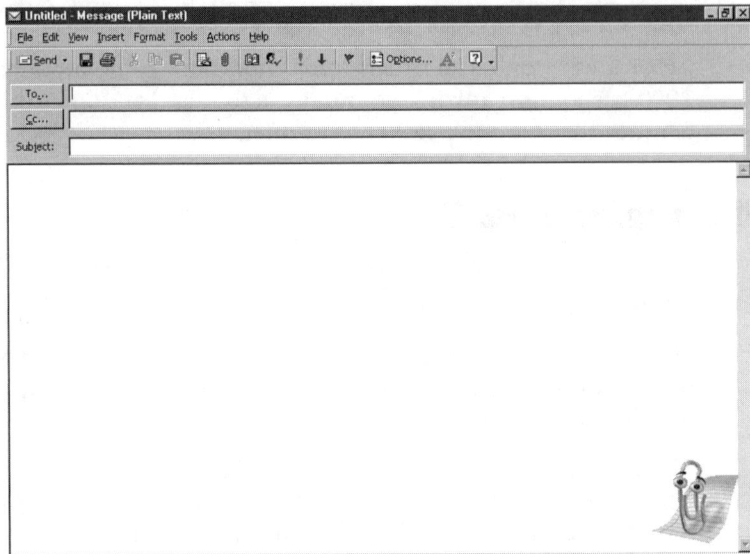

Outlook's email window looks like those in many other email programs.

Using your modem, you can send faxes from your computer to a fax machine or another computer with fax software. You can also receive faxes from anyone and print them out using your very own printer. You can schedule faxes to be sent at a certain time, and you can send them to one person or a large group of people.

Contacts

This appears to imply that there are two locations for addresses, an address book and contacts. That is not necessary with Outlook 2000. All addresses plus distribution lists can be in your contacts. You can add categories to break out personal from business, or you can create another contact folder and store items separately.

Just about everyone has an address book, in one form or another. Whether it's that naughty little black book or your Christmas card list, a well-organized address book is a useful thing to have.

Using Outlook, you can build your own personal address book using Contacts. You can fill it with the names of the people you contact the most. You can even fill it with the names of everyone you know, if that's what you want to do.

Outlook makes it easy to add the names, addresses, phone and fax numbers, email addresses, and more. You can put them in one at a time, or you may be able to import them electronically if you already have an address book set up through another service.

Once you've entered the names and addresses, you can use them for traditional reasons, like sending out holiday greetings or catching up with old friends on the phone. But you can also use them to send emails, faxes, and much, much more.

Although you don't have to use contact lists for business reasons, that's by far the most common use for them.

Along with the usual information, such as name, address, phone, fax, and email, you can also put in a job title, company name, and Web site address for your contact, as you can see in the figure below.

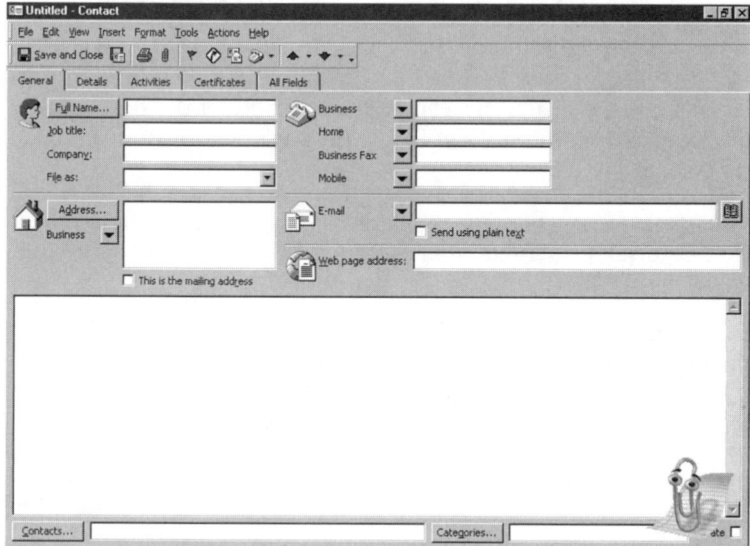

Entering a contact is as simple as filling in this form.

And there are spaces for comments or notes and a categories area that you can use to group your contact lists. Outlook makes it easy to enter and edit all of this information.

There are a number of different ways to view your contact lists as well. You can view them as address cards, and you can also sort them in a number of ways:

- By phone number
- By country
- By company
- By the categories you defined when you entered the information into the database
- By the date you're next supposed to follow up with the contact

Once you've got your contacts entered, you can use Outlook to perform a variety of functions that will improve your business communications. You can schedule a meeting by sending an invitation you created using your contact list. If you have people who work for you, you can assign tasks to them using Outlook and your contact list. You can send emails to your contacts, or a single email to every contact in a certain group. You can even use the popular Letter Wizard in Microsoft Word in conjunction with your Outlook contact list to send a letter to one or more of your contacts.

And, in one of the ultimate examples of how deeply you can integrate Outlook into your life, you can even use it in association with Microsoft Internet Explorer 5 to find a road map on the Internet to a contacts' address.

Calendar

Life is a tangled web, but Outlook has enough features to help you make some sense out of your day-to-day existence.

For example, let's say you've successfully scheduled a meeting with a couple of important contacts using Outlook's contact list. You need to make a note of the date and time of that meeting, or else you'll be the only invitee who doesn't show up. What's the solution? Outlook's calendar, of course!

The centerpiece of any organizer is its calendar because that's where you actually schedule your time. Using Outlook's calendar, you can go well beyond the basics of time management.

Unlike most paper calendars, Outlook's calendar lets you schedule appointments well in advance. For example, if your brother has finally proposed to his fiance but the wedding isn't until 2002, you can put the date down in Outlook. Then, if the wedding date gets moved, you can easily move it within your Outlook calendar.

When you're working with the calendar, you can view your appointments in a number of different ways. You can look at a single date in detail, take a week-at-a-time view, or get the overview for an entire month.

You can also use the calendar to build a to-do list, and you can easily display it so you can track your progress toward your goals. For example, if you have a weekly appointment with your chiropractor, you can easily schedule it as a recurring appointment well into the future. Similarly, if you have a staff meeting every Monday morning, put it on your calendar and you'll never overlook it.

Notes

When your spouse calls to remind you that your daughter's school conference is tonight, you probably just write yourself a quick little sticky note. Outlook's notes function serves this purpose. It's a place for you to jot down quick things that don't really fit into another category—they aren't appointments, meetings, or tasks, but they are important.

An Outlook note can be as brief or as lengthy as you want it to be, and you can store it in the Notes folder. You can view your notes in a number of different ways, and they can be sorted by a variety of categories, including by the date they were created and by subject matter.

Reading Newsgroups

Newcomers to the Internet often don't know anything about newsgroups because they're an underrated (and underadvertised) aspect of the Internet. Newsgroups are like bulletin boards, organized by subject matter, that allow people with common interests to share their knowledge (or lack thereof) with each other.

Outlook, through Outlook Express, offers a full-featured newsreader that allows you to use newsgroups to their fullest. You can sort through the massive lists of newsgroups to find just the ones that might interest you. Then you can read the messages in the newsgroups you like and post messages of your own.

Other Outlook Features

There are many more features in Outlook. Some of these features will be more useful to you than others, depending upon your personal needs, but they're all valuable. You'll learn more about these features throughout this book.

What Outlook Can't Do for You

Outlook is a wonderful, full-featured program that can help you make sense of your cluttered personal and professional life. But it's not a miracle worker. One way or another, you'll need to get involved in the process. You'll get out of Outlook only what you put into it, just as with any other personal information manager. Outlook won't help you keep track of your contacts, for example, if you don't do a good job of entering them in the first place.

But what you'll probably find is that Outlook makes being organized so easy that you'll find yourself being more dedicated to making it work than ever before.

Be Prepared: What You Need to Run Outlook

Outlook can be installed completely on its own and is a self-sufficient program. But because it is usually installed as part of the Microsoft Office suite of applications, it's best to look at the requirements for running the entire Office suite. Besides, Outlook functions at its best when it's integrated with the rest of Office.

The following is the recommended configuration for running Office:

- A Pentium (or equivalent) computer with 32MB of RAM
- Roughly 200MB of available hard disk space for the typical installation
- A CD-ROM drive
- A VGA or higher resolution video adapter (Super VGA, 256-color recommended)
- A mouse
- 9600 baud or higher modem (28,800 or higher recommended)
- Windows 95 or later, or Windows NT Workstation 4.0 with Service Pack 3.0 installed

The Least You Need to Know

- Outlook is a personal information manager (PIM) that helps you get a handle on your everyday life.
- Outlook can help you organize your email, your personal (and/or business) contact information, your calendar, even your tasks.
- Outlook is not a miracle worker, however. If you are disorganized in how you use Outlook, you won't be any more organized than you were before you had it.

Chapter 2

How Do I Get This Thing Configured?

In This Chapter

- The configuration decision
- Internet only email
- Corporate workgroup mode
- Configuring your email account
- Sharing information on the Internet

Okay, so you've got an idea now of what Outlook has to offer. Pretty neat, huh?

Well, you're not going to get very far unless you actually install the software in that big gray box on your desk and get it configured properly.

Many of you probably already have the software installed, most likely as part of the Microsoft Office suite of applications. You may have it on your home computer, your work computer, or both. This chapter is all about configuring your new version of Outlook. By the time we're done, you'll be set up and ready to run (and once it's actually configured, it'll be easier for you to follow along with the rest of the book).

Firing It Up

The first time you start Outlook, you will have to make a couple of decisions that will impact the way Outlook is installed. These decisions will also affect how your program looks and operates and the type of features it will have to offer.

The Configuration Decision

When Outlook is installed, so is the latest version of Microsoft's Web browser, Internet Explorer 5. This is a great feature if you're just getting started with the Internet (or with computers) because it gives you a top-of-the-line browser to use to view Web pages.

If you already have Internet Explorer installed on your computer, this new version will replace it automatically. However, if you prefer to use a different Web browser (such as Netscape) to surf the Internet, you still can.

You are not required to choose Internet Explorer as your default Web browser. It is merely installed so that you'll be able to use all of Outlook's functions, which include the ability to view Web pages.

Also, if you have a previous version of Outlook installed on your computer, it will be replaced by Outlook 2000.

Why Do I Need Internet Explorer with Outlook?

Outlook offers the ability to view Web pages, but it needs Internet Explorer to be able to display them for you. In other words, without Internet Explorer installed on your computer, you would not be able to view Web pages in Outlook.

Pick a Mode, Any Mode

Decisions, decisions, decisions.

When you first start Outlook, you'll be asked to choose how you would like to configure your email. There are three choices.

First, you can choose not to use Outlook for email at all. This is not a great idea, because Outlook is an outstanding program for handling email and offers several features that help make the busy emailer's life easier.

Once you've decided that Outlook is your best choice for email, you must choose whether you are going to use the Internet Only option or the Corporate or Workgroup option for configuring your email.

Upgraders Take Note

If you have a previous version of Outlook installed on your computer, the first time you start Outlook 2000 a window appears that asks you if you used the older version to read email. If you did, Outlook 2000 can use the same settings you used for that email setup. That saves you the trouble of going through all of the email setup options.

In many cases the decision of which configuration to use is made for you. For example, if your computer is connected to a corporate network and you'll be using email to send messages within the company as well as to outsiders, you'll probably need to choose the Corporate configuration.

If you're using Outlook at home or for business reasons but are connecting to the Internet by the modem in your computer (rather than through your company's server), you'll want to pick the Internet Only configuration. The decision is made in the dialog box seen in the following figure.

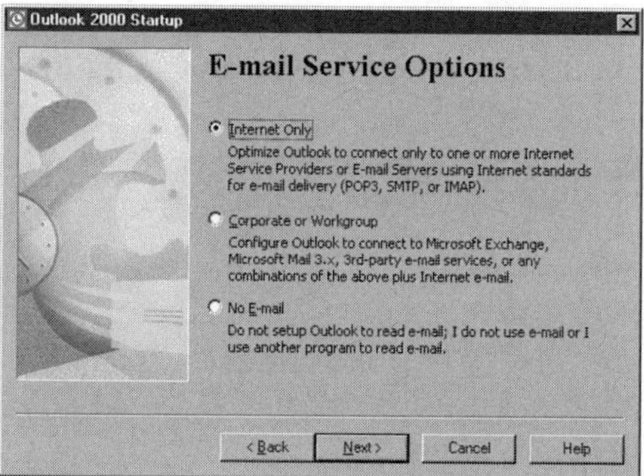

During installation, you'll be required to select the type of email configuration you would like to use.

The vast majority of features you'll use in Outlook won't be affected by this all-important configuration decision. Your Address Book, Contact Lists, Calendar, Journals, Notes, and Tasks will look and operate exactly the same, regardless of your choice of email configuration.

In fact, the only features that will be different between the two configurations are email and fax service. Among the differences are the type of formatting you can apply to your outgoing emails and the way in which you can share your Outlook information with other users.

But the biggest difference is one you'll never really see. The different configurations tell your computer how you communicate with the Internet, a bunch of technical gobbledygook that *you* don't really need to worry about, but which is very important to your computer's ability to complete its work successfully.

Be Careful!

Before you install any program in the workplace, you should check with your system administrator (or at the very least, your boss). That way, you can be certain that you are choosing the best configuration for your computer's setup. For example, some companies have internal networks that are set up in such a way that you don't have to select the Corporate mode of Outlook. You're better off asking and getting the right information.

Setting Up Internet Only Email

Once you've made the decision to go with Internet Only email, you'll have to configure your email account so that Outlook knows where to go to get your messages.

If you were already set up with an Internet account—that is, you're upgrading to this version of Outlook or using Outlook to replace another email client—you can easily import your email information to upgrade to Outlook 2000.

The first time you start Outlook 2000, you will be routed into the Startup Wizard, which walks you through this process. If you have another email program such as Outlook Express or Eudora installed on your computer, the Startup Wizard will prompt you with a screen that looks like the one in the following figure.

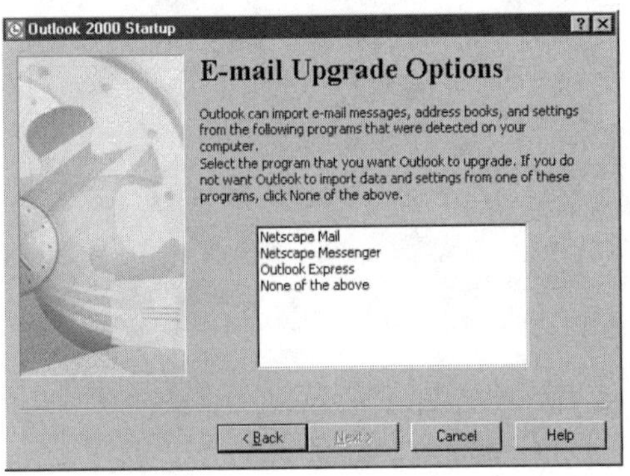

You can import your old email settings into Outlook 2000.

You Need Internet Access First!

Before you go ahead with configuring your Internet Only email service, you must have an account with an Internet service provider (ISP). There are many local and national companies from which to choose, but you'll need some setup information from that company before you can proceed. For example, you'll need an email address, the names of your mail servers, and more.

As you can see, you are asked to select the email client from which you would like to import the data. Simply select the email client you were using, and the settings from your previous account will be copied within Outlook. If you haven't been using this computer for email, select None of the above and Outlook will start completely fresh.

Modern technology is a wonderful thing, isn't it? However, if you haven't used this computer for email in the past (for example, if you just purchased the computer or have never had an Internet connection before), the Internet Connection Wizard will appear during this Startup Wizard process. It will help you set up your email service.

It's not necessary for you to do this when you use Outlook for the first time, but you might as well get it out of the way. After all, if you don't want to set up your account now, what the heck are you reading this section for?

The Internet Connection Wizard walks you through the entire process. If you decide to put it off, you can always get back to it later. To get to it, just click the Tools menu, and select Accounts. Then click on Add and you'll be ready to start.

The first question the Internet Connection Wizard asks is for your name, as in the following figure. Type the name that most people call you (be that your formal name or a nickname).

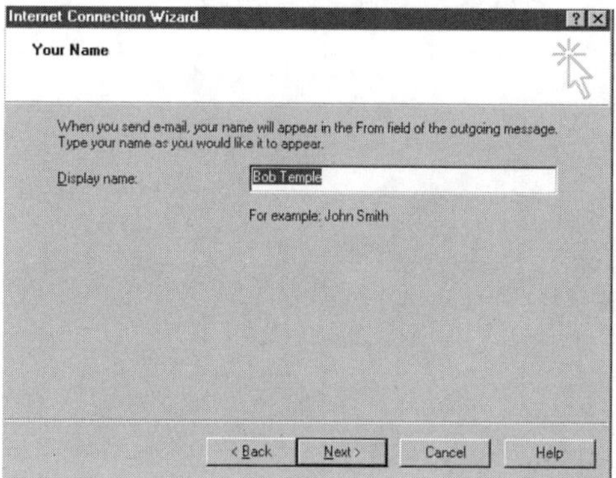

Type the name you want people to call you.

This is the name that will appear with your emails when you send them. After that, however, the questions get a little trickier. After each window is completed, click the Next button to move on. Let's take a look at these screens:

- *Your email address* This is the address people will use to send mail to you. In most cases, this is something like `yourname@yourcompany.com`. For example, my email address is `btemple@reditorial.com` (`reditorial` is the domain name for my company, Red Line Editorial).
- *Your POP3 server* This is the address of the computer through which you will be receiving mail. POP3 stands for Post Office Protocol version 3, which is a group of rules that your ISP uses to transfer mail between its computers and yours. This address should be provided to you by your ISP, whether it's a private company or the one for which you work.
- *Your SMTP server* This is the address of the computer through which you will send mail to others. SMTP stands for Simple Mail Transfer Protocol, which is a set of rules that Internet computers use to exchange mail between themselves. This address should also be provided by your ISP or network administrator.
- *Internet mail logon* This is the username and password that you use to log on to your ISP's computer.
- *Connection type* Your choices are pretty simple: You can connect using your phone line or your company's network, or you can do it manually.

If you're using a home computer and you connect to the Internet using your modem, you should select your phone line as the option. That way, your computer will automatically dial into your ISP whenever you select Send and Receive. If you connect manually, you'll have to connect to your ISP separately before checking mail using Outlook. The following figure shows the dialog box in which you make this selection.

Make this selection if you connect to the Internet using your computer's modem.

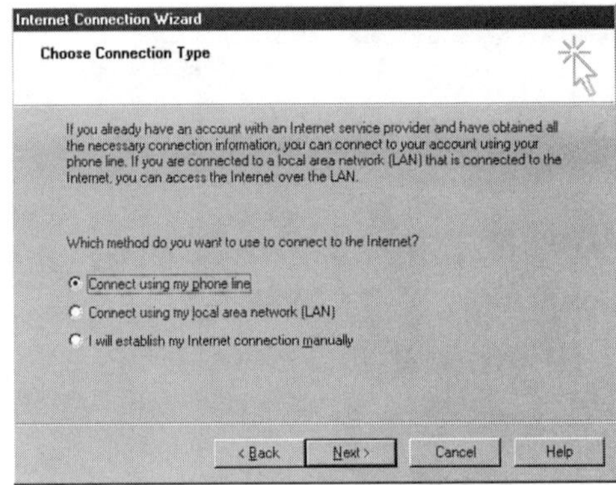

If you choose to connect to the Internet using your phone line, you'll be asked to select an existing dial-up connection or to create a new one to connect to the Internet.

➤ *Dial-Up connection*   f you have an existing Internet account that you used with other software (say, a browser like Internet Explorer or another email program), you can select an existing connection, and it will be configured automatically.

However, if you're connecting to the Internet for the first time using this computer, you should set up a new dial-up connection.

This process is very easy. You'll just need to provide the username and password of your Internet connection and the telephone number your computer should use to dial into your ISP's computer, as you see in the following figure.

Set up a new Internet connection if you don't already have one.

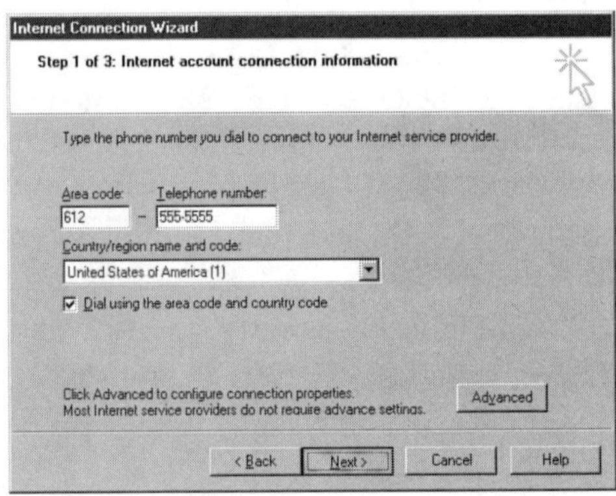

Finally, you'll need to give a name to your connection. I usually use the name of the ISP, but you can call it whatever you want.

You're done! Once all of these steps have been completed, you're ready to send and receive messages using the Internet. The mechanics of email are covered in Part 2, "Get a Life: Talking to the Outside World."

When you select Internet Only for your email service, you can also choose the ability to send and receive faxes using a software program called WinFax. The basic version of this program (WinFax Starter Edition) is installed with Outlook. It may be basic, but WinFax allows you to send and receive faxes via your computer, which is about as technical as it needs to be.

Using this software is covered in Chapter 13, "Just the Fax."

Setting Up Your Email in Corporate Mode

Before you select the Corporate mode for email configuration, it is strongly recommended that you meet with your company's network administrator in order to ensure that this is the proper selection to make.

If your network administrator advised you to select the Corporate mode for email configuration, then that person probably also set you up with a mail account.

If you work for a nice company, you got to select your own username and password. If you work for a mean company that assigns such things, you should immediately begin to search for a nice company for which to work. Just kidding.

It is an advantage to be able to use the Corporate configuration, because Outlook offers some advanced features for Corporate mode users, such as the ability to share your calendar and other Outlook folders on your network. This is covered in the next section.

Corporate or Not?

Many companies that have internal networks and provide Internet access still don't have corporate email networks. For example, my company has its own domain name and many people with email accounts, and the company offers Internet access to employees. However, my company doesn't have its own Internet server, so when I send an email message to a co-worker, it goes out to our ISP's computer, where my co-worker connects to pick it up. Therefore, we should use the Internet Only mode for email.

Using the Corporate configuration doesn't necessarily mean you can only send email within your company. If you would like to be able to send and receive email over the Internet (to users outside of your company), you can create an Internet email account in addition to your corporate one.

You can add an Internet email account at any time. The process is very similar to doing it in Internet Only mode, as described earlier in this chapter. Only the beginning step is different. To start the process, click the Tools menu and then click Services. In the Services dialog box, click Add and proceed as you would for an Internet Only configuration.

Sharing Information on the Internet

Outlook offers the ability to share information over the Internet in ways other than email. For example, you can share specific folders or files, and in some cases you can share your contact lists and more as well. What you can share and how you share it depend on the type of configuration you chose at installation.

Microsoft Exchange Server, a program that many corporations use on their internal networks, allows your calendar and contact lists to be placed into a public folder. Many corporations find this valuable because it allows employees to easily find out if others are available for a meeting, for example. It also allows you to set up the ability for others (such as your secretary) to check your calendar and access your email, among other things.

Public or Private

With Microsoft Exchange Server, each user's messages, calendar information, contacts, tasks, and so on are stored in private folders. Similar types of information can also be stored in public folders. If you want to share a folder, simply provide permissions to those with whom you want to share it. Start with a simple right-click on the folder you want to share. Then click the Permissions tab and assign permissions to the desired individual.

Your calendar information is maintained in a hidden public folder. When you book time in your calendar, an entry is written in this hidden public folder. The time is marked as booked for you, but no details are given. This way, when a user wants to book a meeting with others in the company, the program only needs to check one location to see if any of the invitees are busy.

Microsoft Exchange Server also allows you to share items from outside of Outlook. For example, if you're working on a presentation with a co-worker, you can allow that person to have access to the folder in which you are keeping your presentation documents. That way, you each can monitor the changes the other has made.

Outlook 2000 also includes a new feature called Net Folders, which allows users to share Calendar and Contact information over the Internet with other Outlook users.

The Least You Need to Know

- Outlook 2000's Internet Only configuration works best for those who use their modem to connect to the Internet.
- Outlook 2000's Corporate mode works best for people who have internal email networks at their place of business.
- You need Internet access before you can configure your Internet Only email account in Outlook.
- You can share Outlook information with others using either the Corporate or the Internet Only mode.

Chapter 3

Please, No Flash Photography on This Tour

In This Chapter

- Launching Outlook
- Taking a tour of the Outlook window
- Finding shortcuts to common tasks
- Outlook's major features
- Exiting Outlook

You've got Outlook safely installed on your hard drive, probably with a bunch of its Office-mates. Your email configuration is all set up. What now?

Well, you could just sit there looking at your desktop and letting all of Outlook's features go to waste, or you could launch Outlook on your own and just start playing around until you're comfortable with it. But if you were going to do either of these, you probably wouldn't have purchased this book, right?

Outlook is the kind of program that you probably won't be able to live without, once you get used to it. You can run your entire computer from Outlook, keeping track of your files and folders as well as your calendar and contacts. It's the kind of program that you can make your home, so to speak. But if you're going to move into the Outlook environment, you'll want to take a little tour of the place and see its major features.

That's what this chapter is all about. It's a kind of open house for Outlook—a chance for you to stop on by, check out all the different rooms, see the views, even try out an appliance or two. You'll get no high-pressure sales push here. The best news is that you've already qualified for the place, or you wouldn't have a copy of it installed on your computer. You can move in anytime you like!

Launching Outlook

Like any good house, there are lots of points of entry into Outlook 2000. But it might be time to call an end to the house analogy here. When you enter a house through a different door, you're in a different place; in Outlook, no matter how you go in, you start in the same spot.

There are three basic ways to enter Microsoft Outlook. None of them are all that difficult, and one is really no better than the others. It's all a matter of personal choice.

- *The icon on the desktop* It doesn't get much simpler than this. During install, a shortcut icon called Microsoft Outlook was dropped on your desktop without your consent. A little rude, maybe, but it was done nonetheless. Double-click on it to launch Outlook. If you don't like shortcut icons on your desktop, you can drag it to the trash and it'll be gone for good. You can then start Outlook in one of the other two ways.
- *The Office Shortcut toolbar* If you installed the full Microsoft Office suite and not just Outlook, you were allowed to choose whether you wanted an Office Shortcut toolbar installed on your desktop. If you installed the toolbar, you can launch Outlook from it by clicking on the Outlook icon.
- *The Start menu* This is probably the way you launch most of your programs, unless you're a big proponent of the icons-on-the-desktop method. Simply click the Start button, click Programs, and then click Microsoft Outlook.

As stated, it doesn't really matter which way you start Outlook. Some people really like a clean desktop, so they get rid of the Outlook icon and the Office Shortcut toolbar. They must then launch the program from the Start menu. Others like to do a quick double-click from the desktop rather than having to hunt down Microsoft Outlook from a long list of programs on their hard drives. If you like living on the edge, you can even alternate between the different ways. Wouldn't that be exciting? Regardless, Outlook's first screen will probably look like the one in the following figure.

In some cases, however, you may jump directly into Outlook's Inbox when you launch the program.

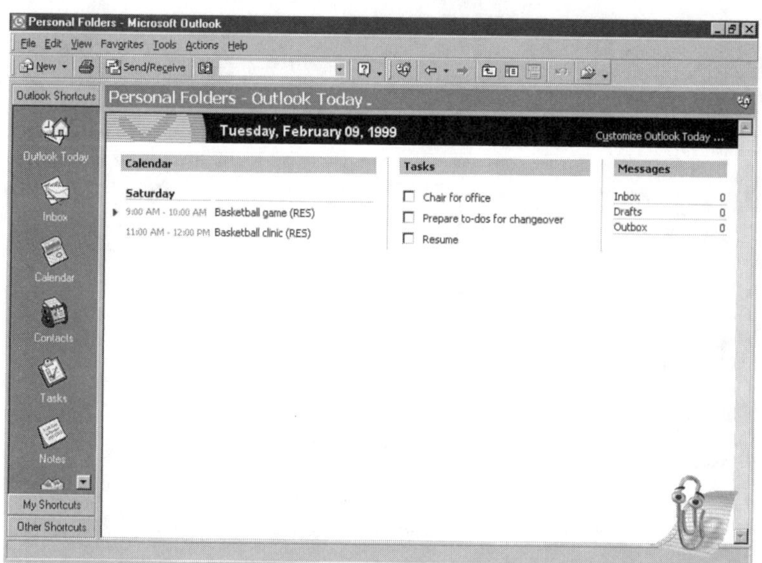

Outlook's opening screen will be the same no matter how you start the program.

Take a Look Around the Outlook Window

The major part of the Outlook window at startup is Outlook Today.

Outlook Today is a summary of the day's events. It's a great tool for a busy person, whether she's a business professional or a homemaker. It immediately displays any appointments you have for the current day, any tasks that you have to attend to, and the number of email messages that have arrived or are waiting to be sent. If Outlook doesn't launch the Outlook Today folder when it starts, click on the Outlook Today icon in the Outlook Bar on the left. It should be the top icon in the list.

Personally, I love using it at the start of each business day. I come into work, start up my computer and open Outlook, and have a quick, at-a-glance view of the day ahead, as you can see in the following figure.

A Couple of Possibilities

Two things may be slightly different on your screen than on the one in the following figure. First, your screen may not be maximized—that is, it may not take up the entire screen. If not, click the Maximize button, which is the second from the right in the upper-right corner of the Outlook window. Second, the Office Assistant may appear. He looks like a paper clip (although he sometimes changes shape into a bicycle) and generally appears in the lower-right corner. The Office Assistant is an important component of Outlook and is covered in detail in Chapter 4, "Stopping to Ask Directions."

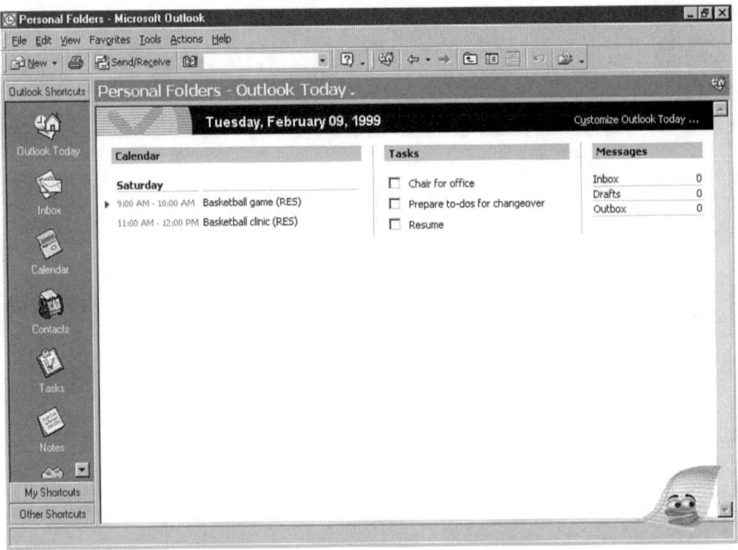

Today's appointments and more are shown in Outlook Today.

Down the left edge of the window is the Outlook Bar, which offers quick access to Outlook's most commonly used features. It also gives you access to other files on your computer and more. (This is covered in more detail in the next section of this chapter.)

Menu Bar

At the top of the window is a menu bar, which most programs now have. The menus from which you can choose—File, Edit, View, Favorites, Tools, Actions, and Help—are all discussed in detail at one point or another in this book.

Standard Outlook Toolbar

Just below the menu bar is the Standard Outlook toolbar, which offers some quick ways to perform different tasks in the program.

The most often used button on this toolbar is probably the New menu button on the far left. It offers a long list of choices for making additions to Outlook, as you can see in the following figure.

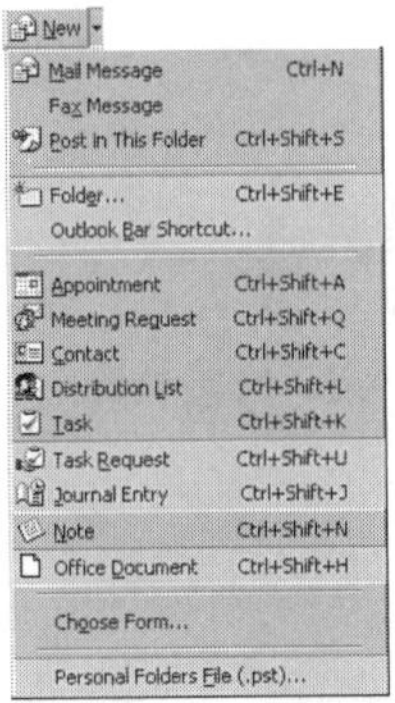

The New menu gives quick access to a long list of items.

IntelliSense Menus

Microsoft Office 2000 features a different type of menu system than in previous versions of the software. If you haven't experimented with the menu system in Word, Excel, or one of the other Office programs, now is a good time to start.

You'll be able to tell an IntelliSense menu by the two down arrows at the bottom of the menu. When you click on those arrows, the menu displays more options. The menu is also expanded if you leave your pointer on the menu name for a few seconds.

IntelliSense menus are designed to "sense" which options on a menu you use most. As you use certain options more and more, they are "promoted" up the list, moving lesser-used choices below the arrows. The goal is to leave you with a shorter menu made up of only the options you use most.

The additional menu items that appear after you click the down arrows appear to be blanked out, but they're actually operational.

The New menu is for adding things quickly: a new email message you'd like to send, a new appointment on the calendar, a new contact for your list, a new note or journal entry, or even a way to open a new document in a different Office program.

Also on the Standard Outlook toolbar are a printing button, a button to quickly send and receive email, and a button for quick access to your address book or your contacts list. And at the very end is a button with a question mark. This button gives you access to the toolbar itself so you can remove the buttons you won't use or add buttons you'd like to see.

Leave it to Microsoft to offer a great toolbar, plus the option to customize it to your own tastes.

Finding Shortcuts Wherever Possible

If you're anything like me, when you were a kid your mom asked you to do the dishes a lot. And there were probably a few times when you did less than a complete job and then jumped on the couch to watch a little *Gilligan's Island*. That's called taking a shortcut. (And if you're anything like me, you occasionally spent a little time without the television after that, with no Mary Ann to comfort you.)

The shortcuts you'll find within Outlook won't get you in trouble. In fact, they'll help you get jobs done fast and done *well,* which I'm sure your mother would appreciate.

The Outlook Bar, which runs down the left side of the Outlook screen, contains a large number of shortcuts designed to make you more productive. Your shortcuts are divided into three different categories—Outlook Shortcuts, My Shortcuts, and Other. Try not to feel too bad for Other, because it packs some punch even if it doesn't get an important-sounding name. As you're about to see, the Outlook Bar's shortcuts can trim time off your Outlook tasks and can also help you run your entire computer.

Each of the three shortcut menus has a header button you can click to access the menu. For example, in the following figure the Outlook Shortcuts bar is open, while My Shortcuts and Other are in the bottom-left corner, closed.

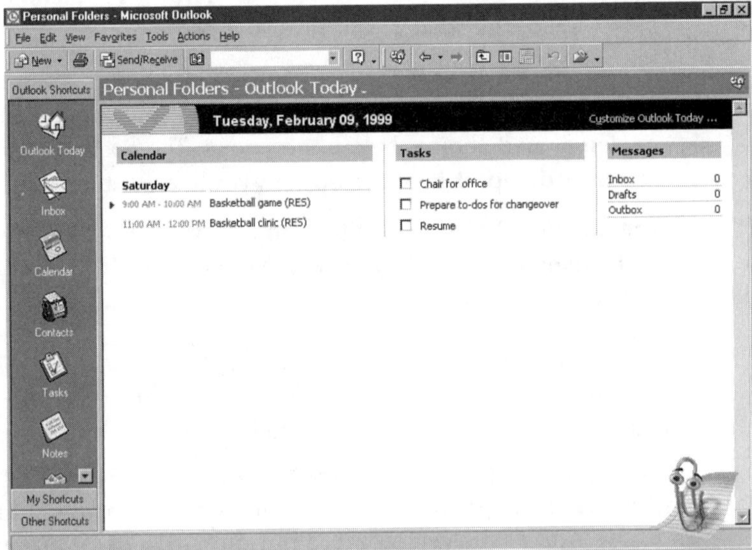

To open a shortcut menu, just click on its button in the Outlook Bar.

All you have to do to open the My Shortcut bar is click on it. The three bars stay in the same order, with Outlook Shortcuts on top, but the My Shortcuts bar is open.

Now let's take a look at what's available from each of these shortcut menus. Later in this book, you'll learn how to modify these menus and add shortcuts to the folders you use most, thus making Outlook an even more functional and useful program.

Outlook Shortcuts

This menu bar gives you quick access to the features of the Outlook program itself. Typically it consists of eight icons, and you won't be able to see them all at once. You should see either a down arrow at the bottom of the bar or an up arrow at the top. Just click it to see the rest of the icons:

- *Outlook Today* As noted earlier, Outlook Today gives you a quick glance at your calendar, tasks, and messages for the day.
- *Inbox* This is the place where your incoming email and fax messages will appear.
- *Calendar* This button takes you to your daily calendar, which opens in the day-at-a-glance view on today's date.
- *Contacts* Clicking here opens your list of contacts and a menu that allows you to search alphabetically.
- *Tasks* Opens your lists of tasks, generally sorted by due date. You can change the order in which these tasks are displayed, however.
- *Notes* Opens any notes you have created and allows you to quickly create new ones.
- *Deleted Items* These are the Outlook items that you have discarded, such as emails you have read and deleted. They remain here until you empty it.

My Shortcuts

When you start up Outlook, the My Shortcuts bar displays four icons that all have to do with your email setup: Drafts, Sent Items, Outbox, and Deleted Items. Clicking on any of these icons shows you the contents of the folder. For example, if you click on the Sent Items button, you see the list of email you've sent, as shown in the following figure.

New Button Alert!

Your New button in the upper-left corner is super-smart. If you click the little arrow next to it, you get a full list of its features. However, when you click the word "New," the result is different depending upon which window you're in. For example, if you're in Calendar and click New, you're ready to enter a new appointment. If you're in Contacts and click New, however, you're ready to enter a new contact. Cool, huh?

Other Shortcuts

The Other shortcuts offer you a link between your Outlook program and your computer as a whole.

You'll see an icon for My Computer, which allows you to see and open files that are stored on your hard drive, floppy drive, CD-ROM drive, and so on. You'll also see folders for My Documents (sometimes called Personal) and Favorites. This is a great menu bar to personalize by adding the folders that you access the most. We'll cover customizing these menu bars later in this book in Chapter 5, "Fun with Files and Folders."

The Sent Items shortcut shows the emails you've sent to others.

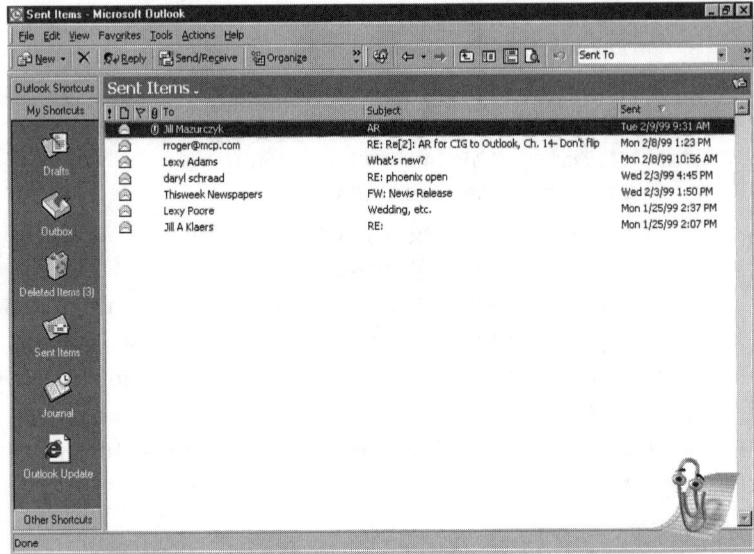

Starting Outlook's Major Features

Back in Chapter 1, "Where to Begin?," we took a look at what Outlook can do for you. Nobody likes a tease, so I'm prepared to show you how to get going with the program. You thought I'd never get there, didn't you?

Outlook has tons of features, but there are really four main areas that just about everybody deals with on a regular basis: Email, Calendar, Contacts, and Tasks. All of these are covered in at least one full chapter in this book, and some are covered over a series of chapters. This section is by no means a full-length look at these topics; it's a quick-start lesson. You'll also see how these features are integrated into Outlook and how they interact with all of the other features.

Email

Email is everywhere throughout Outlook. Take a look again at the Outlook Today window that greets you at startup (click on Outlook Today in the Outlook Shortcuts bar if it's not currently visible on your screen). There are plenty of places to access email.

Right below Outlook Today in the Shortcuts menu is the shortcut to the Inbox. Click it to see the list of messages you have already received. You can also get to the Inbox by clicking Inbox beneath the Messages header in the Outlook Today main window. Also under the Messages header, you can click Drafts to see any messages you've started but haven't finished or Outbox to see messages you've written but haven't sent.

If you click the New button, it opens the window where you can compose a new email message. If you click the Send/Receive button, your computer sends any messages you've written and checks your server for new messages (it will dial out through your modem if necessary, unless you chose manual dialing during setup).

And remember, if you display the My Shortcuts bar, you'll see all of your email folders.

Calendar

The Calendar is a full-featured tool that allows you to do much more than you might expect. That is, it's more than just a way to remind you of your appointments (although it does that, too).

In the Outlook Today window, you can see your appointments for today or for a few days out. To make a new appointment, click the Calendar button in the Outlook Shortcuts window. It should open a window with a one-day view of today's date. (If not, click the 1-Day button near the top of the screen, and then click today's date in the month-view calendar at the upper-right of the screen.) Then click in any of the half-hour blocks on today's calendar. The block turns blue. Then type in the information about your appointment.

Once you've finished typing your appointment, click your Enter button and then click Outlook Today from the Outlook Shortcuts bar. You'll see your appointment listed in the Calendar portion of Outlook Today, just as in the following figure.

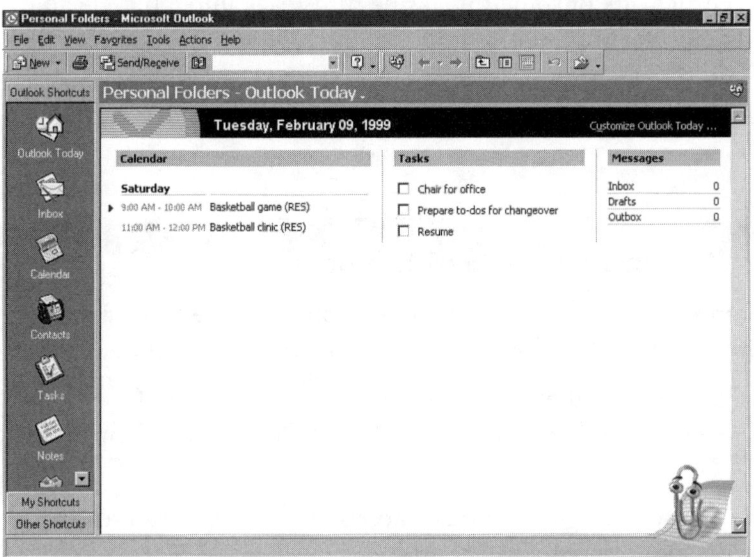

Appointments show up in the Outlook Today window.

Contacts

Click the Contacts button on the Outlook Shortcuts bar to open your list of contacts. If you'd like to enter a new contact, just click the New button from the toolbar above.

From the Contacts window, you can send your contact an email message, schedule an appointment with that contact, or assign the contact to handle a task for you.

Tasks

Your tasks also appear in the Outlook Today window, and they can be sorted by due date or a number of other means.

Click Tasks in the Outlook Shortcuts menu to see the full list of tasks that are awaiting action. To enter a new task, just click the New button from the toolbar above. Once you've entered the task, return to the Outlook Today window by clicking Outlook Today from the Outlook Shortcuts bar. Your new task will appear.

Once a task is completed, just click the box next to it and a strikethrough will show that you no longer need to worry about it.

Exiting Outlook

Exiting Outlook is just like exiting about a million other programs on your PC. Simply click that little X in the upper-right corner of your screen. The Office Assistant will probably give you a little wink or something as he turns back into a bicycle and rides away. There's more on the Office Assistant in the next chapter.

If you have any items pending, such as an email you haven't saved or an appointment that hasn't been fully entered, Outlook will ask if you want to save your changes before you exit.

The Least You Need to Know

- You can start Outlook from the icon on your desktop, from the Start menu, or from the Office Shortcut bar if you accepted it during installation.
- Once you're inside Outlook, there are several ways to access each of Outlook's features—from the New menu, from the Outlook Bar, or from Outlook Today.
- Outlook's three shortcut bars give you quick access to Outlook's features and to other folders on your computer's hard drive.
- Outlook's four most-used features—Email, Calendar, Contacts, and Tasks—are fully integrated with each other and are easily accessed from a variety of places within the program.

WELL, YOU CAN'T GET THERE FROM HERE...

Chapter 4

Stopping to Ask Directions

In This Chapter

- The Office Assistant
- How to search for help
- Asking questions
- The What's This? tool
- Getting help online
- Microsoft's Faxback service

You're probably not the kind of person who would buy a software program, try to figure out how to install it without reading the directions, and then try to figure out all of its wonderful features just by poking around.

Those are the kind of people who get into trouble. They create important documents and later can't find them. Their computers freeze on them at the most inopportune time. (Is there ever a *good* time?) Perhaps most importantly, they waste countless hours trying to figure out how to do the simplest of tasks.

I'm no psychic, but I'm guessing that's not the kind of person you are. If you were, you wouldn't have purchased this book in the first place, right?

In all seriousness, it is a good idea to experiment (to a degree) with any software program. And since we've covered Outlook's major offerings and even shown you a little about how to get into the major features of the program, you might decide to leave the nest for a minute or two to see what you can find.

That's not a problem. Whether you always ask for directions or only occasionally do, this is an important chapter for you. Even if you read this book cover to cover, follow every recommendation, and practice, practice, practice, there's going to come a time when you need a little more help.

Outlook—and the rest of the Microsoft Office suite of applications—has an animated helper for you, plus the usual complement of help menus. You can also find help on the Internet, through America Online, or from Microsoft itself.

The Office Assistant

We've discussed the Office Assistant briefly in the previous chapters, but now it's time for you to become better acquainted with the little fellow shown in the following figure.

He normally appears as a paper clip with eyes, but he changes shape depending upon what you're doing. He sits there on a piece of paper, just waiting for you to ask for his help. If he isn't visible for some reason, all you need to do is click the Office Assistant button on the toolbar. (It looks like a cartoon balloon with a question mark inside it.)

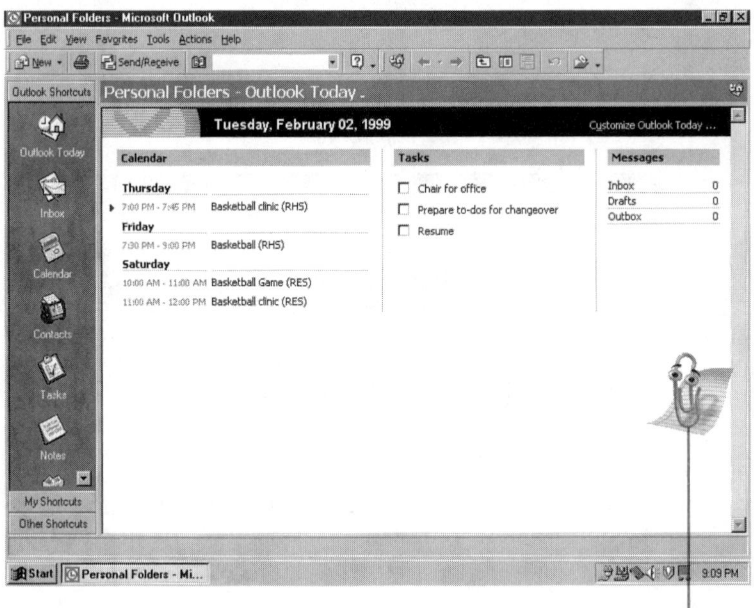

The Office Assistant is ready to help when needed.

The Office Assistant is designed for the computer user who doesn't necessarily have tons of experience navigating through help menus, in which the topic you're looking for might not be indexed under the title you'd expect.

Asking a Question

Asking for help from the Office Assistant is easy because you can simply type in the question you'd like to have answered.

For example, let's say you're wondering how to delete an appointment from your calendar. To activate the Office Assistant, click on it once. A word balloon appears above the Office Assistant and asks you what you would like to do, as shown in the following figure. Type your question in the box provided, and then click the Search button. For example, your question might be, "How do I delete an appointment from my calendar?"

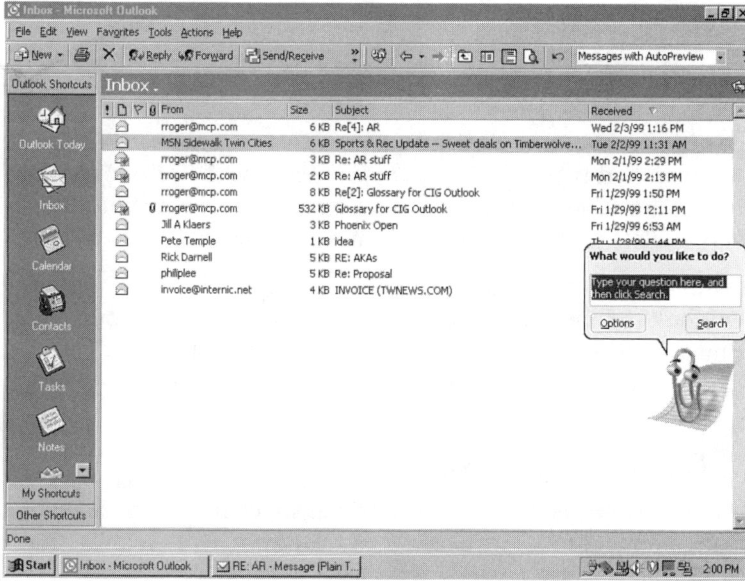

Type your question and the Office Assistant will search for possible answers.

The Office Assistant pulls out the keywords in your sentence and brings up help topics that match. For example, the Office Assistant's response to the preceding question appears in the following figure.

At least one of these topic headers will probably contain information that will answer our question. The others may or may not, but you'll probably click the one that best fits your question.

The question in the example is pretty basic. As you ask more detailed questions, however, some of the answers may not be even close to what you're asking about. In those cases, you may want to shorten your question to just the essential keywords.

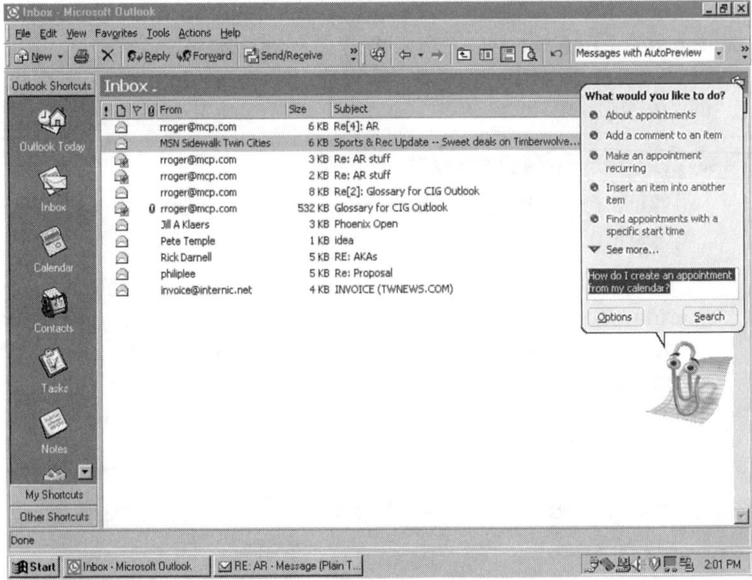

The Office Assistant brings up help topics based on the question you asked.

(Unlike the editors of this book, the Office Assistant doesn't mind sentence fragments.) In our example, if you had typed "delete appointment" in the preceding example, you would have gotten almost exactly the same topic headers as you did when you typed "How do I delete an appointment from my calendar?".

Once you've picked the topic header you think will most closely match your answer, just click it once. The Outlook Help window will open on the right side of your screen, condensing the main Outlook window into a smaller area on the left. The Help window is where the full answer to your question will be displayed.

Playing with the Office Assistant

Your Office Assistant can be customized to fit your personal style. You can make all kinds of changes, including changes to the appearance of the animated creature that serves you.

If you're interested in making changes, just click the Office Assistant and then click the Options button. You'll see the Office Assistant window. Or, you can right-click on the Office Assistant and choose options from the menu that appears.

The window opens automatically with the Options tab selected, as shown in the following figure. Here you can change basic Office Assistant settings, such as when you would like automatic help from the Office Assistant, whether you want it to respond to the F1 key, and so on.

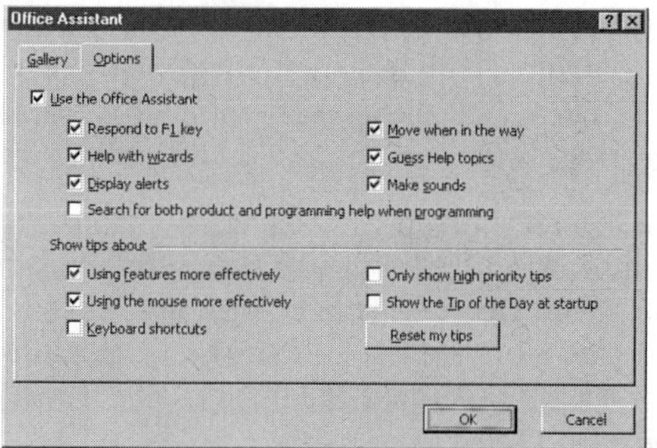

In the Office Assistant window, you can change the way your Office Assistant looks and responds.

The top check box, Use the Office Assistant, is selected. If you're uncomfortable having an animated creature watching your every move, just deselect that box and the Office Assistant will go away. Later, when you want it back, just pull down the Help menu and select Show Office Assistant.

You can also decide when (or if) you want the Office Assistant to offer friendly advice when you're working with a wizard. And the Office Assistant can be used to display alerts to you.

One feature I believe is very helpful is the Move when in the way check box. This automatically moves the Office Assistant when your cursor comes near him. For example, as you're typing an email, the Office Assistant will stay out of your way.

The Gallery tab is where the real fun happens. Here you find out that your paper clip friend's name is Clippit. Click the Next button to see the other characters from which you can choose. My personal favorite is the Genius, who looks like a little animated Albert Einstein. (It makes me feel like I've got a really smart guy helping me out.) You can also change your Assistant by right-clicking on the Assistant and selecting Choose Assistant. If you want to see your Assistant move, right-click on it and select Animate.

Getting Help the Traditional Way

What if you're a little old-fashioned? What if you don't want some animated doodad answering questions as if it were a living, breathing thing? If so, Outlook lets you get rid of the Office Assistant and still get the help you need.

First, you must disable the Office Assistant as you did in the previous section: Click on it once, click Options, and then deselect the Use the Office Assistant button. Then click OK. The Office Assistant is now disabled.

A First Time for Everything

The first time you use Outlook Help, it may take a while to load all the topics. You may even be asked to reinsert your Office CD-ROM. Just give it a minute and it will be ready to go!

To get help now, you'll need to work from the Help menu. Click Help and then click Microsoft Outlook Help. Once again, the Help window is displayed on the screen, covering up the main Outlook program.

The top-left button in the Outlook Help window (see the following figure) is the show/hide button. If you don't see three tabs titled Contents, Answer Wizard, and Index on the left side of the Outlook Help window, click the show/hide button and it will display them for you.

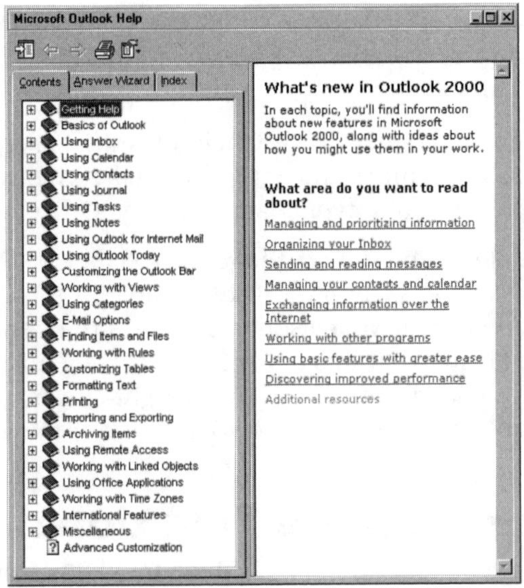

The Outlook Help window offers assistance in the traditional way.

Each of these tabs offers help to Outlook users, and the one you choose to use depends on your personal preference. Here's a quick look at how they work:

- *Contents* If you were searching for a topic in this book, would you go to the table of contents at the front or the index at the back? If you're more likely to use the table of contents, the Contents tab is for you. The topics aren't organized alphabetically, so you have to scan through the list to find the one you're looking for. Once you find it, click the plus sign next to it and the subcategories will be displayed.
- *Answer Wizard* This works very much like your Office Assistant. You type in a question or a series of keywords, and it brings up a list of topics from which to choose.
- *Index* This one is for the people who use the index at the back of the book when they're looking for help. The list is organized by topic, in alphabetical order. You can scroll down the list and double-click the topic you want. Or, you can type in a keyword and click Search, to get a list of possible matches. Double-click the topic from the bottom window and your answers will appear in the right-hand pane.

What's This?

Sometimes, you can search for help all you want and still won't find the exact thing you're looking for. The What's This? tool can help.

With What's This?, you can point your mouse directly at the thing that's driving you crazy and get a quick explanation of what it is. You'll even get a suggestion about how you might be able to better use it.

To access What's This?, pull down the Help menu and click the What's This? button. Your pointer will now have a large question mark riding on it, but not all the time. Only certain aspects of Outlook can respond to the What's This? query, so if you move your pointer over a button or area that is not covered, your pointer will appear as normal. When the question mark appears, you can click on the object and a help box will appear with information about that topic.

In the following figure, the folder banner is clicked and the What's This? help box explains what a folder banner is and what it does. It also gives another use for the folder banner, just in case you're interested.

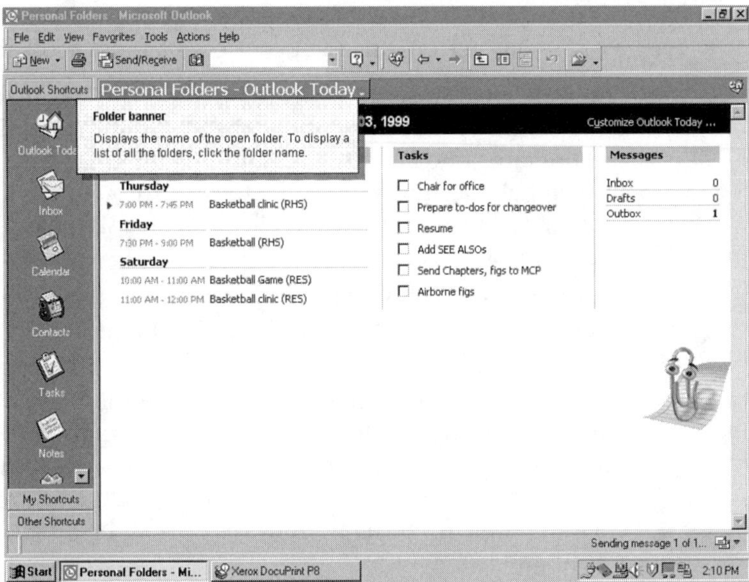

Using What's This? to get basic information is quick and easy.

Getting Help Online

Not surprisingly, Microsoft makes it easy for you to get help on the Web for all of its programs. In the new Office 2000, it's easier than ever because they've added an Office on the Web selection.

From the Help menu, simply click Office on the Web. If you have an Internet connection, you'll be taken directly to your default Web browser and sent to Microsoft's Office Update home page. From there, click the Search button to search for the product you need help with—in this case, Outlook.

Even better, though, is to go to the Microsoft Knowledge Base. This is the same database that Microsoft's technical support people use when you call them on the phone. The Microsoft Knowledge Base's Web address is `www.support.microsoft.com`.

This is a great place to go if Outlook isn't functioning properly in a certain area. Every bug that's reported to technical support is documented here, so you're likely to find an explanation for your problem, if not a solution for it.

Using Microsoft's Faxback Service

If you have access to a fax machine, you can use it to retrieve information directly from Microsoft. Microsoft's faxback service is called FastTips, and it can be reached at 1-800-936-4100. On your first call, you can order a "map" of Outlook that will give you codes to help you order the fax that answers your question (with a second call). It may not be the quickest or easiest method to get answers, but it works.

The Least You Need to Know

- The Office Assistant answers questions written in complete sentences (or with keywords) and gives you plenty of options to solve your problem.
- The Office Assistant can be customized to operate in specific ways, to disappear, and even to change its appearance.
- Outlook offers traditional help through Microsoft Outlook Help on the Help menu. You can use three different tabs: Contents, Answer Wizard, and Index.
- The What's This? option allows you to point to an object with your pointer and find out what it is, how it works, and some options for different ways to use it.
- You can get help from Microsoft on the Internet, either from Microsoft's Knowledge Base or the Office on the Web link from Outlook's Help menu.
- You can have answers to questions automatically faxed to you by using FastTips, Microsoft's faxback service.

Chapter 5

Fun with Files and Folders

In This Chapter

- Selecting, moving, and copying files
- Creating new folders
- Renaming files and folders
- Different ways to view your files
- Adding folders to the Outlook Bar
- File management tools

If you've spent any time at all working (or playing) on your computer, you know that everything is based on a system of files and folders.

You write a letter to Mom, and it's a file saved into a folder. You figure out the family budget, and it's a file saved into a folder. And then comes the biggie—you created a file a week ago and now you have no idea where it is.

If you could only remember the name of that folder.

Outlook is no different. Whether you've created a list of tasks or contacts, entered a bunch of information into a calendar, or sent emails to 100 people, you've created files, saved files, moved files, and deleted files—perhaps without even knowing you were doing it.

What to do with all these files and folders? How can you find the important ones easily? How can you create your own system of folders in order to better organize your files? Can Outlook help you with files and folders that are used in other programs? Do you like movies about gladiators?

Oops, forget that last one.

Truth be told, Outlook is designed to be much more than just another program that takes up space on your computer while helping you perform a function or two. If you let it, Outlook can help you manage every single file in your computer.

You've already learned some basics about how Outlook can help you organize your appointments, your contacts, your tasks, your email. But Outlook can also help you keep your computer under control. In fact, Outlook can become an indispensable part of the everyday use of your computer.

Keeping an Eye on Your Files and Folders

If you're a computer veteran, you've probably spent a lot of time rummaging through your lists of files and folders. You may even have learned how to move, delete, copy, and rename them. Outlook can help you do all of that, and you may find that using Outlook for those tasks will make it even easier for you.

Before we can go too far, however, we need to show you how to find the files and folders that already exist on your computer's hard drive.

You may remember from our tour of Outlook back in Chapter 3, "Please, No Flash Photography on This Tour," that one of the tabs on your Outlook Bar will lead you into the guts of your computer. Each of the three tabs located there—Outlook Shortcuts, My Shortcuts, and Other—leads you into your files and folders. Let's take a quick look back at them.

Outlook Shortcuts

They don't look like folders, but each of those eight icons in the Outlook Shortcuts bar is, in fact, a folder that contains some of your files.

For example, take the Inbox. When you click it, you see a list of emails you have received and not yet deleted. Each of those emails is a file, and from the Inbox window you can move, copy, forward, delete, and so on any or all of those files.

When you click on most of these buttons, however, you won't see files. For example, if you click on Contacts, you get a list of your contacts, but not really a list of files. Still, you are working with files in each of those places.

The other two menus on the Outlook Bar are better examples of files and folders.

My Shortcuts

As you probably remember from Chapter 3, My Shortcuts contains some of the folders you use in email—Drafts, Sent Items, Outbox, and Deleted Items.

Click on any of these buttons and you will see a list of files—that is, if you have any files in any of these folders.

We won't spend a lot of time on this area, because it is covered in detail in Chapter 11, "Managing Much Mail." But the principles of working with files and folders that we will cover in this chapter apply to the files and folders in My Shortcuts as well.

Other Shortcuts

If I could change any single thing about Outlook, it would be the name of this shortcut bar. "Other" sounds so unimportant, like it contains items that are so unnecessary that they can't be grouped under a *real* category name. Might as well just call it "Miscellaneous."

One click on this shortcut bar's header (just click the word "Other") and you will quickly discover that it is very important, indeed.

Typically, you'll see three buttons in this bar—My Computer, My Documents, and Favorites—as you can see in the following figure.

- *My Computer* Here's why I don't think this shortcut bar should be called Other. The My Computer button is the same as the one on your Desktop. It leads you to the folders that contain every single file on your computer—all your Outlook files as well as any file created by any other program. Sounds a bit more important than "other," doesn't it?
- *My Documents* If you've spent any time working in any of the other Microsoft Office programs, you've probably noticed that when you go to save a document, the program defaults to save the file in a folder called My Documents. That's the folder you're looking at right now. The Personal folder is actually located on your hard drive, most likely inside your Microsoft Office folder. This button gives you a shortcut to it.

- *Favorites* This folder contains shortcuts to the Web sites that are your favorites. In the Microsoft Internet Explorer Web browser, you can save a site you would like to revisit by adding it to your list of favorites. When you do so, it appears in this folder.

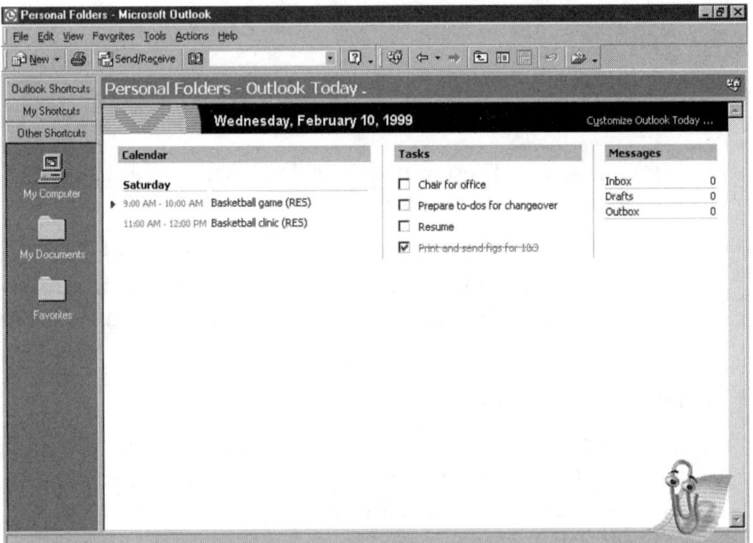

The Other shortcut bar, on the far left, contains three buttons by default.

Getting That Custom Fit

On any of these shortcut menus, you can make changes. You can add new folders, and you can move, delete, or rename existing ones. This is a great way for you to personalize Outlook and optimize your time in your busy schedule.

Some people don't want to spend much time messing around with that kind of thing. After all, Microsoft has created so many different ways to do various things in these programs that there's no need to change anything, right? Well, the reason the program's designers give you so many options is because different people have different tastes. But even with the multitude of options they present, they can't please everyone. They give you the option to make your own rules and design your own layout for the program, so that you'll love it all the more.

Adding shortcuts is covered later in this chapter.

Checking In on Your Outlook Folders

Now that you've seen the folders in the Outlook Bar, it's time to see them working within Outlook.

To begin, let's take a look at the files and folders you use when you are working with Outlook. If you are working on a standalone computer (such as a home computer), these files are stored on your hard drive. If you are using Outlook in a networked computer system (such as you might have on your computer at work), your Outlook files might be stored on the network server or they might still be on the hard drive in the computer on which you work. (Check with your system administrator if you are not sure.)

In Outlook, you can create new folders, change the order of the folders on the Outlook Bar, rename folders, copy them, delete them, and more.

Let's give it a try!

To begin, we'll need to be able to see the folders themselves, not just the buttons on the Outlook Bar that lead you to them. To do this, we need to change your Outlook screen to Folder List view.

First, click the View button. Then click Folder List. You will note that the main portion of your Outlook screen is resized, and a new panel appears. Since Outlook Today is the default view, you will probably see only one folder listed, called Outlook Today. To the left of it should be a plus sign in a little box. Click on the plus sign, and a list of subfolders within the Outlook Today folder is displayed, as you see in this figure.

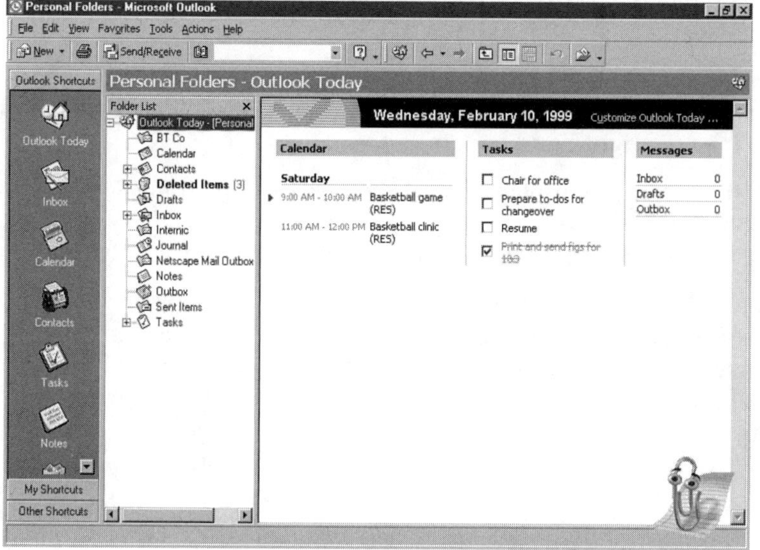

The Folder List is in the center panel.

Each of the items listed under Outlook Today is a folder. And, if any of them has folders contained within it, it will have the little box with the plus sign next to its name.

Do Not Be Afraid

Since everyone's configuration is different and everyone has used different programs before, your folder list inside your Outlook Today folder may be very different from what you see in the figure. Some things should be constant—you should have a folder for each of the main Outlook features, such as Calendar, Contacts, and so on. But you probably won't have a folder called BT Co in yours, because that was a folder I added manually to my setup. So don't be worried if things don't look exactly the same on your computer as they do in the figure.

So, what's all this plus-minus stuff mean? It's simple, really. If a folder has a plus sign next to it, the folder has subfolders within it that are not currently displayed. If a folder has a minus sign next to it, the folder contains subfolders, and they are all currently displayed. As you can see, the Outlook Today folder now has a minus sign next to it because all of its subfolders are being shown. If you click the minus sign, all of the subfolders will be hidden.

When you have all of the subfolders displayed, a single click on any folder name will display the contents of that folder. For example, if you click on the Calendar folder, the Calendar will pop into the right-hand window.

Let's say, for example, that I want to display a list of the files that are in my Sent Items folder (these are emails that I have sent to other people). If I single-click the Sent Items folder, the complete list of files is displayed, as you can see in the following figure.

The purpose of the folder list is to allow you to make changes to the organizational system of your folders. It's your chance to customize your stuff. If you use this tool to create a huge bureaucracy within your computer, working with your files will be like trying to fight City Hall. If you use the tools wisely, you'll turn into a regular speed demon on your computer.

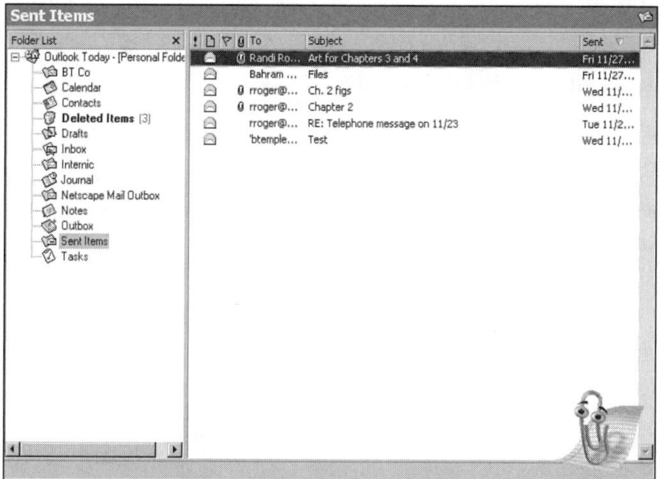

Single-clicking any of the folder names will display the contents of the folder in the right-hand pane.

Make Room for Subfolders

Technically speaking (and I know you love it when I get technical), every folder on your computer is a subfolder to the almighty C: drive, which is the granddaddy of all folders.

In Outlook however, there are top-level folders, which are the ones that contain major aspects of the program. Your Calendar, Contacts, and Tasks folders are all top-level folders. You cannot make changes to top-level folders. For example, you can't delete your Calendar folder, because then you wouldn't have a place to store your Calendar.

Why Do I Need Subfolders?

You might not, but chances are good that they will help you remain organized. For example, do you think it would be easier to keep all of your email in one big Inbox folder or to sort it out, based on whether it's work related or personal? That's a good example of how a well-designed system of subfolders can help you.

But you don't have to spend a ton of time worrying about how to set up your subfolder system. Subfolders can be deleted, renamed, and so on, so your subfolder setup is usually a work in progress anyway.

Creating a new folder is simple. Let's say, for the sake of our learning experience here, that you want to create two folders within your Tasks folder so that you can keep your personal tasks separate from your business tasks.

There are precisely two ways to create a new folder, and this way we can learn both of them!

First, let's get into the Tasks folder by single-clicking on the word Tasks in the folder list. You'll note that your task list appears on the right side of your screen, and the word Tasks is highlighted in the folder list. Now, from the File menu above, select Folder, then New Folder.

A dialog box appears that looks like the one in this figure.

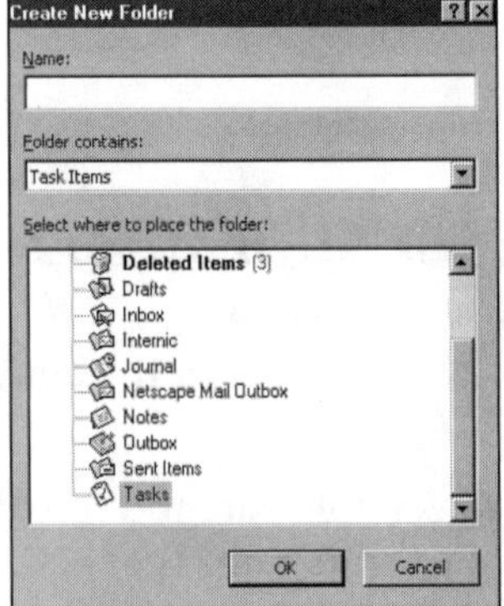

Fill in the necessary information to add a subfolder.

First, you are asked to name the subfolder. Let's call it Personal. The second box asks what type of information will be stored in this folder. It defaults to whatever the upper-level folder contains, but you can change it from the drop-down menu. For our purposes here, leave it at selecting task information. Finally, you are asked into which folder to place the subfolder. Make sure Tasks is highlighted and click OK.

You will note that in the main folder list, the Tasks folder now has a plus sign next to it, indicating that it has a subfolder that is not displayed. Your Office Assistant, if you are using it, asks you at this point if you'd like to add a shortcut to this new folder on the Outlook Bar. At this point, click No. (We'll cover this later.)

To add our other subfolder, right-click on Tasks in the folder list, then click New Folder. Repeat the above steps, this time calling the new subfolder Business.

Once you have completed that, click the plus sign next to the Tasks folder, and you will see that our two new folders have been successfully added to our folder hierarchy, as in the next figure.

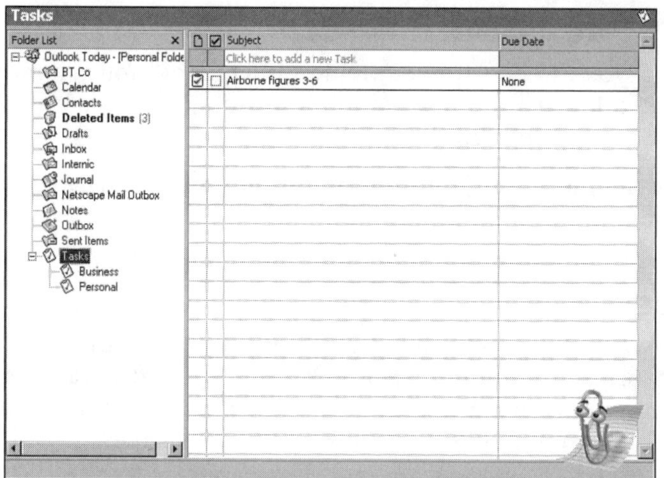

The two new subfolders are now listed under Tasks.

Make a Shortcut

In our little exercise, you saw that when you add a new subfolder, Outlook's Office Assistant immediately asks you if you would like to make a shortcut to that folder on the Outlook Bar. Had you clicked Yes, it would have prompted for where you would like the shortcut to be located.

There are a couple of other ways to create shortcuts that are just as easy:

- *The drag-and-drop method* You can click and drag any folder icon from the folder list into the Outlook Bar. Simply open whichever of the Outlook shortcut bars you would like to use for a home for your shortcut, click on the folder name, and drag it into the shortcut bar. You can even place it at any spot on the bar you want.
- *Click right* Another way to create an Outlook Bar shortcut is to right-click anywhere within the shortcut bar and choose Outlook Bar Shortcut. Then, identify the folder for which you want to create the shortcut, and it will appear.
- *Ordering from the menu* You can also create a new Outlook Bar shortcut from the File menu at the top of the screen. From the File menu, select New, then select Outlook Bar Shortcut. (Remember, because of the new Intellisense menu system, this choice may be hidden under the down-pointing double arrows in the New menu.) You will then be presented with a dialog box in which you will tell Outlook how and where you want the shortcut to be displayed.

Playing with Your Files and Folders

There's all kinds of fun stuff you can do with your folders in Outlook. You can move, copy, and rename your Outlook folders (except the top-level ones). And you can use Outlook to modify the rest of the folders in your computer as well.

Just be careful, because moving, renaming, deleting, and so on can become addictive, just like Internet chat rooms.

Copying and Moving

We're not going to go crazy here explaining all the different ways to do this. Suffice it to say there's a simple way (if you trust your drag-and-drop ability) and a drawn-out way of doing it. The drawn-out way involves your Edit menu and its Move and Copy functions. You can use them if you like, but the following way is much easier and quicker.

To move a file or folder, simply click it and drag it to the place you would like to store it. Remember, if you are moving it from one subfolder to another, make sure both folder names are displayed in the folder list, so that you can drop it in the right place.

To copy a file or folder, simply press Ctrl and drag it to the place you would like to copy it.

You can also move or copy a folder by right-clicking on the folder name, then selecting Move *Folder Name* or Copy *Folder Name*, whichever is appropriate.

When you copy or move a folder, all its contents go with it, but it retains its original purpose. For example, if we moved those Task folders we created earlier into a Calendar folder, they would still be Task folders, not Calendar folders.

Renaming

To rename a folder, all you have to do is right-click on the folder name in the folder list, then select Rename *Folder Name*. You will revert to the folder list; the name of the folder will be selected and a cursor will appear in the box. Just type in the new name for the folder.

As you can see in the following figure, I right-clicked the Business folder we created earlier, then changed its name to Work (isn't that clever?).

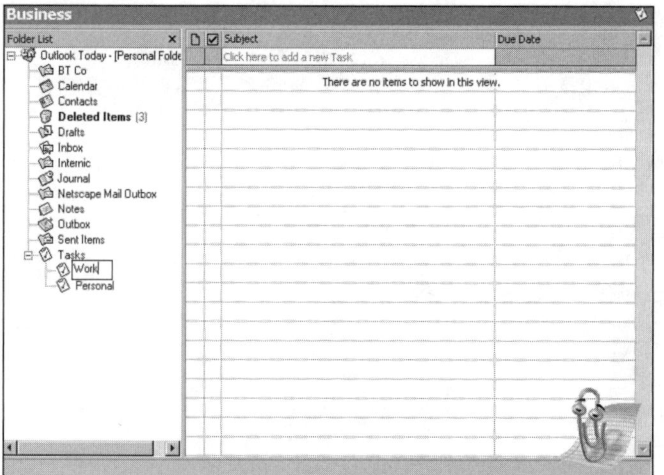

Right-clicking on the folder name in the list allows you to change its name.

Deleting and Undeleting

Deleting a folder may seem like a snap—and it is—but the folder isn't really *gone* until you tell the program you really want it gone. This is Microsoft's little way of saving those of us who have a tendency to accidentally hit the ol' Delete key at the most inopportune times.

To delete a file or folder from the folder list, simply select it and either press your Delete key or click the delete button on the toolbar above (the one that looks like a hand-drawn *X*).

Outlook never asks you if you are "sure," as some other programs do. But you do have a chance to get that information back, if you so desire.

All deleted items are actually sent to the Deleted Items folder (a fitting place for them). You can get to the Deleted Items folder by selecting it from the folder list or from the shortcut to it on the Outlook Bar.

You can retrieve a folder or a file by dragging it back into another folder. If you're sure you really want it gone, however, select it from the Deleted Items list and click the delete button (or hit your Delete key). This time, the Office Assistant does ask if you are sure you want to permanently delete the item, as you can see from the following figure.

The Office Assistant gives you one last chance to bail out of a delete.

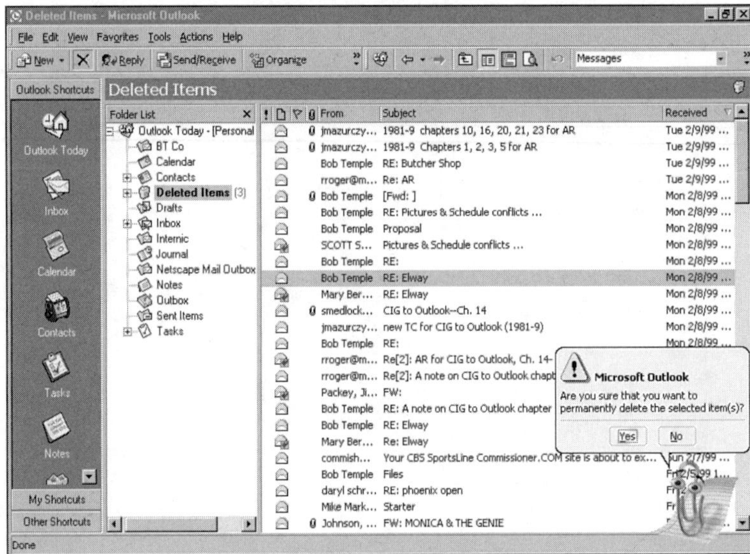

Click Yes and it's gone for good.

Keep Deleted Items Clean!

Your Deleted Items folder fills up rapidly with discarded email, completed tasks, cancelled appointments, and so on. A full Deleted Items folder only drags down your performance.

You'll want to remember to go into your Deleted Items folder on a regular basis to clean things out. I do it every Monday morning, if not more often, to clear out last week's garbage. Just make sure you aren't deleting anything important.

You can delete multiple items easily. To delete the entire list, highlight any of the files and press Ctrl+A. That will select your entire list, and you can just click the delete button or your Delete key. Or, you can enter the Tools menu, then select Empty Deleted Items folder. You can also do this by right-clicking on the Deleted Items icon in the Outlook Bar and selecting Empty Deleted Items folder.

To select a range of files, highlight the top file in the list and then Shift+click the bottom file. Everything between will be selected, and you can then delete them all.

If you want to delete 10 files on a list of 20 but the 10 aren't all in order, just Ctrl+click on each of the filenames you want to delete, and only those files will be selected. Then delete them.

Finally, you can tell Outlook to empty your deleted items every time you exit Outlook. To do this, open the Tools menu, choose Options, then click the Other tab. Check the box next to Empty the Deleted Items folder upon exiting, and it will be done.

The Least You Need to Know

- Outlook can be used not only to manage its own files, but also to manage the entire file system for your computer.
- There are several ways to move, copy, rename, and delete your files and folders. Outlook makes it all very easy.
- Creating new subfolders in your folder list is easy, and can help you to better organize your system of files, making you more productive.
- Creating shortcuts to folders on the Outlook Bar is another way to improve your productivity. You can even select where on the shortcut list you would like the new folder to appear.
- Deleted files and folders aren't really removed from your system until you clear them from the Deleted Items folder. This should be done regularly to avoid having the folder get overrun with old items that are of no use to you anymore.

Chapter 6

Tool Time

In This Chapter

- The Magical Mystery Outlook Bar
- Looking at views
- Creating custom views
- Options and services
- Navigating your computer through Outlook
- Outlook Today

The first part of this book has been a get-acquainted session to help you get used to the way Outlook looks, feels, and acts. Just as today is the first day of the rest of your life, this is the final chapter of the first part of this book.

We've already covered a number of different ways to customize Outlook to your own tastes. In this chapter, we'll look at a couple of other ways to set things up your way so that when we move into specific areas of Outlook, you'll already have things arranged the way you like them. Some of this information might be review, and some will be new, but it's all relevant.

Have you ever purchased a computer program and liked the way it worked, but not the way it looked or the manner in which it displayed information? The designers at Microsoft anticipated this in their design of Outlook. They've allowed you to change a great many things so that the program is set up the way you want it to be.

The Magical Mystery Outlook Bar

Chapter 3, "Please, No Flash Photography on This Tour," covered the default buttons on your Outlook Bar in detail. If you need a quick review of their various purposes, now would be a good time to look at that chapter again.

In Chapter 5, "Fun with Files and Folders," you learned how to add buttons to the Outlook Bar. These buttons serve as shortcuts to files and services within Outlook.

The reason that the heading for this section is "The Magical Mystery Outlook Bar," however, is that the Outlook Bar can be whatever you want it to be. It is strongly recommended that you customize the Outlook Bar. You'll find that it will greatly improve your productivity.

Let's take a look at email, for instance. Most people keep their email separated into separate folders, one for business and one for personal messages. If you set up these folders as shortcuts on your Outlook Bar, you'll be able to quickly access those messages whenever you need them. And you can view the messages you want without having to wade through other messages.

Sure, you can view all your folders anytime you want by using the Folder List view, but that takes up a chunk of your screen that could be better used for something like Outlook Today or whichever Outlook feature you're currently using. In fact, that's the whole reason for having shortcuts on the Outlook Bar—they don't take up much space, and they speed up your access to important files and folders.

What's Your View?

As mentioned, Outlook lets you customize things the way you want to see them. One way to do this is through Views. You'll have to play around with Views for a while until you find out which appearance and setup is most pleasing to you.

The Advanced Toolbar

The best way to work with Views is on the Advanced toolbar. You'll remember from the discussion of toolbars in Chapter 3 that directly beneath the menu bar is the Standard toolbar. The Advanced toolbar offers additional choices that are, ahem, more advanced. To see the Advanced toolbar, just right-click on any spot on the Standard toolbar and click Advanced in the box that appears. In the following figure Outlook Today is displayed, and you can see that both the Standard toolbar and Advanced toolbar fit easily on one line.

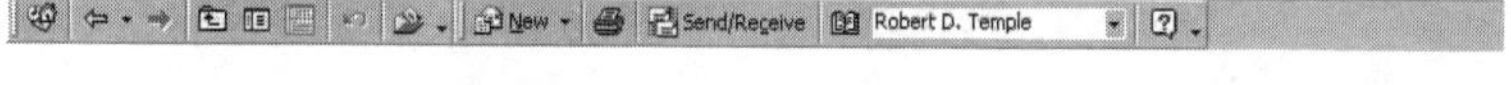

The Advanced toolbar shares space with the Standard toolbar.

The Advanced toolbar has additional offerings, depending upon which folder you're in, and all the buttons may not fit on the toolbar. For example, click on Calendar. You can see double arrows at the ends of both the Advanced and Standard toolbars, indicating that there are additional buttons you cannot see.

There are a couple of options to fix this situation:

- *Move a toolbar* You can move either toolbar by clicking and dragging on the vertical line at its far left (the line that appears to be sticking out). You can switch one of the toolbars from left to right, or move one to the side or the bottom of your screen. This will open up more room so that all the buttons are visible.
- *Close the Standard toolbar* If you decide the Advanced toolbar is more valuable to you, close the Standard toolbar. Just right-click on the toolbar and select Standard. To reopen it, repeat this process.
- *Close individual buttons* Beneath the double arrow on each toolbar is a little down arrow, indicating a drop-down menu. Clicking on it displays not only the buttons you can't currently see, but also an Add/Remove Buttons option. Select that and then select any buttons you don't use until your toolbars are short enough to display all the buttons you need. Be careful not to remove buttons that you might need later.

Once you've opened the Advanced toolbar for one of your folders, it will remain open for all of your folders until you close it. For example, if you open the Advanced toolbar for the Inbox and you switch to the Calendar, you will still see the Advanced toolbar but the buttons will have changed to those for the Calendar.

The Current View

Depending on the folder you're in, there may be many, many buttons on your Advanced toolbar. Each of them will have a window that displays the current view and a drop-down box to change the view for that folder. That window is called Current View.

Here you can select how you want information in each folder to be presented to you. In the following figure, you can see the choices for viewing the contents of the Inbox. To do this, click on your Inbox button on your Outlook Bar, and then pull down the Current View window.

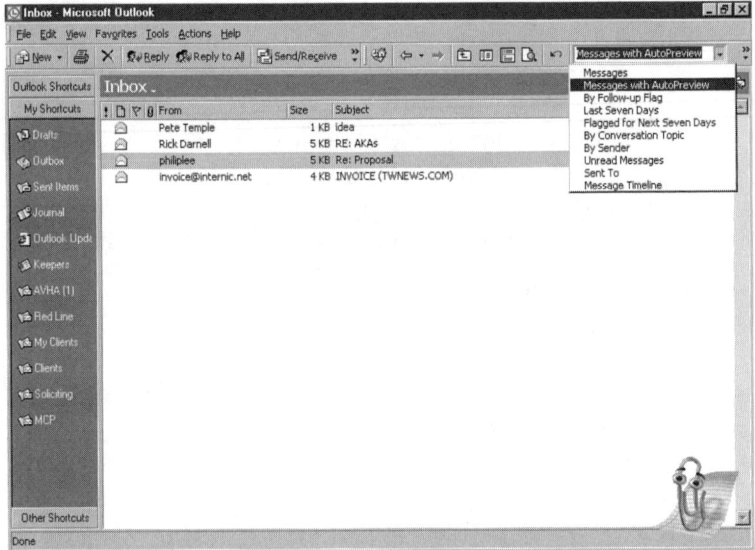

Use the Current View window on the Advanced toolbar to change how a folder's contents are displayed.

Your View May Be Different

If you've moved one of the toolbars or deleted any buttons, your screen may look a little bit different than the figure here. However, the only way you wouldn't be able to change your view with your screen is if you deleted the Current View window from the toolbar.

We could go through all of the options for the Current View for each of the folders in Outlook, but that would make for a really long chapter and might put you to sleep. Instead, we'll cover the different views for each folder as we discuss each of the folders later in this book.

Going with Custom Options

Don't like any of the views that the folks at Microsoft have designed for you? Well, make your own darn view, you picky son of a gun.

If there are certain things you want to view in certain ways, you can go right ahead and set them up yourself. However, be aware that this process can get complicated. You should thoroughly check out the existing views to make sure they don't meet your needs before you try to create your own views. Or, rather than creating your own view from scratch, you might find it easier to customize an existing view.

Creating a New View

First, open the View menu, select Current View, and then select Define Views. In the dialog box that appears, click New. The Create a New View dialog box appears in the following figure.

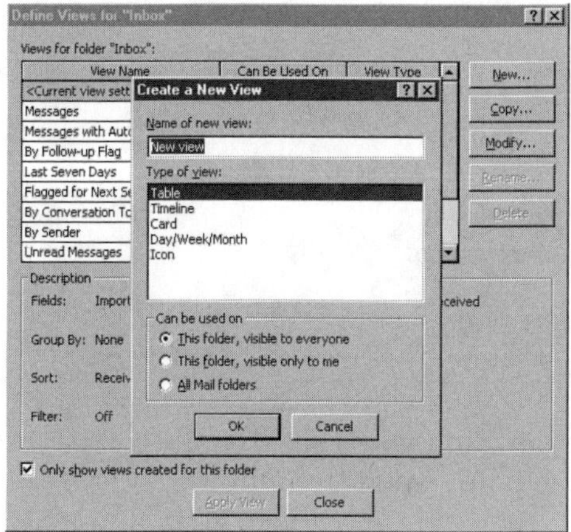

You can name your new view and select the type of view you would like.

You can enter a name for your view and select the type of view you would like it to be. At the bottom of the dialog box, you're also asked to choose where within Outlook you can use this view—in all of your folders or only certain ones. For example, if you have several different mail folders, you might want to allow the view to be used in each of them.

When you've made these choices, click OK to bring up the Settings box. Here you can choose which fields you would like to be included in your view. (Fields are like subject headings.) When you click the Fields button, you're given a list from which to choose. You can also specify the order in which you want your fields to appear.

Customizing an Existing View

Need to make a little adjustment here or there to make a view great? Here's a little example of how to do it.

Let's say that you really love the way your Inbox displays messages in the Messages with Auto Preview view, except for one little thing—you wish that the size of the message was displayed.

Outlook can help. First, open your Inbox and make sure your view is set to Messages with Auto Preview. From the View menu, select Current View and then Customize Current View. You'll get the same dialog box you did when you created your own view.

You want to add the Size field to your view, so click the Fields button. Find the Size field in the left window, select it, and then click Add to move it over to the end of your list. Now you can move the Size field to any point in the view you would like. In the right window, click and drag Size up the list. A dotted red line appears. Move Size up until the dotted line is between From and Subject, and then release. Your screen should look like the one in the following figure.

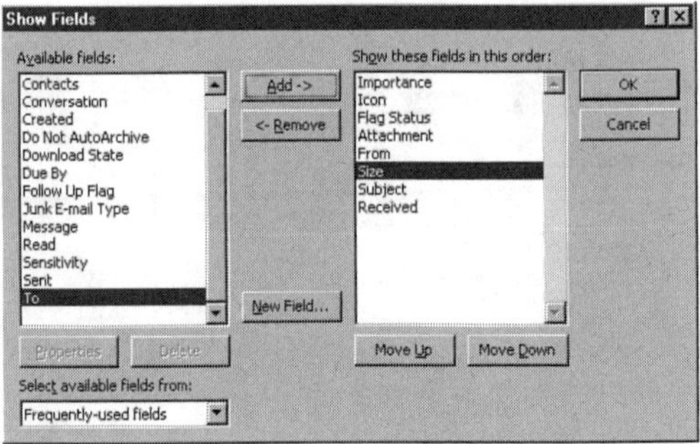

Adding Size to this view includes being able to place it at the exact point you would like to see it.

You're done! Click OK, click OK again, and you'll see that the size of each message in your Inbox is displayed right at the point where you put it.

Sorting and Grouping

You'll also find it useful to be able to sort your views and group them. For example, in your Inbox, you can have your messages displayed in the order in which they were received, alphabetically by the name of the person who sent them, and so on.

To sort or group, you'll again need to open the View menu, select Current View, and then select Customize Current View. Depending on what you would like to do, click either the Sort or Group By button. A dialog box will present you with your options.

What's Your Preference?

By now you're probably wishing that Microsoft didn't give you any choices at all. "Just give me the program and let me use it already!"

Well, guess what? There are even *more* choices you can make! The beauty of all of this, however, is that you don't *have* to make any changes or choices at all. You can leave everything at its default setting if you want. Again, these are just options—take them or leave them.

You can use the Preferences tab to make changes to the basic setup of any of the five main areas (folders) of Outlook: Email, Calendar, Contacts, Journals, and Notes. To get to the Preferences tab, select Options from the Tools menu. You'll see the Preferences tab, just like the one in the following figure.

The Preferences tab is neatly divided into the five main areas of Outlook. Some preferences can be set on this tab, and others must be set after clicking the appropriate button. Here's a quick look at what you can do in each of these areas:

- *Email* The most important area in the E-mail Options window is the Message Handling area. Here you can make some important decisions, such as whether to keep a copy of any message you send in the Sent Items folder (most people do). You can also decide how you want your messages to be formatted when you're replying to or forwarding a message.

- *Calendar* On the main Preferences tab, you can select the amount of time before an upcoming appointment that you'll get a reminder. Inside Calendar Options is a really neat feature for people with abnormal workweeks. If your workweek is something other than Monday–Friday from 8–5, make those changes here to block out your work hours. You can also decide if you want your calendar displayed as Sunday–Saturday, or if you want the weekends displayed together in a Monday–Sunday format.
- *Tasks* There's not much here. All you can do is change the color of tasks that are overdue or have been completed.
- *Contacts and the Journal* In Contact Options, you can change how the name is displayed (last name first or first name first). In Journal Options, there are many different choices. These are covered in Chapter 19, "The Long and Short of It: The Journal and Notes."
- *Notes* You can change the color, font, and size of the note itself.

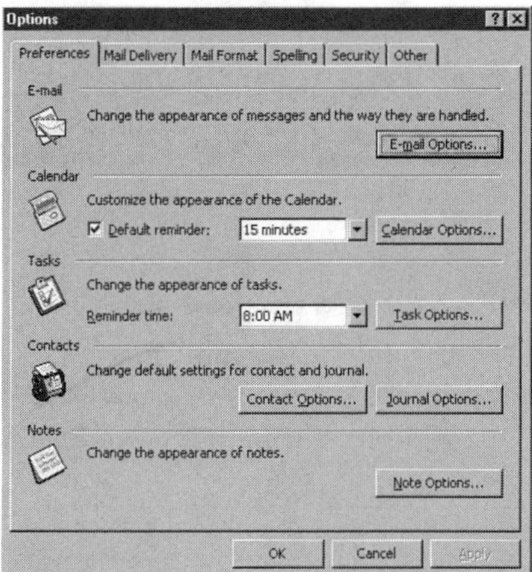

Use the Preferences tab to change the setup of any of the five main areas of Outlook.

Navigating Your Computer Through Outlook

You can also use Outlook to view the files created in other programs on your computer. You've probably worked with the My Computer icon on your desktop to delete a file, to copy from a floppy disk, or something else. You can do the same things without ever leaving Outlook.

From the Other shortcuts bar, simply click the My Computer icon. From that point, you're working on your files just as you would be if you were on your desktop. For example, you can delete any unwanted files by highlighting them and pressing the Delete key. These files are then sent to your Recycle Bin on your desktop (not to the Deleted Items folder within Outlook, because these aren't Outlook files).

This functionality makes Outlook an even more useful program. Once you're comfortable with Outlook, you can use it as a form of "home base" from which to do *all* of your computing work.

Customizing Outlook Today

You've already learned about the merits of Outlook Today, which provides a great at-a-glance view of upcoming appointments and tasks, plus the messages that are waiting for you.

You can also make changes to the types and amount of information presented in Outlook Today, and to the look of the page itself. To begin, get back to Outlook Today by clicking the Outlook Today button on the Outlook Shortcuts bar. Near the top of the Outlook Today window, click Customize Outlook Today. This opens the Customize Outlook Today window, as seen in the following figure.

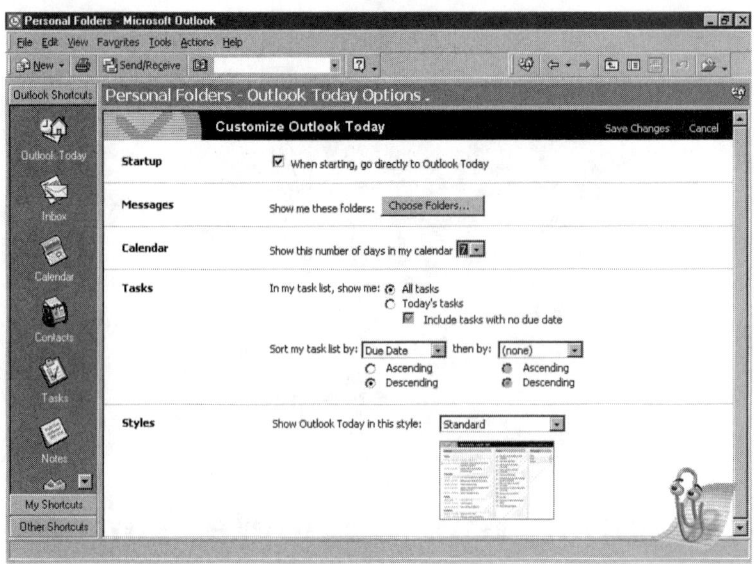

Customizing Outlook Today to your tastes makes it more functional.

First, you can decide whether you want Outlook Today to be displayed automatically when you open Outlook. (As you might guess, I leave this checked.)

You can also decide which folders are displayed in the Messages list, how many days of the Calendar you would like to be displayed, which tasks you would like to see, and how you would like them sorted. Finally, you can pick the layout style you like for the page. Go ahead and experiment with this a little; you'll find one you like, I'm sure.

The Least You Need to Know

- Adding folders to the Outlook Bar gives you quick access to the files they contain.
- You can alter the view of each of the five main areas of Outlook. You can display the information differently or display more or less information.
- You can create your own views or customize the existing ones within Outlook.
- You can set preferences in each of the five main areas to determine how certain things are handled. These preferences can easily be changed at any time.
- You can use Outlook to manage files and folders that weren't created in Outlook, just as you would if you were working on your desktop.
- You can customize Outlook Today to suit your needs.

Part 2

Get a Life: Talking to the Outside World

Email has become such a vital part of everyday life that many people check it even before they read the morning paper. Email has woven its way into the fabric of modern life, and it's woven into the fabric of Outlook, too. In this part we'll cover email and Outlook's handling of it, from top to bottom. First, we'll give you some background on email itself. Then we'll cover the basics of how to use Outlook to send and receive email. Finally, we'll cover some more advanced topics, such as handling email messages, managing mail folders, and sending and receiving attachments.

Chapter 7

What's the Big Deal About Email?

In This Chapter

- Why so many people use email
- Everyday uses of email
- What is email?
- How email works
- Anatomy of an email address
- What you need in order to use email

When Macintosh launched the iMac in 1998, they came out with a series of clever commercials. (I know I probably shouldn't mention Macs in a book about a Microsoft product, buy hey, they're partners now, right?) One of those commercials starred Jeff Goldblum, one of my personal favorites. In it he waxed poetic about email: "Just what *is* this email, anyway? I don't have an email."

The message was that you could buy the computer and be emailing messages around the world within seconds. Of course, it's not that simple.

You don't have to worry about buying the computer, because you've already got one. And although getting a computer set up and running is a trillion times easier today than it was 10 years ago, getting started with email still requires a little bit more than plugging a phone line into the back of your computer.

Email is an electronic form of regular mail (the "e" stands for "electronic"). This chapter covers email from the ground floor—all the basic information you need to understand before you ever start emailing people.

That said, you should also know that this chapter isn't really Outlook specific. That is, the information presented here can be used regardless of what program you're using to send and receive your email.

This also means that if you're already an email veteran, you can approach this chapter in one of two ways: You can use it as a refresher (you may even learn something), or you can ignore it altogether and move ahead a few pages to Chapter 8, "Basic Training for Emailers." It's your call.

Why Is Everyone Except You Already Using Email?

The answer is pretty straightforward: Email is easy, useful, fun, and cheap.

Any questions?

There's really little question that email is the most popular feature of the Internet. Virtually every person who has Internet access also has some type of email account—meaning that there are as many as 150 million emailers out there. (Some days, it seems like they are all sending me email at work, too.)

Email allows you to communicate almost instantaneously with people all over the world. It can save you the cost of postage or long-distance phone calls, and it can also save you time.

For many people, email is free—their employers provide them with addresses. You can also get free email accounts through a number of Web sites, including Yahoo! and Hotmail. However, you'll have to have an Internet account through an Internet service provider (ISP). This usually costs around $20 per month. Many ISPs give you a free email account when you sign up for Internet access.

Later in this chapter, we'll go into more detail about what you'll need to be able to use email.

The aspect of the Internet that is growing fastest is the World Wide Web, but not everybody uses it.

Internet Versus WWW

When people talk about the Internet, most of the time they are referring to the World Wide Web. However, the two terms are not interchangeable. Call me a techno-geek if you want, but technically speaking, the Web is merely one aspect of the Internet. Other components that make up the Internet are File Transfer Protocol (FTP), Gopher, newsgroups, and so on.

The World Wide Web is the most popular of these components, without a doubt. Think of it this way: Everything that's on the Web is on the Internet, but not everything that's on the Internet is on the Web.

The Many Everyday Applications of Email

To better understand why email is so popular, let's take a look at some everyday uses for it.

There's no way to list all the possible applications of email. The following are just some common ones:

- *Saving money on long distance* When you use email to communicate with distant friends, relatives, and business contacts, you do lose a little of the personal touch. However, the cost savings makes up for this. You pay a flat monthly fee, usually very small. Sending long emails costs the same as sending short ones.
- *Smart business communications* All businesses can benefit from communicating with customers quickly and cost-effectively. Sending a quick thank-you or follow-up to a customer improves communication and service. But internal email also improves productivity. Sending a quick note down to Jim in Purchasing helps cut down on wasted time.
- *Sending files* You can attach files to your email messages, such as proposals for customers, reports for your boss, and pictures of the kids for Grandma. I use this a lot. For example, when I'm done writing this chapter, I'll email it to my editor. It'll be emailed around to several people before it finally finds its way into print.
- *Subscribing to mailing lists* You can subscribe to email mailing lists, each devoted to a particular topic. For example, if you're a stamp collector, you can subscribe to a philately (stamp collecting)

How Email Got My Brother Married

My older brother, Pete, has a story that is a perfect example of the many benefits of email. He's engaged to a woman he probably never would have gotten to know if not for email.

No, he didn't meet her in a chat room. They met the old-fashioned way—in a bar. But Pete lived in Minnesota, and they met in Iowa, where she lives. How many times have there been long-distance relationships like this that start over a weekend but then fizzle?

Through the magic of email, they were able to communicate inexpensively every single day between visits. The number of in-person visits grew over time, as did the commitment, with email keeping things rolling. Finally, they became engaged, and Pete's now an Iowa resident. (No, he didn't propose by email—although it would have been fitting.)

They both agree that without the cheap method of communication that email provided, they probably wouldn't have been able to keep the relationship going.

mailing list to receive email from other subscribers. Many people use these to increase their involvement in a hobby.

- *Joking around* One of the great things about email is that you can pass along the latest joke you heard without the boss getting on your case (unless s/he hears you laughing at your computer screen, of course). The jokes I receive have usually been passed along by many people before I get them because it's so easy to forward messages.

There are many other uses for email, of course. Once you're up and running with email, you'll probably find a few new uses of your own!

How Does Email Work?

Email is a lot like regular mail, only faster and cheaper. You can write a formal letter in email, or you can just drop a note with a quick thank-you or question. Regular mail can be delivered to anyone with an address; email can go to anyone with an email address.

The way email is delivered is much like regular mail, too. When you send a letter across the country, first it goes from your house to your local post office. Then it's sent to several other points before arriving at the post office closest to the recipient's home. That post office makes a final check to ensure that the address is valid. If the address is not valid, it is returned to you, the sender. If the address is valid, the message is delivered to your recipient's mailbox. There, the recipient picks it up and opens it.

With email, your message bounces from your computer to your ISP's computer and through several other relay points before it lands in your recipient's mail server. That computer checks the address to make sure it's valid. If not, the message is bounced back to you. If so, the mail server drops the message in the recipient's mailbox. Your recipient then opens it.

Because of the speed of email, some computer types now refer to regular mail as "snail mail." But what makes email so fast?

The best answer is that it is completely automated. When you click the Send button in Outlook, your email is launched immediately. Assuming all the computers between your ISP and your recipient's ISP are working properly, your message will be delivered almost instantaneously. Sometimes it takes a few minutes, and other times it can take a day or so, such as when either your mail server or your recipient's aren't working properly. Even then, though, it's faster than regular mail.

If you're on your company's network and you send an email to a coworker on the same network, there's a good chance it will be delivered instantaneously.

The key component of email, just like regular mail, is the address. One key difference between the two is this: If you make a minor mistake in the address on a regular letter, the post office will still *try* to deliver it, and often it will find the right home. However, if any part of an email address is incorrect—even capitalization in some cases—the email won't be delivered. With email, you'll never get the benefit of the doubt from a letter carrier who's been on the route for years and knows the people by name.

Dot-com This, Dot-com That

Since those email addresses are so darn important, it's probably a good idea to learn a little bit about how they work—about what all this dot-com business means, anyway. The best way to look at it is probably to use the snail mail example again.

Your email address is just like your snail-mail address, starting out very specifically and becoming more general as you go. For example, a snail-mail letter sent to your home starts with your name, which is very specific. Then comes your street, which is a little more general. Then comes your city, which is very general. Then comes the state, which is extremely general. (For the sake of this example, let's forget the zip code.)

So it is with an email address. Mine is

`btemple@reditorial.com`

The `.com` part of the address is the most general, kind of like the city or state in which you live. When a message is sent by email, the computers will first route the message in reference to the `.com`, an extension that is specific to commercial entities in the United States. Next, they will attempt to route the message to the computer that hosts the `reditorial` domain name. Once it finds that computer, all that's left is to find the right mailbox in which to drop the message. It will find mine, `btemple`, and deposit the message there.

What's the . For?

One of the most common things that non-computer users poke fun at is the "dot" in the middle of email and Web site addresses. Everything's "dot-this" and "dot-that." But what are all these "dots" for?

It's simple, really. You can't have spaces in Internet addresses because a computer reads a space as marking the end of the address. So periods are used instead.

Thank goodness we don't have to do that in books, because otherwise `my.writing.would.look.like.this.`

In some large corporations, if you are sending a message to another employee of the company who has the same domain name you do, you might only have to type in your recipient's username for the address. Similarly, if you're a member of an online service like America Online and you're sending a message to another member of the same service, you need only use the username.

Some email addresses are very long, however. Whatever you do, make sure you get the address exactly correct, including any punctuation. Otherwise the message won't be delivered.

Getting Set Up with an Internet Service Provider (ISP)

If you're a corporate user who's using Outlook at the office in Corporate Workgroup mode, you probably won't need to get set up with an ISP. If not, read on.

An ISP is a company that gives its members access to the Internet for a monthly fee. It can be a small local company or a huge corporation. (For example, America Online is an ISP.) Typically, you pay a monthly fee in exchange for access to the Internet and an email account. Your provider should give you all the information you need to use Outlook as your email program.

If you already have Outlook installed and are now setting up your email connection, you'll need to establish an account within Outlook. To do that, open the Tools menu and select Accounts. Then follow the instructions for setting up an account, just as you did in Chapter 2, "How Do I Get This Thing Configured?"

The Least You Need to Know

- The email phenomenon is much more than a fad. Email has become a vital part of everyday life for millions of people around the world.
- Email can be used as an inexpensive, long-distance tool to quickly send brief messages, send documents, subscribe to mailing lists, and much, much more.
- Email works much like regular mail. It moves from your computer through a number of others before arriving at the address of the recipient.
- An email address must be exactly correct or the message will be returned.
- Internet service providers (ISPs) offer Internet access and email for a monthly fee.

Chapter 8

Basic Training for Emailers

In This Chapter

- The ins and outs of the Inbox
- Outlook's email folders
- Buttons, bells, and whistles
- Setting it up your way
- Inbox views
- Email etiquette

I know, I know, I know. You're really anxious to get emailing because you haven't chatted with your mother-in-law in a while, and with email, you can do it all the time. Just think of the fun. Every time you connect with your Internet service provider (ISP), there could be a message waiting for you from her… or maybe from your boss… or maybe even the IRS! (I happen to be one of those rare breeds who likes both his mother-in-law and his boss, and I've got nothing but the utmost respect for the IRS. But you get the point.)

However, there are still a few things we need to cover before we get to sending and receiving messages. First, you need to understand how Outlook handles email, what the various buttons and symbols mean, and the etiquette that goes with email (like never talking when your partner is in his backswing).

The Inbox Isn't Always First

There's a way to file incoming messages before they ever reach the Inbox. You can program Outlook to file all incoming messages from, say, your boss into a folder that is just for business messages. This will be covered in detail in Chapter 11, "Managing Much Mail."

We'll also talk a little about setting up Outlook's preferences so that email is handled the way you would like it to be. Finally, we'll look at the many different ways you can view the Outlook Inbox, to give you an idea of which one might best suit your needs.

Outlook's Inbox

It seems somehow ironic that a program called *Out*look would have an *In*box as one of its major features. The Inbox is the crux of the email portion of Outlook. It's where all of your incoming email messages and faxes are stored until you decide what to do with them.

The Inbox is so ingrained into the Outlook system that you can't swing a dead cat without hitting a button that leads you to it. (I would never say such a thing, of course, being the animal lover that I am.) As you use Outlook Today, there are usually two entry points for the Inbox onscreen at any given moment. You can click Inbox in the Messages menu within Outlook Today, or you can click the Inbox button on the Outlook Shortcuts bar.

Well, don't just sit there. Go ahead and click one of them to open your Inbox. It should look a little bit like the following figure.

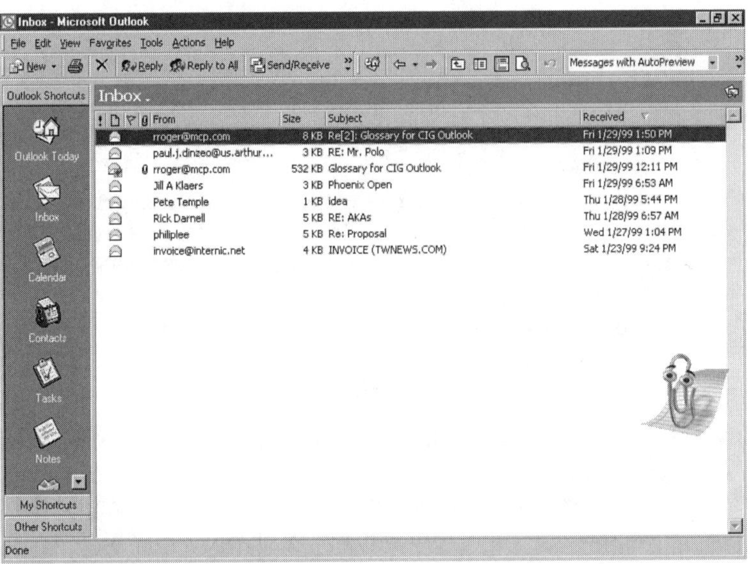

The Inbox is home to all your incoming mail messages and faxes.

The Inbox shown here is mine, and it contains a number of messages. These messages will sit here in the Inbox until I decide what to do with them—delete them, file them in a different folder, or whatever.

We'll talk more about views later in this chapter, but you should note that in the upper-right corner of the figure, the Inbox is being viewed in Messages with AutoPreview.

In this option, all unread messages are displayed with the first three lines of text visible until you open and read the entire message.

Now let's take a look at some of the other features of the Inbox window. They're discussed as they appear in the Inbox before you've customized the window. Later in this chapter, we'll talk about how you can change the Inbox to suit your needs.

Good Field, No Hit

You may remember from our discussion of views in Chapter 6, "Tool Time," that different fields can be included in the Inbox. At that time you added the Size field to the Inbox, and you can see that it's still there in the preceding figure.

Fielding

A *field* is a specific type of information that you want to appear in your view of a folder. For example, if you wanted to see the size of any incoming messages, you would want the Size field to appear in your view.

For now, let's ignore those funny little icons to the left of the Inbox header and instead focus on the main fields. We won't cover Size here, because you added that one already. Only the following three are defaulted into your Inbox—there are several others you can add:

- *From* This is the person who sent you the message, obviously. Typically you'll see the person's email address. However, if that email address can be found anywhere in your contact list, Outlook converts it to the name of that person.
- *Subject* Whenever you send an email to someone, you type a subject for the message. This field shows the subjects of the emails.
- *Received* This is the date and time the message was received by your mail server (the computer at your ISP that routes your mail to you). It is *not* the time you retrieved the message. This is important to remember because it gives you a better indication of when the sender actually sent the message.

One important thing to remember is that you can sort the information in the Inbox window by any of these fields. For example, if you want your messages to be sorted alphabetically by the sender's name, click on the From portion of the header. If you want to sort the messages by the time they were received, click on the Received portion of the header. Whichever field name has a little arrow inside of it is the field by which the folder is presently being sorted. Click that field again and the list (and the arrow) will invert.

Let's say you want to sort your Inbox by the time the messages were received, so you click on the Received portion of the header. If you see a down-pointing arrow, the newest message is at the top of the list. Click again and the arrow points up, meaning that the oldest message is now at the top of the list, as in the following figure.

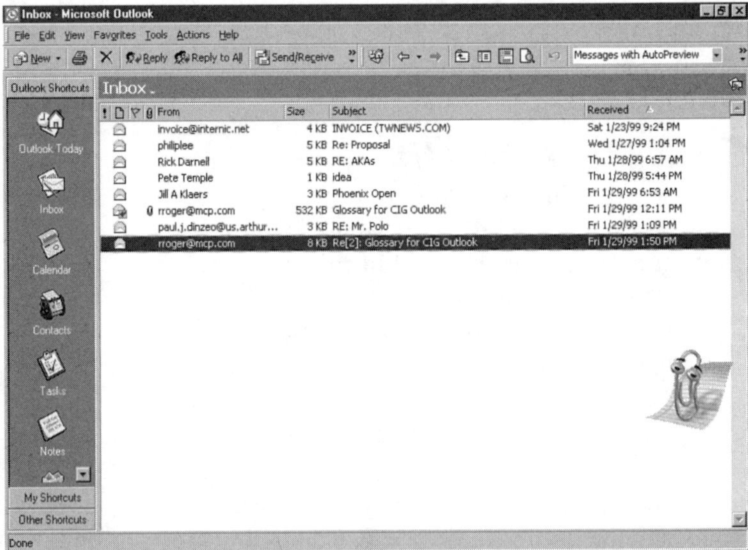

This Inbox is sorted by the time the messages are received, as you can see by the arrow next to Received.

Bells and Whistles (and Flags and Stuff)

To the left of all those large fields are four smaller ones that are also important—maybe even *more* important—to your Inbox. These are the little codes that help you prioritize the messages you've received:

- *Importance* The exclamation point to the far left of the header row indicates the importance of the message you've received. This can be set by the sender or by you, using the Rules Wizard. Similarly, when you send messages to others, you can determine their importance. It's a way of drawing the recipient's attention to the email. Unfortunately, I'm blessed with a number of friends who believe "high importance" means a particularly funny joke.

  If the sender has determined that the message is of high importance, an exclamation point appears in this field. If she sent the message with low importance, a down-arrow appears. If she sent it with normal importance, nothing appears in this field.

  As you can see from the following figure, one of the messages in my Inbox was sent with high importance and the rest were sent with normal importance.

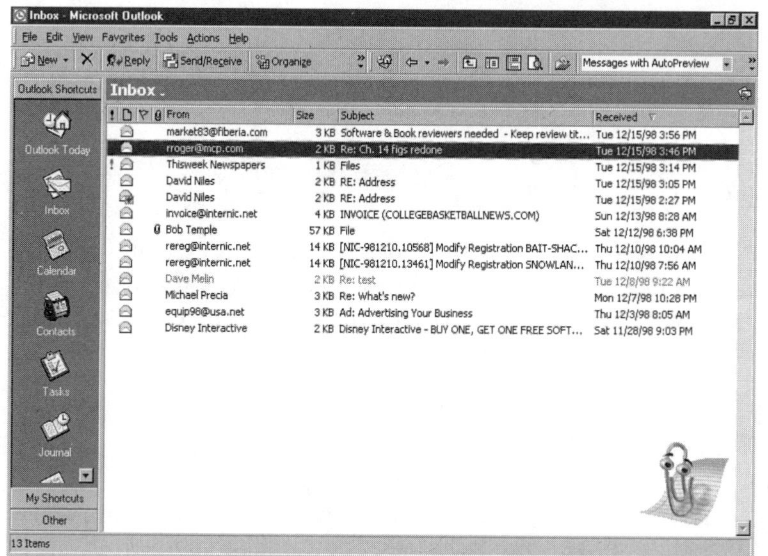

One message in this Inbox was sent with high importance.

- *Envelope icon* There will always be an icon in this field for each of your messages. This field reacts to how you handle a message, but you cannot set it. It simply tells you the status of your message. If it appears as a closed envelope, it's a message you haven't read. If it appears as an open envelope, it's a message you have read. If it appears as an open envelope with a left-pointing arrow on it, it's a message you've read and replied to. If it has a right-pointing arrow, it's a message you've forwarded.

  In the preceding figure there is one message I've replied to, and the rest are messages I've read.

- *Flagging* You can flag certain messages that you want to handle in a specific way, or as a means of categorizing them. For example, you can flag messages you want to forward or that you need to follow up.

  The most common use for this is the follow-up function. When you have a message open, there's a flag button in your toolbar. Click it to get a dialog box where you can determine the reason for the flag and a due date, if needed (see the following figure).

- *Attachments* The little paperclip icon indicates whether the email you received came with any attached documents. If a paperclip appears in this field, there's at least one document attached to the email. Attachments are covered in detail in Chapter 12, "Add-Ons: Attachments to Email."

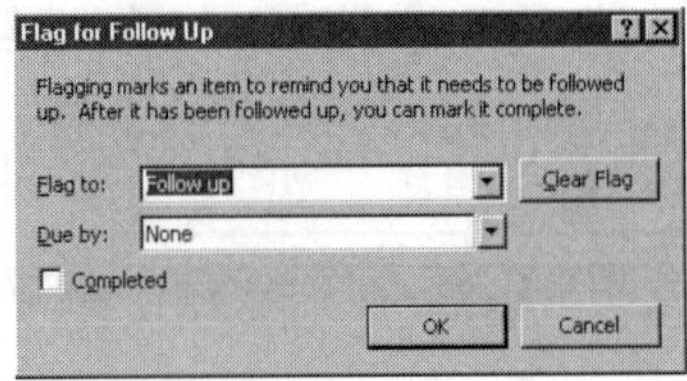

Flagging messages helps you prioritize them.

You can sort the list of messages in your Inbox by any of these fields as well. For example, if you sort them by flag, the messages you've flagged appear at the top of the list. Or if you sort the messages by importance, the high importance messages are at the top of the list.

Setting It Up Your Way

There are a variety of ways to customize the Inbox window to suit your tastes. As we've discussed, you can add fields to the Inbox window to display information at a glance that you might need to evaluate your messages. You can also change the view—the way the Inbox displays the messages themselves.

Now it's time to take a more in-depth look at these two features, plus a few more.

Adding/Removing Fields

In the previous section of this chapter, we covered the seven basic fields that are displayed in the Inbox by default. Any of these seven can be removed from the window, and there are many others that can be added.

To add or remove a field from the Inbox window, right-click on the field row of the Inbox, and then pick Customize Current View from the menu that appears. Click Fields, and you'll get a window like the one in the following figure.

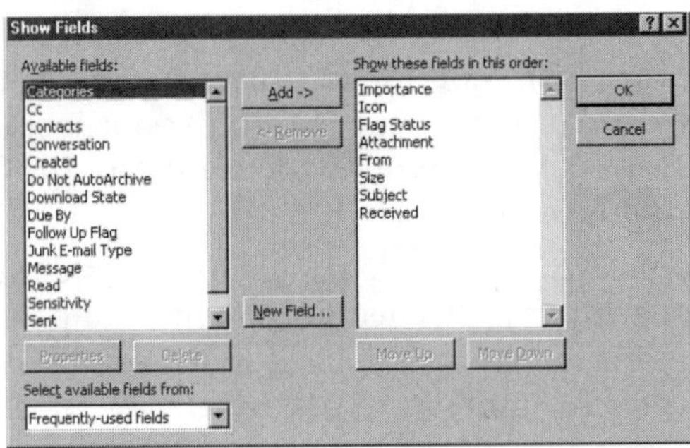

There are a myriad of fields that you can add to your Inbox.

On the left are the fields you can add to your Inbox. On the right are the fields you've already added to your Inbox. (The extra one in the figure is Size, which you added in a previous chapter.)

The list is fairly extensive, but there's more. In the bottom-left corner of the window is the Select available fields from: drop-down menu. It's currently set to Frequently-used Fields, but there are many, many more. Pull down that menu and select All Fields, and you'll have too many to bother counting.

To make matters worse (better?), you can even add your own field by clicking the New Field button. You can then name the field and determine the format and type of information that you want to display. To add a field, just highlight it and click the Add button. To remove one, highlight its name in the right panel and click Remove.

You should be careful about how many fields you add, because having a bunch of fields that you don't need will only muddy up your Inbox.

Changing the View

In this case, "view" refers to the manner in which the messages are displayed. There are several ways to view your messages, including some that actually sort out the messages for you a little bit.

There are two ways to change the view. You can use the Advanced toolbar or you can use the View menu. If you want the Advanced toolbar to be displayed, right-click on your current toolbar and then click Advanced. The Current View window is a drop-down window.

If you use the View menu, select Current View from the list and you'll get the same choices as those in the drop-down menu. Here's a look at all of the choices:

- *Messages* Displays the messages in list form in the top half of the window, as shown in the following figure. Whichever message you highlight is displayed in its entirety at the bottom of the window.

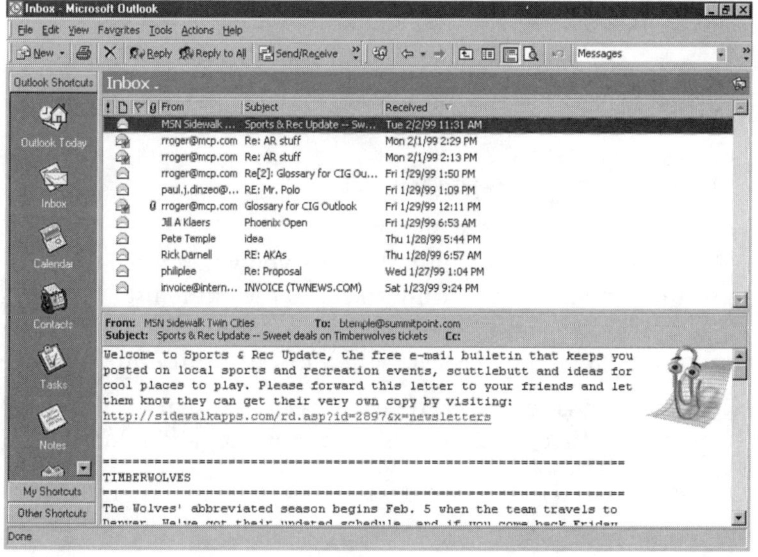

The Messages view displays one message at the bottom of the screen.

- *Messages with Auto Preview* The same list view as Messages except that when an unread message is in your list, you see the first few lines of it.
- *By Follow-up Flag* Sorted into groups based on the type of follow-up flag you've chosen.
- *Last Seven Days* Shows only those messages received in the last week.
- *Flagged for Next Seven Days* Shows only the messages you've flagged that must be followed up in the next week.
- *By Conversation Topic* Sometimes you'll get an email conversation going back and forth with someone. If several messages are part of the same conversation (they have the same subject), they're grouped together.
- *By Sender* Messages are grouped by the person who sent them, as in the following figure.

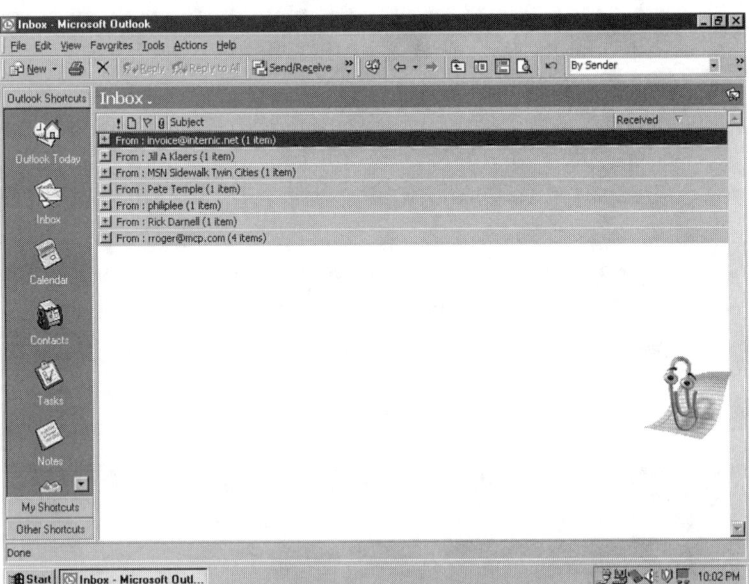

Messages viewed By Sender.

- *Unread Messages* Shows only messages you haven't read.
- *Sent To* Sorted by the name of the recipient.
- *Message Timeline* This one is just plain weird. It shows you when the messages were received on a sort of timeline, which only confuses the entire list.

Of these choices, the two most popular are Messages and Messages with Auto Preview.

In any of the views in which the list is sorted, each group has a plus sign to the left of it. Click it to reveal the contents of that group (just like viewing files and folders).

Other Settings

There are a number of other ways you can sort and view your messages, but we're concentrating on the basics for now.

When you display your list of messages as a table (such as with Messages or Messages with Auto Preview), you can adjust the width of the fields easily. Simply move your cursor to the line that divides any two fields and a left- and right-pointing arrow appears. Drag it to the left or right as you see fit. This will adjust the fields so that more or less of the information is displayed.

More settings can be found in the Customize Current View window. Right-click on any field name, click Customize Current View, and select Other Settings from the View Summary box. You'll get a window like the one in the following figure.

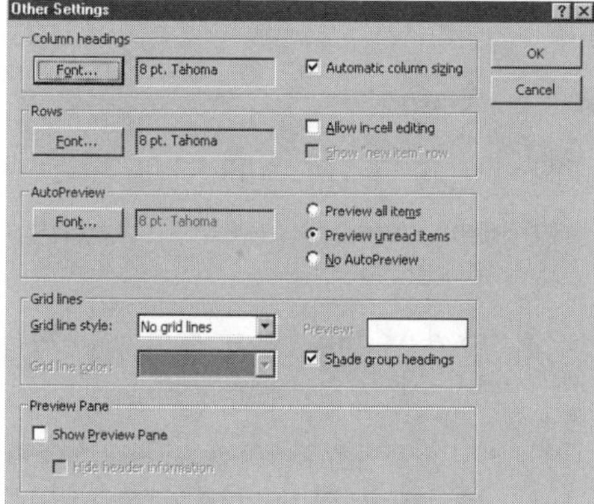

Set your preferences for typeface and more.

Here you can set your choices for typeface and size for your column headings, rows, and auto preview. You can also decide whether you want gridlines to be displayed, how to display them, and more.

Email Etiquette

Email is nothing like golf—there's no formal etiquette to follow and no written rules. Common sense dictates much of what happens by email, and sometimes trial and error takes precedence.

The basics of email etiquette should be the same as with all of our interpersonal communications—be polite, and treat others as you would like to be treated. Because email is a little impersonal, some people forget that they're sending their messages to another human being.

Here are a few specifics to remember:

- *Emoticons* These are the little punctuation marks that, when grouped together, make an expression like this—:) (a smiley face). They're cute but they're overused, and they should be used sparingly.
- *Abbreviations* Lots of people use abbreviations to shorten emails, but again, overuse is annoying. FYI, abbreviations should be curtailed ASAP.
- *Don't yell* Using all caps may add emphasis, but some people in the online world view it as YELLING. Be careful how you use them.
- *Don't spam* Spamming is sending the same email (such as a solicitation) to many, many people. Doing so can disable smaller servers and anger many, many people. Another type of spamming is sending the same mail over and over, such as jokes and virus hoaxes, to the same person.

The Least You Need to Know

- Outlook's Inbox displays the messages you've received by email and by fax.
- By default, the Inbox comes with seven fields displayed—Importance, Icon, Flag, Attachment, From, Subject, and Received.
- You can add more fields and/or remove existing fields from your Inbox at any time. You can even invent your own fields to be displayed.
- You can view the Inbox in a number of different ways, including several that categorize your messages for you. The two most common ways of viewing the Inbox are Messages and Messages with Auto Preview.

Chapter 9

Drop Me a Line

In This Chapter

- Composing that first email
- Formatting email and adding your signature
- Checking your spelling
- Using stationery
- Checking for mail
- Reading your mail
- Replying and forwarding
- Retrieving erroneous mailings

There are some technologically challenged people who pine for the old days, when the phrase "drop me a line" meant to call on the telephone. There's a new millennium on the horizon, people, and it's time to get with the program. Today, when someone tells you to drop them a line, they're as likely to mean "send me an email."

I'd say we've spent enough time goofing around with email. The stuff we've covered so far has been an important foundation for your future as an emailer, but it's time to get serious here and start pumping out the mail.

While we're at it, we'll work on receiving email, too. And we'll investigate a few of the doodads that Outlook offers for sprucing up your email.

Connections and Being Connected

You'll need an Internet connection to be able to send and receive email. However, you don't have to be connected to the Internet when you compose your email. You can write as many emails as you like while you're offline, and Outlook will send them the next time you're connected.

Composing That First Email

Nervous? With eight chapters of build-up behind you, that's understandable. But the time has finally come—let's send an email.

Before you can send an email to anyone, however, you need his or her email address. You can send a message to one person or one thousand, but you've got to have the email addresses to do it. If you're just getting started, you might not have anybody else's email addresses. But there's *one* person whose email address you know: yourself.

That's right. You're going to start by sending an email to yourself.

Starting in either Outlook Today or the Inbox window, click the New button in the upper-left corner of the screen. This will automatically open a new message window, as shown in the following figure.

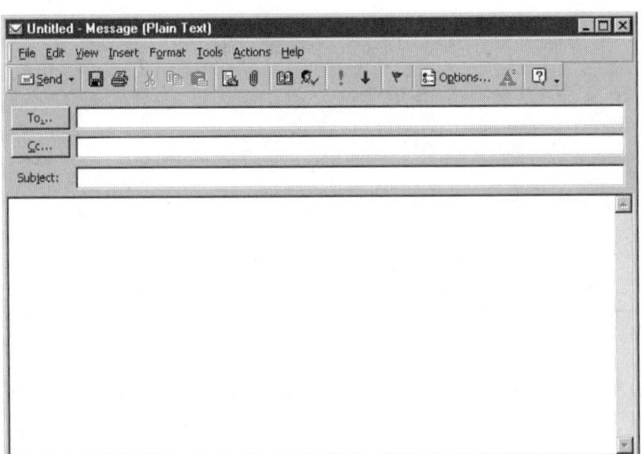

The new message window is where you'll compose your email.

First, you'll need to type in the address of the person to whom you're sending the email. Click in the space next to the To: button, and then type in your email address. Remember, email addresses can't have spaces in them, and it's extremely important to get the address exactly correct.

In the Subject: area, type a subject for your message, something like "Test." (You can move between fields by clicking them with your mouse or by using your Tab key.)

Next, go to the big window at the bottom. Here's where you type the text of your message. Try to be funny, because I know you appreciate a little humor now and again.

If you want to send a copy of this message to another person, type his or her address in the Cc: area. You can even send blind carbon copies to people (the other recipients won't know that the Bcc: person got the message). If the Bcc: field isn't visible in your new message window, choose Bcc: Field from the View menu.

Address Helper

Note that the To: and Cc: fields (and the Bcc: field, if visible) are buttons. Once you've built an address book, you can click this button to automatically enter the address of a recipient.

Even though we haven't covered the Address Book feature of Outlook yet, you might have entries in it. If you've previously used a different email program, your saved addresses from that program were probably brought into Outlook during installation. To check, click your To: button. If you want to send the message to someone on your list, highlight their entry in your list and click the appropriate button (either To:, Cc:, or Bcc:). Then click OK and their name will appear in the field you selected for them.

As you can see from the following figure, I've added myself as a Cc: recipient of the message by choosing my entry in the Address Book.

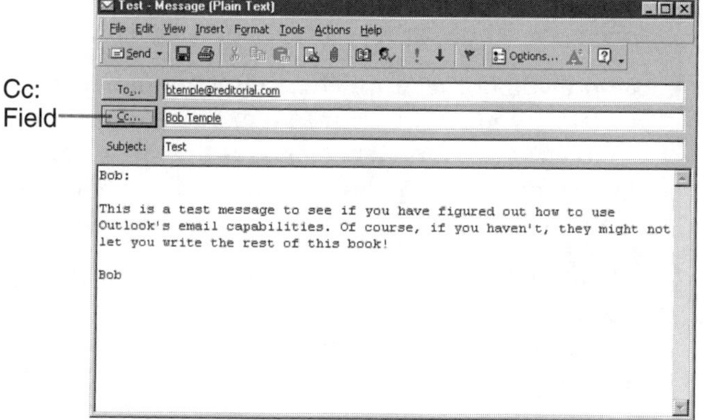

Entries copied from your address book appear as names, not email addresses.

Also note that in the Cc: field it shows my name, not my email address. That's because you copied it from the Address Book. It's a way of making it easier to understand. The message will still be sent to my email address, but showing my name will help you when you refer to the message later. When you look in your list of sent messages, you'll see the names of the people you sent the messages to, not their email addresses. That way, you can tell at a glance to whom the messages went.

Your message is ready to go. If you don't want to do any special formatting or other stuff with this message, you can click the Send button now. The message won't actually be sent over the Internet yet, but it will be placed in your Outbox. To complete the sending process, click the Send/Receive button on your Standard toolbar. If you're connected to the Internet, the message will be sent immediately. If not, Outlook will dial up your Internet service provider and send the message on its way.

Are They as Advanced as You Are?

By using Outlook 2000, you're using one of the most advanced, full-featured email clients available. Unfortunately, that can cause problems when you attempt to communicate with someone who has an email client that's not so advanced. In some email clients, formatted messages appear garbled, with odd characters showing up. Really antique email programs can't even handle some characters, like quotation marks. For the most part, however, a formatted message sent to someone with an older email client will still be legible. They just won't see the benefits of all the formatting you applied.

Formatting and Other Options

If you've spent any time working with Word or another word processing program (who hasn't?), you've probably formatted text. Even changing a type's font or size is considered formatting, so it can be pretty basic. You can apply basic formatting or more advanced formatting to your messages if you're so inclined. You can also flag your messages or rate their importance before sending them.

There are a number of reasons why you might want to apply a little formatting to your text: to add emphasis, to make a point more clear, or even to make the whole thing a little more attractive.

Before you bother applying a bunch of fancy formatting, you might want to make sure that your recipient can even view messages that are formatted. Even today, many people use text-only email programs.

In Outlook 2000, you can send messages as plain text, HTML, or Rich Text Format (RTF). You make this choice in the Format menu of your new message window.

Keeping It Plain

If you're a normal, average, peanut-butter-and-jelly kind of person, you should use plain text for sending messages.

Actually, it's a good idea to leave your default setting at plain text (also referred to as text-only) in some programs and only format messages to people who you know can view all of the options you've added.

All email programs can view any message you send as plain text.

The Rich Get Richer

Most people who want to format messages bypass RTF and go straight to HTML, because HTML offers all the options of RTF plus a few more.

RTF allows you to format messages with things like bold type, italics, different fonts and font sizes, and so on. This is pretty easy to do once you've opened the Formatting toolbar.

First, with the message open on your screen, click Rich Text from the Format menu. The appearance of the message should change (the font should be different; usually Arial). To view the Formatting toolbar, open the View menu, select Toolbars, and then click the Formatting button.

You can make formatting changes in one of two ways: by highlighting text you want to format and clicking the appropriate formatting button or by clicking the formatting button before you enter the text you want to format.

My email to myself has already been typed, and I wanted to put the word "Outlook" in boldface. So I highlighted the word and clicked the Bold button. Then, I changed the type to a much larger size, and added a bulleted list. The result is the email you see in the following figure.

HTML, Baby

HTML stands for *Hypertext Markup Language,* the language of the Web. You can memorize that if you really want to be considered a geek. Otherwise, let's just move on.

When you format your messages with HTML, you can do all of the things you can in RTF and more. Again, you have to be certain that your recipient can view your HTML coding—anyone else you know who's using Outlook 2000 certainly can.

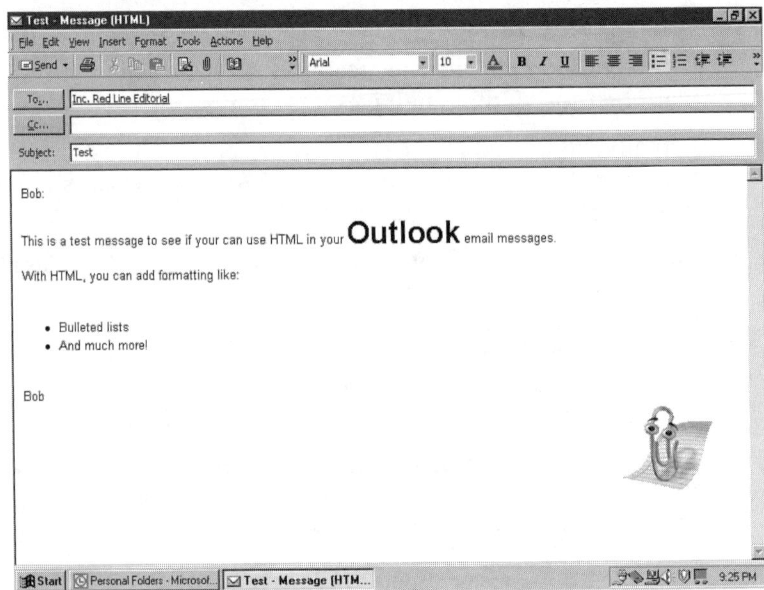

Adding formatting is easy with RTF and the Formatting toolbar.

There are many nice features of HTML formatting, but here are the two most common:

- *Hyperlinks* When you send an email in HTML and include a Web site address or an email address, it automatically becomes a hyperlink. So, if you're sending a friend the address of a Web site he should check out, he can just click on that address and his Web browser will automatically find the site for him. If you send an email address, the recipient can click on it and his email program will open a new message window with that email address already in the To: window.
- *Pictures* With the price of scanners and digital cameras falling virtually by the day, attaching photographs to email is becoming more commonplace. If I had a dollar for every friend who's emailed a picture of their new baby to Grandma and Grandpa, I'd have, well, two dollars. But you get the picture (pardon the pun).

Let's send an HTML email. First, send that other one to yourself (by pressing the Send button) if you haven't already. Then click the New button again, enter an email address and subject (send it to yourself again), and then choose HTML from the Format window.

If you want to change the font and type size, go ahead. Then type yourself a message that includes a Web site address or email address. Once you've typed the address, Outlook automatically turns it into a link and underlines it for you, as you see in the following figure.

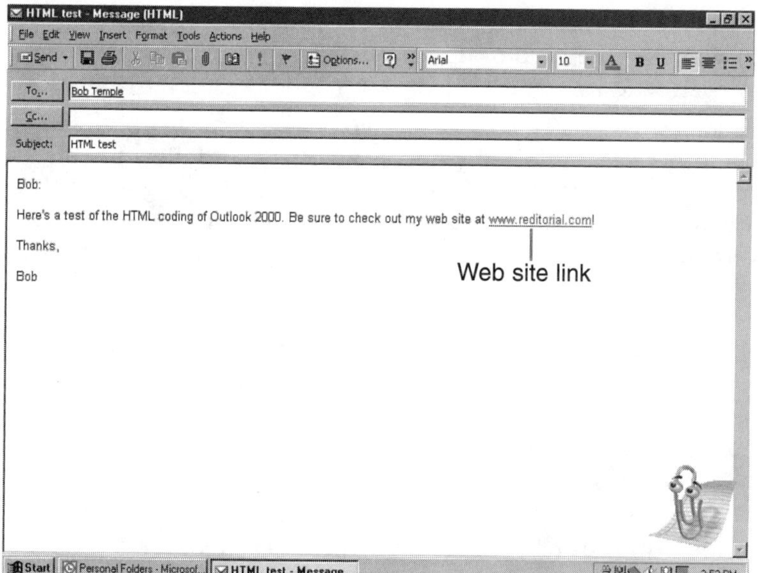

In HTML, Web site addresses and email addresses appear as hyperlinks.

Signing Off

Many people like to add special signatures to their emails. This is particularly useful if you want to put your name, title, company, Web site address, or other information at the end of all your business emails, but you don't want to have to type it every time.

In the Inbox, open the Tools menu, select Options, and then click the Mail Format tab. Click on Signature Picker, and then click New. You'll be asked to create a name for your signature. Then click OK and enter the text for your signature.

Then, when you've typed your email, click the Signature button in the message window and it will drop your signature in automatically!

Other Options

The Standard toolbar contains a few other ways to adjust your email before you send it. Here's a quick look at those features:

- *Importance: High* That red exclamation mark in your toolbar codes your message as being of high importance. Some people (my friends, for example) use this as a source of humor, sending jokes and then disguising them as being important. I prefer that people use this button a little more judiciously.

- *Importance: Low* The blue, down-pointing arrow codes the message as being of low importance. (I don't see the need of this, personally. If something is that unimportant, why even send it?)
- *Flag* You can flag a message you've already received, or you can flag a message you're sending to another person. When you flag a message for follow-up, it's to remind yourself (or the recipient) that you need to check on the progress of this message at a later date. For example, if you send a message asking for a project to be done by a certain time, the flag will remind the recipient to check on the project's progress later.

These are some of the little extras that Outlook adds to help draw attention to particular messages. It's yet another way Outlook helps you stay organized.

Checking Your Spelling

It's always a good idea to check your spelling before you send an email, especially if it's business-related. Misspelled words reflect poorly on you and can even alter a client's opinion of your company.

If that HTML-formatted message you created is still open on your screen (and it should be, because you haven't sent it), you can easily check the spelling. From the Tools menu, click Spelling. Outlook will immediately being checking your message. When it finds a problem, it will pop open a window like the one in the following figure.

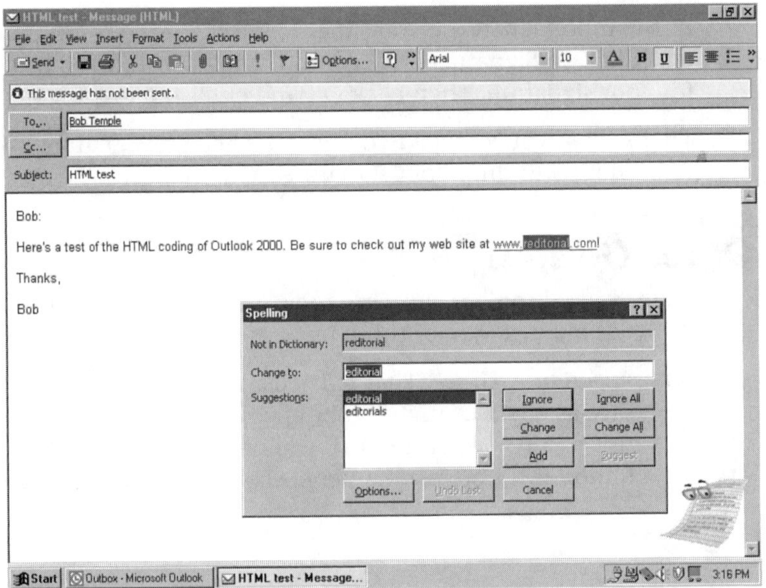

The spell checker in Outlook even checks the spelling in Web addresses.

You can set Outlook to always check your spelling before sending by opening the Tools menu, selecting Options, then clicking the Spelling tab. Then, check the Always Check Spelling Before Sending box, and Outlook will check all outgoing messages before they get sent.

Sometimes, what the spell checker reports as an error isn't really an error at all, such as in this example. As you can see, it wants to change my domain name, "reditorial," to "editorial" because "reditorial" isn't a word. It is my domain, however, so I don't want to change it. All I have to do is click the Ignore button. If I wanted it to be changed, I would have clicked Change.

If you know that the same word or problem will appear again in that email, you should click Ignore All or Change All. The spell checker will automatically change all references.

Once you've gone through the entire document, your Office Assistant lets you know that the spell checking is complete.

Personalizing with Stationery

Stationery, in terms of email, is basically a background for your message. You can create your own stationery to send messages on, use one of Outlook's prepared stationery choices, use a picture from your hard drive, or simply choose a color for the background.

You can add a picture or color background at any time, including immediately before you send the message. To do this, choose Background from the Format menu, and then select either Picture or Color, whichever is appropriate. If you select Color, Outlook offers you a choice of colors. Just click the one you like best. If you select Picture, you'll have to find the picture on your hard drive by its filename.

If you use one of Outlook's preinstalled stationery options, you'll have to do it before you create the email. From the Inbox, go to the Actions menu and select New Mail Message Using. Then select the More Stationery button and pick the one you like best. Some of these are used for special occasions, like Baby News, but others are just backgrounds from which you can choose.

For example, if you're inviting someone to a party, select Balloon Party Invitation. Your new message window will look like the following figure, and you can enter the specifics for the party in the appropriate areas.

You can also create your own stationery, but that topic is too broad to be covered in a book of this size. To get started, open the Tools menu, click Options, and then pick the Mail Format tab.

In the Send in this message format box, click HTML. Click Stationery Picker, and then click New.

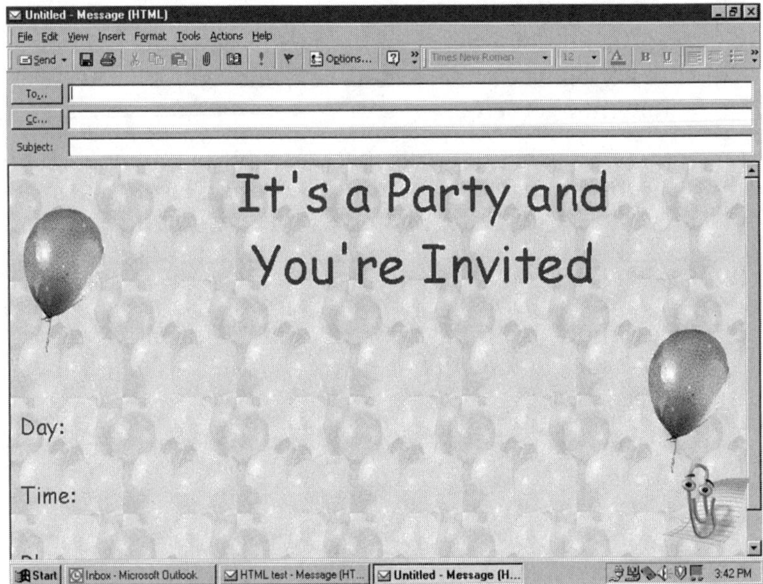

Using stationery allows you to make an email more special.

You're then asked to name your stationery. You can start with blank stationery or customize one of the existing ones. Play with it—it's fun! However, when you selected HTML from the Mail Format tab, that changed the default setting for your email. You should probably go back to the Mail Format tab when you're done creating email and change that default setting back to Plain Text. You'll still be able to access your stationery when you want it (just as we did with the Balloon Party Invitation), but you won't want to send all of your messages in HTML format.

To Send and Receive

All of these messages you've created were moved into the Outbox when you clicked the Send button. In other words, they haven't been *sent* yet.

To send them, you must click the Send/Receive button. Outlook dials your ISP and connects to the Internet. It then sends your outgoing messages and checks for any incoming messages.

Even if you were connected to the Internet when you created the message, it wasn't sent when you clicked Send. You can change that very easily, however. From the Tools menu, select Options. Click the Mail Delivery tab. As you can see in the following figure, there are two boxes under Mail Account Options.

If you check the box called Send messages immediately when connected, your messages will be automatically sent when you click the Send button, as long as you're connected. In the next box, you can determine how often Outlook checks for mail while you're connected. Every 10 or 15 minutes is good. Some combinations of settings allow Outlook to dial out periodically on its own, which you may not like if you are charged by the hour for Internet time.

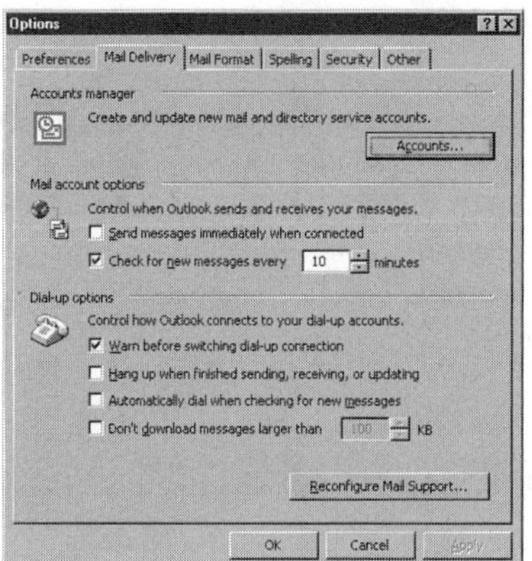

Here you can set options for how and when messages are sent and received.

What's in the Mail?

If Outlook isn't automatically checking your mail at set intervals or if you aren't connected, you can check your mail by clicking the Send/Receive button.

The appearance of your incoming email depends on the view you selected (see Chapter 8, "Basic Training for Emailers"). I view my email with AutoPreview, so my new messages show up with the summary line and three lines of the actual message, as in the following figure.

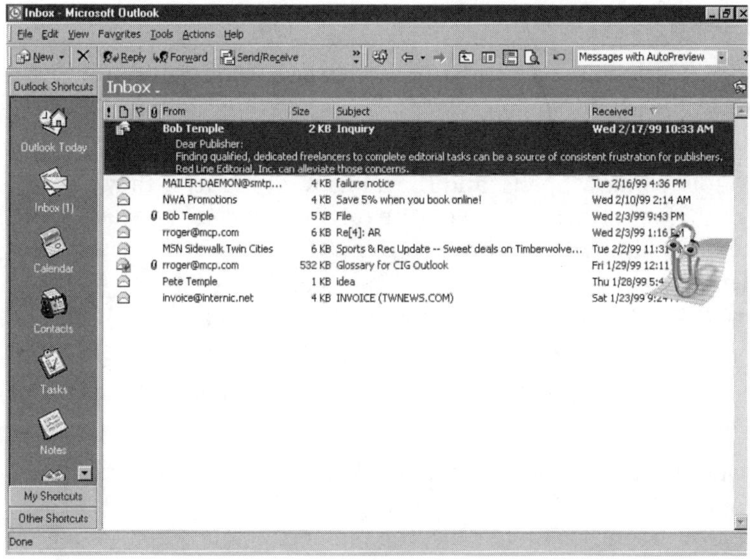

The first three lines of an incoming message appear when you view messages with AutoPreview.

If you use AutoPreview, double-click the message to see the entire message.

If you view your list as Messages, you get the list and the entirety of whichever message is highlighted in the preview pane, as shown in the following figure.

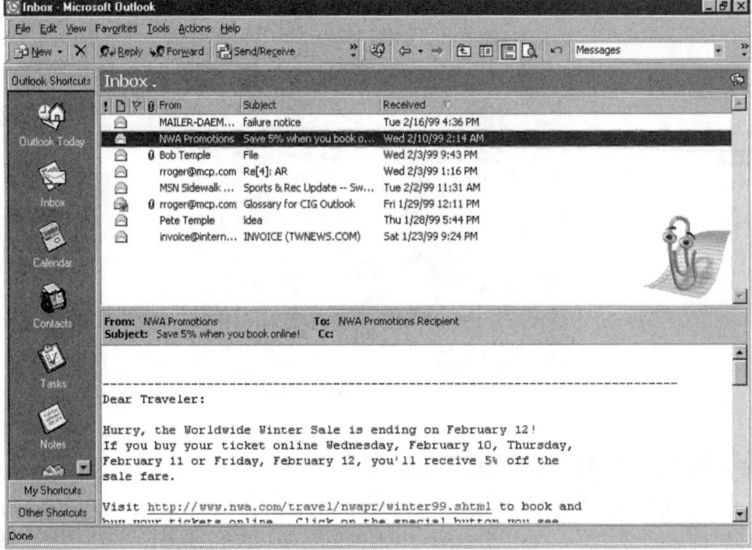

Viewing messages with the Messages view shows the entire message at the bottom of the screen in the preview pane.

If you haven't read a message yet, it appears as bold in your list and the envelope icon is closed. Once you've read it, the envelope icon opens and the message returns to normal font in the list.

Replying and Forwarding

Like most email programs, Outlook makes replying to messages and forwarding them very easy. You can reply to the sender of a message either by highlighting it in the Inbox list and clicking Reply, or by opening the message and clicking Reply.

After the new message reply window opens, and the address (or name, if they appear in your address book) of the person who sent you the original message appears in the To: box. The text of the original message appears in the message window, beneath an Original Message header. This is sent back to remind the recipient what you're responding to. However, if you want to delete this text, you can simply select it and press the Delete key.

Your cursor is ready for you at the top-left corner of the message window. Simply type your reply and click Send.

To forward a message, you must have the original email open (double-click it from the list if you need to open it) or highlighted in the list. Then click the Forward button. A new message window opens that looks like the one in the following figure.

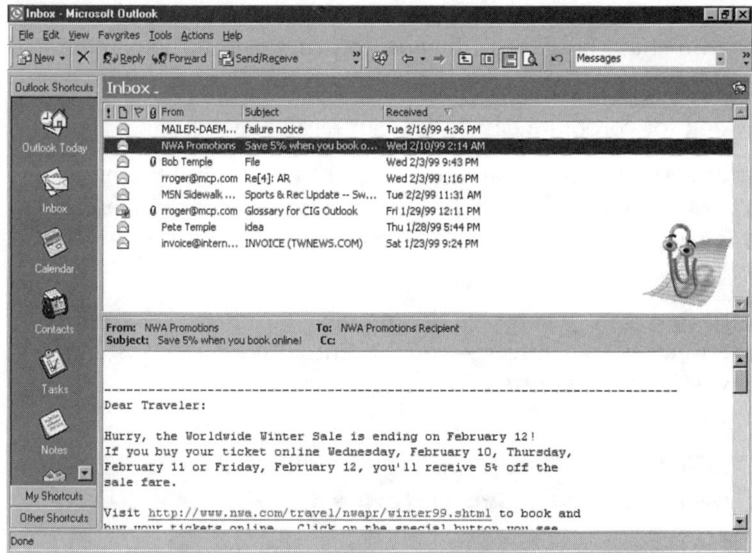

When you forward a message, you can type an introduction above the original message.

Your cursor pops into the To: field so you can quickly type the email address of the recipient.

Again, the text of the original message appears under the Original Message header. You can type an introduction to the email above this text. You might want to do this so the person to whom you're forwarding the message will understand why you're sending it to them.

When you're done, click Send.

Oops! An Error. What Now?

If you've configured Outlook for corporate email, there's an additional trick you can perform—retrieving email you've sent. If you're just a regular Joe using the Internet Only email, however, you can't.

For example, let's say you've sent an email to a co-worker in which you ripped your boss to pieces. Later, when you check your Sent Items menu, you realize that you accidentally put your boss' name in the To: field instead of your co-worker's name.

Is It Too Late?

If that naughty email has already been opened or moved to another folder, you can't recall it. You can only bring it back if it's still in the folder to which it was originally sent.

Suddenly, your entire future depends on getting rid of that message. If you really want to risk your career, you could break into the boss' office, turn on the computer, open the email, and delete it.

Or, if you've set up Outlook for corporate email, you can recall the message.

To recall an email, open the My Shortcuts bar and click Sent Items. Find the message you want to recall and double-click it to open it. In the Tools menu of the message window, click Recall This Message. Then click the Delete Unread Copies of This Message button and click OK.

Finally, click File and then Save so you can save the message with the recall option. Then close the message and cross your fingers—you'll eventually get a message in your Inbox telling you whether your efforts were successful.

The Least You Need to Know

- Composing an email can be extremely easy if you merely type the address of the recipient, a subject, and the message.
- You can add special formatting to an email and even send it in HTML format. You can also use stationery for your message.
- You can add a signature to your emails.
- Use the Send/Receive button to transmit and retrieve your email. You can set up Outlook to retrieve email at specific intervals while you're connected.
- Replying to and forwarding email is available when the message is open.

Chapter 10

Here's Looking Up Your Old Address

In This Chapter

- Why address books are useful
- Making address book entries
- Importing an address book
- Using your address book to send email
- What are distribution lists?
- Why use a distribution list?
- Creating a personal distribution list
- Working with distribution lists

In the last chapter, you learned how to send and receive email. So we're done, right? Heck no. Don't be silly. There's a lot more to learn about email than just how to send and receive it.

In the last chapter, we covered the basics. Now it's time to get a little bit fancier in preparing your mail. You might even find that it's more productive to handle your outgoing mail in the manner we'll cover in this chapter.

What's This About Contacts?

Suddenly the word "contacts" has sneaked into this chapter about address books. Don't worry about it. Contacts are covered in detail in Part 3,"Let's Get Down to Business: Managing Contacts." Technically speaking, there really isn't a difference between a contact and someone listed in your address book. Outlook uses its Contacts list as an address book for email purposes. So, when you're accessing your list of email addresses, you're really working with your Contacts list.

Why Use Address Books?

It's time to send out the annual Christmas cards. That means taking the time to put the addresses on hundreds of envelopes. Do you write out all the addresses from memory? I doubt it, unless you have either a *really* good memory or a *really* short list of friends and relatives.

Instead, you probably grab the family address book. Or maybe in recent years you've entered your Christmas list into a computer program that can turn it into address labels you can stick on the envelopes. Either way, you've organized your address book so that you can quickly and easily find and use the addresses of people you need to get in touch with—even if it's only once a year.

Outlook's address book, found in the Contacts folder, serves the same purpose. It can help you recall the email addresses you need to send messages.

If you think trying to remember people's street addresses or even telephone numbers is difficult, try remembering a few dozen email addresses. All those user names, all those domains—the only good part is that a lot of them end in `.com`.

With Outlook, you don't have to remember any of them. If you're careful about entering them into your address book, you'll be able to live the rest of your life completely oblivious to the email addresses of your friends, relatives, co-workers, and business associates.

Making Address Book Entries

If you're going to use an address book to send email, you're going to need some entries in your Outlook address book.

There are many ways to enter names and email addresses into the address book. You can pick the one that best suits your needs, but they all come in handy, and you'll probably use all of them at various times.

But this chapter is about using address books for email purposes. Let's take a look at a couple of the best ways to enter a name and address into your address book.

It's New (and Improved?)

Outlook's New button is truly a wonderful thing. It's like a good dog. It's reliable—it shows up on every screen, whether you're working in the Inbox, Contacts, the Journal, or even Outlook Today. It might have a different icon on it, but it's there. And it's loyal—it offers the same choices no matter which folder you're working in.

The New button (usually the first button on the left on your Standard toolbar) works two ways. Click the main part of it and you get a New item from whichever folder you're working in. But if you click the down arrow, you get the aforementioned menu that doesn't change. From that menu, select Contact to bring up a Contact dialog box as shown in the following figure.

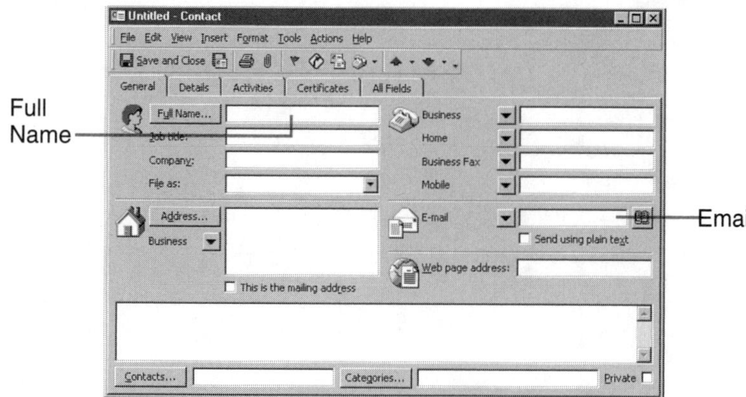

Enter a new contact and it will show up in your address book.

There are five tabs to choose from, with many different things you can enter. You can spend a lot of time creating a new contact, which is why three chapters are devoted to contacts later in this book.

But for now, you're just trying to send email. So stay on the General tab and type in the full name of the person you're adding to your address book. Then click in the Email box and type the person's email address. Then click the Save and Close button and get out of there as fast as you can. We'll revisit it later.

Now the contact is entered, and it will appear in your address book the next time you use it.

Email Interruptus

In the last chapter, you were working on sending email. Maybe when the session was over, you spent a little time practicing by sending emails out to a couple of friends. As you were typing in a friend's email address, you might have had this thought: "I'm gonna be emailing this person a lot now that I have Outlook. How can I save this email address?"

Perhaps the easiest way to make an entry into your address book is to do it right from the email window. To demonstrate, open up the email window as you did in the last chapter. Next, type the person's email address into the To: box in the email window, and then either hit the Tab key or click in any of the other windows. The email address should now be underlined, like a hyperlink.

Once it's underlined, it's ready to be added to your list. Just right-click on the address and a little menu pops up, as in the figure below.

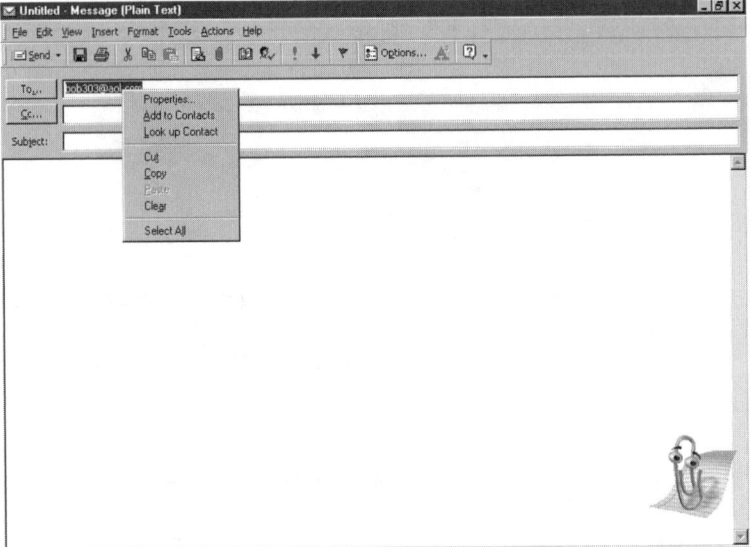

You can add an address while preparing to send an email.

Filter? Is It Dirty?

Lots of computer programs use *filters,* and the term can have very different meanings. For example, a database program will allow you to filter the database to display only the records that meet certain criteria.

In this case, however, a filter allows information from a different program to be reformatted for Outlook. All the naughty, dirty particles are removed from your old address book, leaving only the vital information intact.

Select Add to Contacts. This brings up that now-familiar Contacts screen, except the email address is already in the email window. Usually, Outlook puts whatever is before the @ symbol into the Name field, so you'll probably want to change that. Add or change any other information you want to, and then you're ready to Save and Close.

Importing an Address Book

Many people use other personal information managers on their computers and end up switching to Outlook. If that's the case with you, you've probably taken the time to enter all these names and email addresses into another program. You'd probably like to avoid having to do it again.

The Outlook programmers are so darn smart (and nice) that they've prepared a way for you to do just that. Outlook offers a number of different filters that help you convert your old address book into an Outlook one.

Outlook offers an Import/Export Wizard that will walk you through this entire process. To start it, open the File menu and click Import and Export. You'll get a dialog box like the one in the following figure.

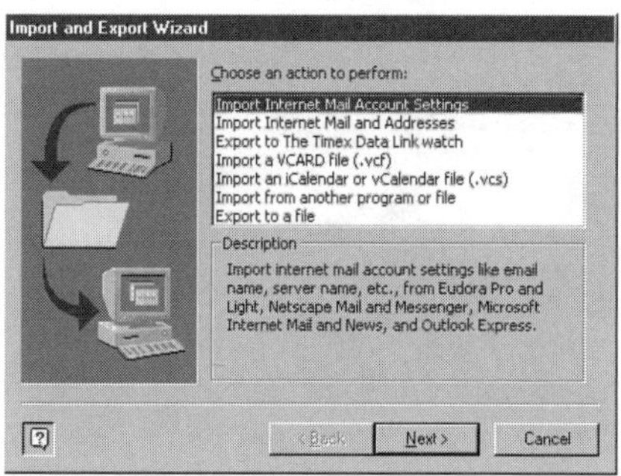

To import addresses from another program, use the Import and Export Wizard.

You'll see a list of options in the Import and Export Wizard dialog box. If the task you're trying to perform isn't listed, click Import from another program or file, and then click Next. You get a long list of programs that are compatible with Outlook. If your old program isn't listed here, you might be out of luck. If it is, highlight it, click Next, and follow the rest of the steps through the wizard.

You will have to know the name of the file from which you are importing, and its location, in order to complete the wizard. When the wizard asks you to select the folder into which you want to place the information, select the Contacts folder.

Take a Letter, Maria

Now comes the easy part. You've got some names listed in your address book, and you'd like to send an email to one of them.

This is simple. Open an email window (a task that should be becoming second nature to you by now). Instead of entering an email address into the To: field, click the To: button. Your address book opens, as seen in the following figure.

Highlight any name on the list, click the To button, and the name moves over to the right. If you'd like to send the message to several people, click their names as well and then click the To button. You can also add names to the Cc and Bcc areas the same way. Heck, why not send the message to everybody you know?

Where's the Address?

When you select a name from your address book to send an email, you'll note that the person's name, not their email address, appears in the To: field in the email window. Don't worry. As long as that name is underlined, it's hyperlinked to that person's email address and the message will be delivered as you want it to be.

Pick a name from your address book and you're ready to go.

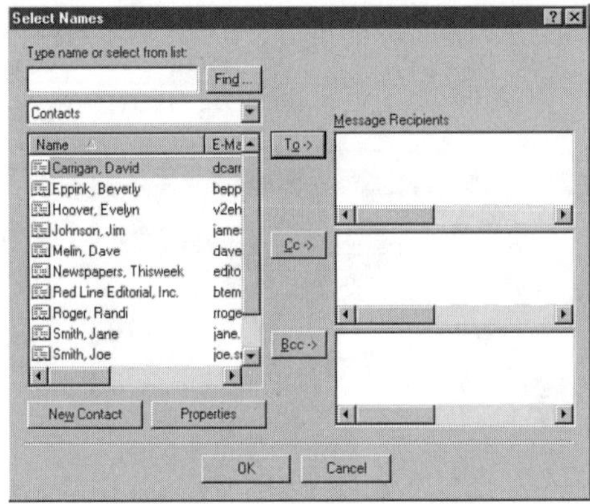

When you're finally done, click the OK button to return to the email window.

Here's my favorite part of this whole address book thing: Once someone is entered in your address book, you don't even have to look up his name in the list again if you don't want to.

For example, let's say I want to send an email to my brother, Pete, who I know is listed in my address book. I can open an email window, type his name (not his email address) in the To: field, and Outlook will find his name in the address book and link it to his email address. I know it's worked when his name is automatically underlined. If the name isn't underlined, you'll have to go into the address book to select the name.

You can even type part of a name, and Outlook will try to figure out who you intended as a recipient. If there is more than one name that matches your partial entry, Outlook will prompt you to make a choice.

Why Send When You Can *Distribute?*

You've got a few names in your address book. That's great. Over time, however, that list is going to grow. If you're anything like me, it'll grow until it's out of control. You'll need to rein it in a little bit.

What do you do when there's a group of people that you email or fax all the time? Maybe you've got a group of co-workers in your department who are all involved in the same project. Maybe you're on the board of the local youth athletic association. Maybe you're serving on a committee at church. Or maybe you're running a fantasy football league. Wouldn't it be nice if you could send off a quick email to everybody in your group without having to search out their addresses from your address book every time?

Of course it would. And Outlook offers a feature called *distribution lists* that is exactly for that purpose. Why not use it?

What Is a Distribution List?

A distribution list is nothing more than a collection of contacts. It simply organizes a group of your contacts into a single entry in your address book. When you need to contact them all, you can use the distribution list to put all of their names (although you won't see them) into your To: field with one click.

Be Careful!

Using distribution lists is easy, once you get them set up. But it's important that you remember who you've included in each list. It's a good idea to check the names on the list quickly before you actually send an email to all of them.

For example, let's say you've got a distribution list made up of your neighbors. When you're planning a surprise party for Shirley next door, you probably don't want to send an email to that distribution list because Shirley will get it. However, you can temporarily remove people from a list if you need to.

Creating a Distribution List

Making a distribution list is very simple. Just open that wonderful New menu and click Distribution List. You'll get a window that looks like the one in the following figure.

First, type a name for the distribution list. I've decided to create a list made up of my clients in the Midwest, so I'm calling it Midwest Clients. Whenever I need to send an email to all of my clients in the Midwest, I can do it easily. Once you've named your distribution list, click the Select Members button.

You'll see a window like the one in the next figure. Your contact list is in the window on the left. To enter names into your distribution list, all you need to do is highlight the name(s) and click the Add button.

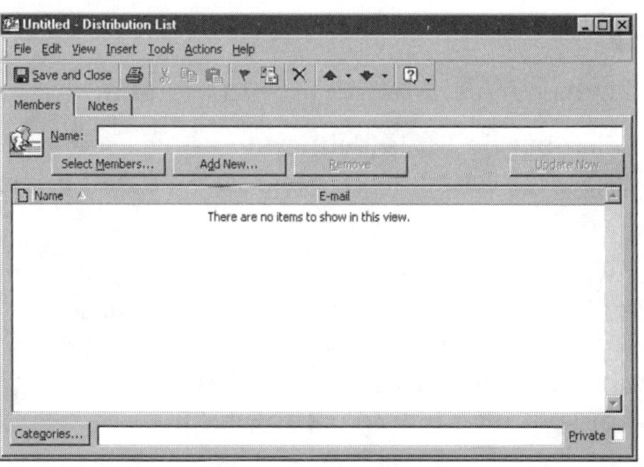

Use this screen to create a distribution list.

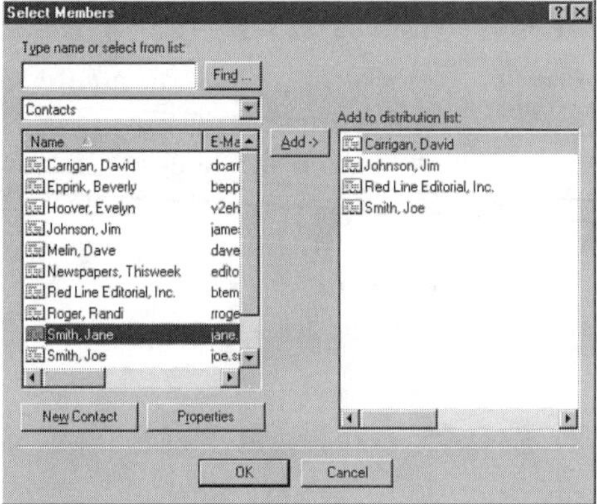

Add names to your distribution list in this window.

When you've made all the entries you need to make in this list, click the OK button and your list is ready to go. You're returned to the Distribution List screen, where you see the names and email addresses of the people you've added.

You can use the Notes tab to type any notes you might want to make about this particular distribution list. When you're done, click the Save and Close button.

Now you can go back in and create as many lists as you want, and your contacts can appear in as many different lists as you like. For example, there might be one person on your contact list who is a friend, a member of your fantasy football league, and a member of your group at work. You might put that person's name into several different groups.

Also note that no matter how many times you add someone's name to a distribution list, they also stay listed individually in your address book. That's because there will probably also be times when you want to send an email to just that one person.

Hey Guys! Guess What?

You've got one list set up, and maybe more. Now it's time to learn how to use them!

This part's really easy. Using a distribution list is identical to using a single entry in your address book. The only difference is that you're sending the email to more than one person.

To begin, open a new message window as you've done many times before. Instead of entering an address into the To: field, click the To: button. Again, you see your address book. Your distribution list should now show up as a boldfaced entry. Highlight it, click the To button, and then click OK. This takes you back to your new message window, and the title of your distribution list appears in the To: field.

If you want to check the names in the distribution list before you send the message, click on the name of the list in the To: field to open a window like the one in the following figure.

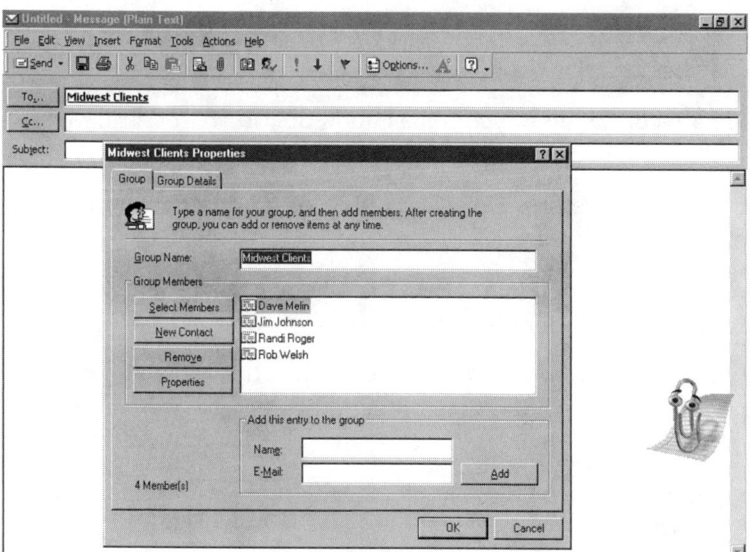

Edit your distribution list here.

At this point, you can add or remove any names you like. To remove a name from the distribution list, highlight it in the list and click Remove. You can add a name by typing the person's name and email address into the fields at the bottom and clicking Add.

No Secrets Here

Just because your To: field has the name of the distribution list and not the names of the individual members, this doesn't mean the recipients of your message won't know who else got it. When they receive the message, they get the full list of recipient's names, not the name of your list. If you don't want them to see all the names, put the distribution list into the Bcc: field, and each recipient will see only his own name.

The Least You Need to Know

- Address books are a record of all of your email addresses, so you don't have to remember them all.
- Address books make sending emails easier because you can enter a contact's address into the To: field with the click of a mouse.
- If you've created an address book in a different program, you can probably import that list of names and addresses into Outlook.
- Making address book entries is simple. You can enter just the name and email address of the person, or you can use the contact list to enter much more information.
- Distribution lists allow you to send a single email to a large group of people with just a click or two.
- Creating distribution lists is easy because you simply select names from your address book.

Chapter 11

Managing Much Mail

In This Chapter

- The mailbox is full
- How to file your mail
- To print or to save?
- Creating an organized mailroom
- Creating a new mail folder
- Different colors and views
- Using the Rules Wizard
- Handling junk mail
- Previewing messages
- How to use filters

Whether you use Outlook's email function for personal mail, business mail, or both, you'll soon find that you're receiving a heck of a lot of it.

Since we just went through the exercise of learning how to send email to a lot of people at once, you'll probably find that they'll all be responding.

And it doesn't take long, once you've got that email address, for people to start finding it. You'll also find that one of the drawbacks of email is that it's so easy and quick that lots of people send you email just for the fun of it.

In addition, you'll probably find yourself on a number of mailing lists, and you'll be getting junk mail, too.

Outlook offers some great resources for sorting your mail. It's easy to create new folders and click and drag messages into them, but Outlook goes well beyond that.

For example, you can program it to automatically take any message you receive from your boss and put it in a special folder before you even see it. (Just don't specify that folder as the Recycle Bin, because that could cost you your job, don't you think?)

File This for Me, Would You?

After all of the different options you've already seen for the various areas of Outlook, especially email, I'm sure you'd be disappointed if you didn't have a ton of different options for organizing your email.

Outlook doesn't disappoint very often. This is another example of Outlook meeting your expectations completely.

Organizing email might sound like a silly waste of time, but if you stop and think about it, it makes a lot of sense.

When you get regular mail at home or at work, do you leave it all in one big pile until it's time to throw it away? Of course not. You sort it out.

Junk mail goes into one pile (or perhaps the circular file), bills go into another, correspondence you might want to respond to goes into another spot, and so on.

It's the same with email. Leaving messages in your Inbox until you're ready to delete them will leave you with a big, unmanageable mess.

So let's take a look at a couple of different ways that you can manage that mess to make some sense of it.

To Print or to Save?

The header above gives you two options for handling your email. There is, of course, a third—deleting it. As you may remember from earlier chapters, deleting email is as simple as highlighting the message and pressing the delete button on your keyboard.

Once you've decided you want to keep the email, you still have a decision to make. You can leave it in your Inbox or save it to another folder. And you can print a copy of it very easily.

If you've decided to print the file, there are a couple of different ways to do it: with the message open on your screen or from a list of messages. To print from the list, simply highlight the message(s) you want to print and click the Print button on the toolbar (it's the one that looks like a printer, fittingly enough).

The message doesn't open; it merely prints.

To print from an open message, you also have two options. You can click the printer icon on the toolbar, if you want to print the message using the default printing options.

However, if you want to change any of the defaults, you'll need to open a Print window before you print. To do that, choose Print from the File menu. A window like the one you see in the figure below will appear.

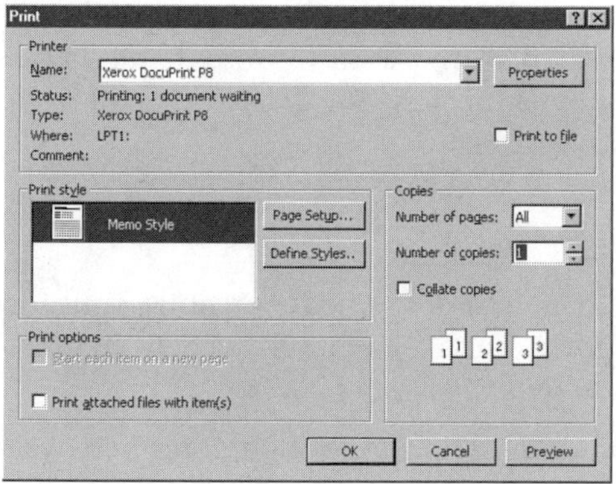

To print without using default settings, open the Print window.

In this window, you can set the printer properties. In the Copies area, you can set the number of copies of the message you would like to print, or you can set the range of pages to print.

Below, in the Print Options area, you can choose to print any files that are attached to the message you're printing.

Click the Preview button if you'd like to see what the page will look like once it's printed. If you like the way it looks, click the Print button, and out it will come!

Saving messages is easy. In fact, it's already done! Any message that comes into the Inbox is automatically saved there. You don't need to make any sort of special effort to let Outlook know that you want a message to be saved.

Once you've read it, all you need to do is close the message by clicking the Close button. And if you're viewing the messages in the preview pane, you don't even need to close them at all!

However, it's saved in the Inbox, which is what we're trying to avoid.

The rest of this chapter is about setting up an organizational system that will keep your emails flowing without getting you confused beyond all help.

More Folders, Please

Outlook offers some excellent features for organizing your incoming messages to make sure you don't end up with a huge pile of them in the Inbox.

Before you get started, however, you might want to take a few minutes to figure out exactly *how* you want your Inbox to be organized. For example, you should decide what folders you want to create and where you want to store them. You should also decide where you'd like to put shortcuts for these folders. Shortcuts will help you gain access to the folders more.

Creating a New Folder

You're going to need some new folders in order to better organize your incoming email. Remember, you've already got an Inbox, an Outbox, a Sent Items folder, a Deleted Items folder, and a Drafts folder.

You can create folders for all kinds of items, but for our purposes here we're going to create email folders.

To create a new folder, open the File menu and select Folder, then select New Folder. A window like the one you see in the following figure opens.

First, you'll need to name the folder. For example, if you were going to create a folder for mail you've received from clients, you might just call it "Clients."

In the Folder Contains area, specify the type of information that will be kept in the folder. You'll want to select Mail Items.

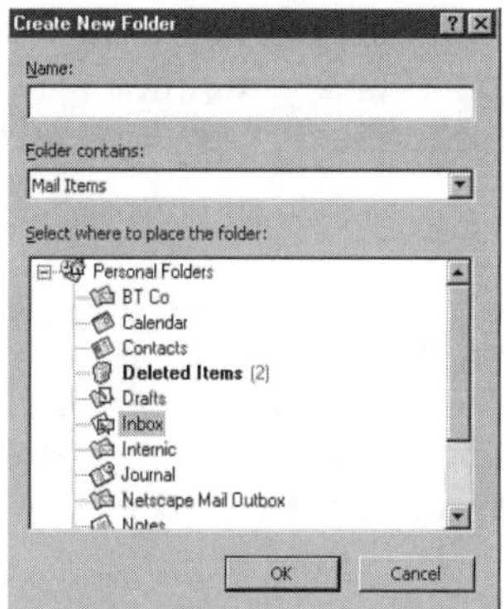

Create a new folder in this window.

Finally, you need to select where to keep the folder. To do this, just double-click the name of the folder in which you would like to place this folder.

Two suggestions here: You might want to make it a subfolder of the Inbox, since this folder will be for handling incoming mail. Or, if you want it to appear on your list of folders along with the Inbox and the other major areas of Outlook, select Personal Folders.

If you're using Outlook in corporate mode, you'll need to select your mailbox and place the subfolder there because your email is probably stored on the server.

What About Other Types of Folders?

If, in the future, you need to create folders for a different purpose, you can do it in this same area. You would then select the appropriate type of information for that folder.

Click OK, and the Personal Assistant will ask if you want to create a shortcut for the folder on the Outlook bar. If you plan to create a large number of new folders, you might not want to muddy up the Outlook bar with icons for each of them. Before adding a shortcut to a folder be sure it's one you'll use a lot.

If you click Yes, the folder icon will show up in the My Shortcuts bar, along with your other email folders such as Inbox, Sent Items, and so on.

The new folder will work just like any of your other mail-related folders. When you have items stored in that folder, you can go in and open them, read them, print them, forward them, reply to them, delete them, and so on.

You can create as many folders as you would like, but be careful—an overabundance of folders can cause just as much confusion as an overabundance of messages in one folder. Again, careful planning is important to making any organizational system work.

Moving Items to the New Folder

Once you have new folders created, you'll need to finish the job of organizing by moving the appropriate items into the correct folders. If you created a shortcut to a folder, simply open your Inbox window and open the Outlook bar that contains the shortcut to the folder (probably the My Shortcuts bar).

Click and drag the file from the Inbox to the Outlook Bar icon representing the folder into which you'd like to move it. The item disappears from the Inbox list and will appear in the new folder when you open it.

To open the new folder, simply click its icon in the Shortcut bar, and it will open, as you see in the figure below.

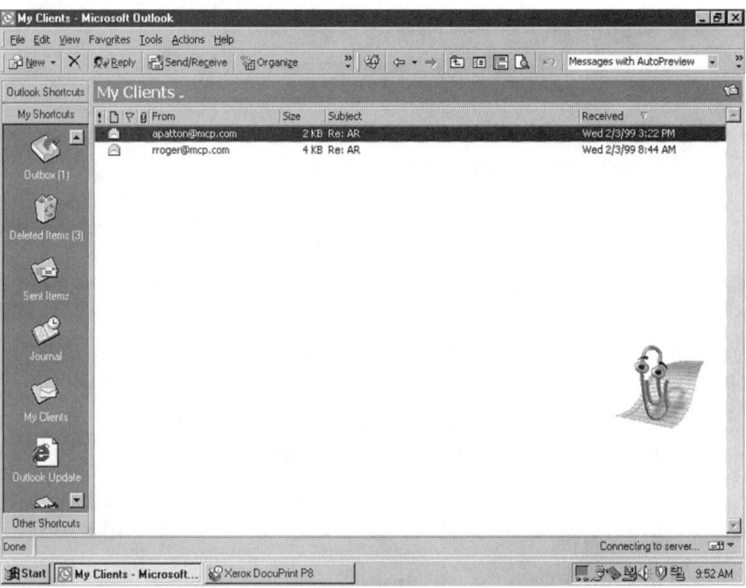

The new folder's contents are displayed, just like your other folders.

If, however, you didn't create the shortcut for the new folder, there are other ways to move a file.

To move a file from a list, simply highlight the file in the list, open the Edit menu, and select Move to Folder. You'll get a window that looks like the one in this figure.

Or, you can choose Folder List from the View menu, and your complete list of folders will be visible. Then, you can drag items onto the folder of your choice.

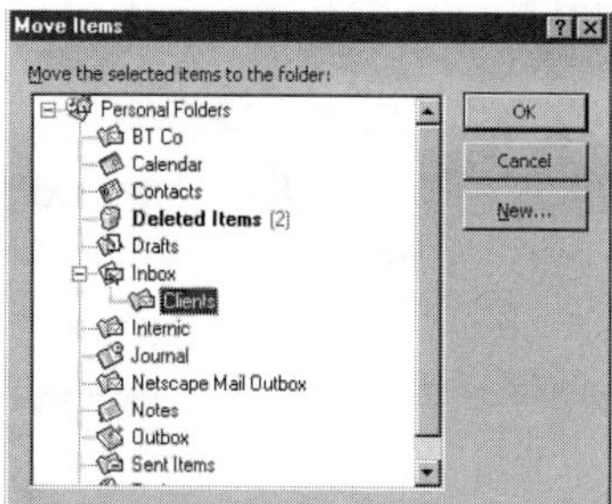

You can also move items using menus instead of clicking and dragging.

Highlight the name of the folder into which you would like to move the item, then click the OK button. The file will be moved.

Sometimes you'll open a message in your Inbox, read it, and want to file it right away. While the message is open, open the File menu and select Move to Folder. You'll be in the same Move Items window we were just in. Use the method already described to move the item.

Organizing Your Organizer

As already stated, Outlook is a personal information manager, which is a fancy way of saying it's an organizer. Now it's time to organize that organizer, using its Organize feature.

Outlook offers an Organizer tool that is great for helping you make sense out of all your email, both incoming and outgoing.

Clicking the Organize button opens up a screen of organizational tools, as seen in the following figure.

Where's the Button?

The Organize button is on the Standard toolbar, but because of some of the other things we've already done in this book, you might not be able to see it. When we opened the Advanced toolbar, it covered part of the Standard toolbar. If you can't see the Organize button, you can slide the Advanced toolbar over to the right by grabbing the vertical bar that separates the two toolbars and sliding it over.

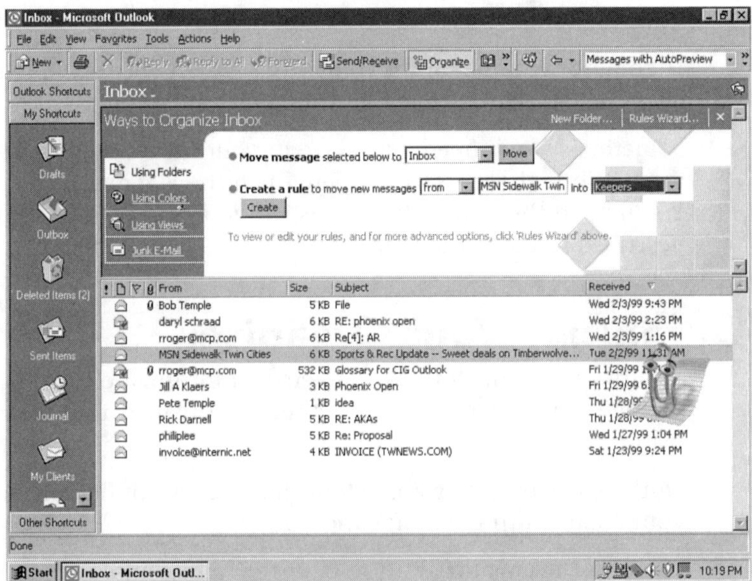

The Organize tool gives you options for cleaning up your Inbox.

On the left side of the Organize window are four tabs that have four different functions. Let's take a quick look at each of them.

More Folder Options

The Using Folders tab gives you a couple options for dealing with folders. Move Message is another way to move a selected message or messages from one folder to another. Highlight the message you want to move, select the folder name from the drop-down menu, then click Move.

Create a Rule is a means of creating universal rules that tell Outlook how to handle certain messages. For example, you might create a rule that any message you get from a specific client should end up in the Clients folder you just created.

To create such a rule, highlight a message from that client in its current folder. The client's name appears in the middle box of the Create a Rule area. Indicate whether the rule is for messages *from* that person or *to* that person (you can do both, but you have to do so with separate rules). Finally, select the folder into which all such messages should be moved. To end the operation, click the Create button.

Rules Wizard

You can create even more technologically advanced rules by using the Rules Wizard.

The Rules Wizard button is in the upper-right portion of the Organize window. The Rules Wizard option also appears in the Tools menu. Take a look at the Rules Wizard—you might find some of the options useful.

Once the rule has been created, any new message you receive from that person will automatically be filed in the folder you selected. You will still be notified that you have unread messages, however.

When you click the Create button, you get a message asking you if you would like to run the rule on the current contents of the folder. This allows you to have Outlook go through your current files and refile them for you.

Color My World

The Using Colors tab gives you another way to make certain messages stand out.

Suppose that you're filing all your mail from clients in a Clients folder. But say you have one or two clients who are particularly important to your company. Wouldn't you like messages from those people to jump out at you a little bit?

It's simple. With the Using Colors tab, you can tell Outlook to display every message you receive from a certain client in fuchsia type, as seen in the figure below.

Tell Outlook to code messages from important clients to appear in red, so they'll stand out better.

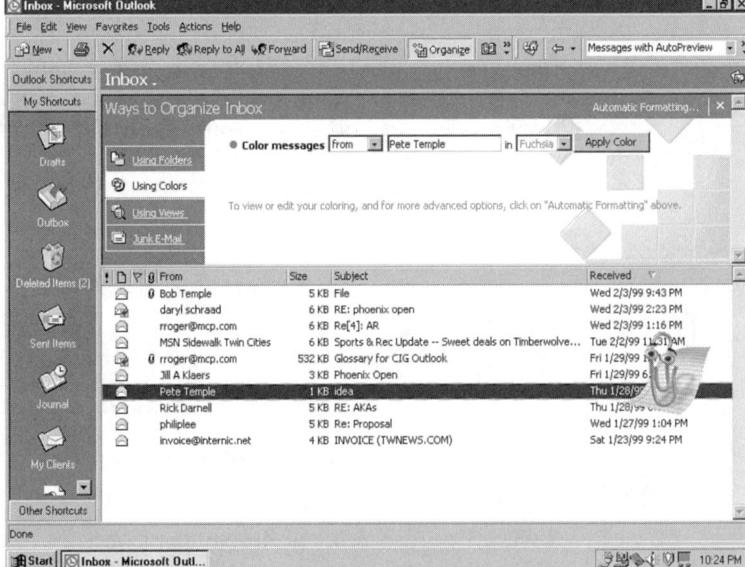

There are a number of colors to choose from, so you can assign a different one to each of your clients. Highlight a message from the person and his or her name will appear in the middle box. Choose the color from the drop-down box and click the Apply Color button. Even messages you've already received from that person will be changed to the color you chose.

Viewmaster

We covered changing your Inbox view back in Chapter 9, "Drop Me a Line." You also can change your view with the Using Views tab on the Organize tool. Click the tab and you'll be presented with a window that displays the different views from which to choose.

Get That Junk Out of Here

Outlook has a built-in function that allows you to filter out junk email before you even open it.

Junk email is fairly easy to recognize. Once you've been emailing for a while, you'll be able to identify it quickly. Using the Junk E-Mail tab, you can tell Outlook to color junk messages in a color you choose. You can do the same for Adult Content messages, as you can see in this figure.

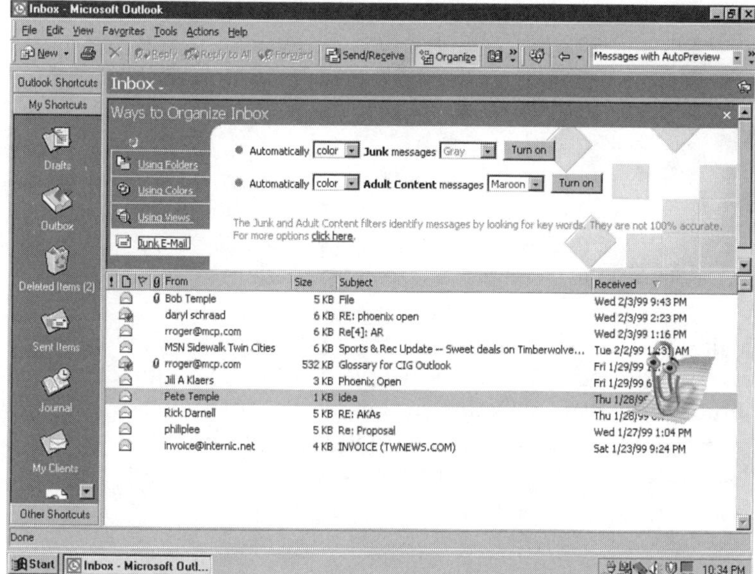

Identify junk email by color in this window.

These filters work by looking for key words in the subject and message body of incoming messages. They are not foolproof, however, so you shouldn't assume that all your messages will be filtered out before you see them.

At the bottom of the Junk E-Mail window there's a link telling you to click here if you want to see further options. Do that and you'll see a window like the one in the following figure.

Set Junk E-Mail options here.

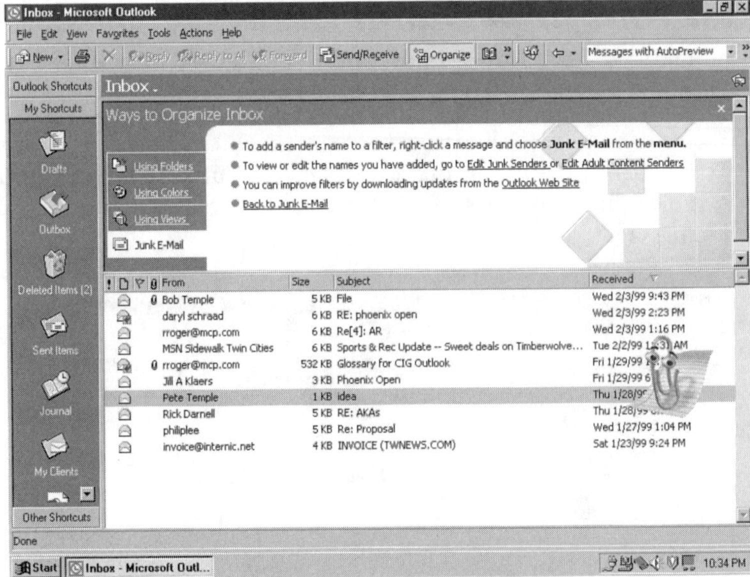

As you can see in the figure, you can customize your Junk E-Mail filters somewhat. For example, you can create and maintain a list of people who send you junk email by right-clicking on a junk message and selecting Junk E-Mail from the menu. Then you can create a rule that would automatically send messages from the people you select to a Junk folder (just don't identify your boss as one of these people, remember?).

Filtering It Out

You can set filters on specific folders to find and display only the messages you want. For example, you can tell Outlook that when you open a certain folder, you only want to see messages from one particular person.

To create a filter, open the folder to which you would like to apply the filter. In the View menu, click Current View, then select Customize Current View. Click Filter, and the Filter window opens, like the one you see in the following figure.

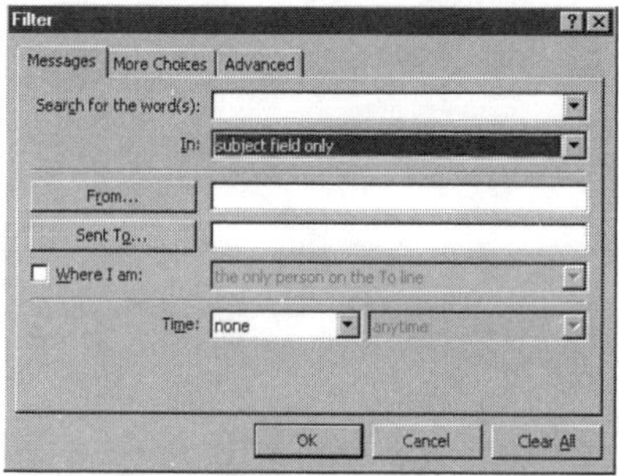

Use filters to display only messages that meet certain criteria.

Fill in the options you want. You can tell Outlook to find certain keywords in the Subject field or in the body of the text. For example, you might display only messages that have the words "peanut butter" in the body of the message. (Why you would want to do that is anyone's guess, but you get the idea.)

Click OK, and the filter is applied. To remove the filter, reopen the Filter window, click Clear All, then OK.

The Least You Need to Know

- Organizing your incoming mail helps you maintain a better handle on a large volume of messages.
- You can print email while it is open or directly from the list of messages in a folder.
- Creating new mail folders is easy and is necessary in order to organize your email.
- The Organize tool helps you set rules for certain folders or for mail received from (or sent to) specific people.
- Outlook offers tools to help you filter out junk email and mail with adult content.
- Filters can be applied to specific folders so that only information that meets criteria you set is displayed.

Chapter 12

Add-Ons: Attachments to Email

In This Chapter

- What can you send?
- Why people send attachments
- How to attach a file
- When it comes to attachments, size matters
- Attaching Outlook items
- How to save and open an attachment you've received

There are times when an email simply isn't enough, such as when you need to send that database of 10,000 records to your corporate office in New York. (Of course, not everybody has a corporate office in New York, but you get the idea.)

You can write an email that's as long as you want. If you've got a long word processing document, you can cut and paste the copy into an email and send it. But there are probably going to be times when you need to send a separate file with an email.

Attachments are a great way to send files quickly and efficiently to another person. They're not difficult to send or receive, and they make great Christmas gifts!

What Can You Send?

Any file on your hard disk, a floppy disk, a Zip disk, a SuperDisk, a Jaz disk—anything short of a Frisbee flying disc—can be sent as an attachment to an email.

The program you use to send the file—in this case, Outlook—doesn't have to be compatible with the file you're sending. You don't even have to have the program that the file was created in installed on your computer in order to send it. On the other hand, you should make sure your recipient can view the file, or else there's really no point in sending it.

You can attach a document from any of the Microsoft Office programs, or from any other computer program. You can attach any other type of file you've created as well. One of the most popular types of non-business files that people are sending as attachments to email are scanned photos of their children. It's a great way to show grandparents and other relatives how big the little ones are getting.

A Case Study in Attaching Files

Sure, it would be nice to send photographs to the grandparents. Yes, it would be handy to be able to send a presentation to a co-worker across town. But can't these things be done the old-fashioned way?

Well, of course they can. But sending things like these as attachments to email is done for the same reason people communicate by email instead of the old-fashioned way: It's convenient, and it's a heck of a lot faster. When time is of the essence, sending attachments becomes even more necessary.

To give you a firsthand example of why files are sent as attachments, consider the following personal story.

In 1995, I wrote my first book for Macmillan Computer Publishing, called *Sports on the Net*. It consisted mostly of reviews of sports-related sites on the Internet. When I wrote it, the Internet was just beginning to really gain popularity. I regularly emailed my contacts at Macmillan with questions, updates on my progress, and the like. But when it came time to send them my chapters, I followed a plan that is antique by today's standards: I saved the files onto floppy disks and sent them by overnight service from my home in the Minneapolis suburbs to their offices in Indianapolis.

This is my third book for Macmillan, and guess how I'm going to send this chapter to Indianapolis when I'm done writing it? That's right—it'll go out as an attachment to an email I'll create in Outlook 2000.

How Do You Do It?

Now that you've seen some of the benefits, it's time to actually send an attached file. After all, you won't see the benefits of sending attachments until you've actually sent and received a few. Before you begin, however, you should make sure you know exactly where the file you want to send is located. You have to show Outlook where the file is located before the program can send the file to your recipient.

The process of sending an attachment is really only an additional step or two in your usual emailing process.

To begin, open the new message window and fill in the To: field, either by typing an email address or by choosing the recipient from your Address Book. Fill in the Subject field as always, and then type your message in the message field. Even though some type of icon will probably show up in the recipient's email program to indicate that there's an attachment, always mention it in your message. (Often, the only reason for sending the email is to send the attachment, so the message might be simply, "Here's the file I promised you.")

Now it's time to attach the file. The easiest way to do this is to click the paper clip button on the toolbar. You can also get into the file attachment area by choosing File from the Insert menu.

It's Only a Copy

When you send a file as an attachment to an email, you're not really sending the original file—you're sending a copy of the file. The original file will remain in the folder from which you sent it.

Keep Those Paper Clips Straight

Whatever you do, don't confuse your paper clips. The big animated one is Clippit, the Personal Assistant in Outlook. The paper clip you should click to attach a file is just a button on the Standard toolbar above.

The folder that opens probably won't be the one that contains the file you want to send. As you can see from the figure, the My Documents folder was the one that opened, but this isn't where the file I want is located.

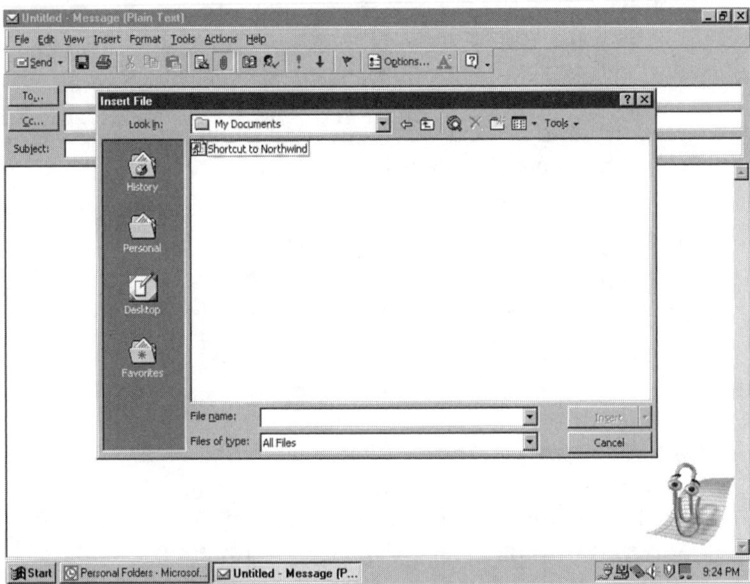

Navigate to the folder that contains the file you would like to attach.

You must lead Outlook directly to the folder with the file you want to send. If the file is located on your desktop (or in a folder on your desktop), just click the Desktop button on the left side of the window and open the appropriate folder. Otherwise, it will require a little more navigation. The fastest way is to open the drop-down menu next to the current folder window.

When you open this window, the current folder is highlighted automatically. If the file I wanted to send was on a floppy disk, I would make sure the disk was inserted into the drive and click the $3\frac{1}{2}$ Floppy (A:) folder. If it was in a file on the hard drive, I would open the C: drive and move to the folder that contained the file.

Once you've found the folder, you can attach the file in one of two ways: You can double-click on the filename, or you can highlight the file and click the Insert button in the lower-right corner of the Insert File window. Either way, you'll jump back to the message window. The attached file will be located in its own window at the very bottom of the screen, as you can see in the following figure.

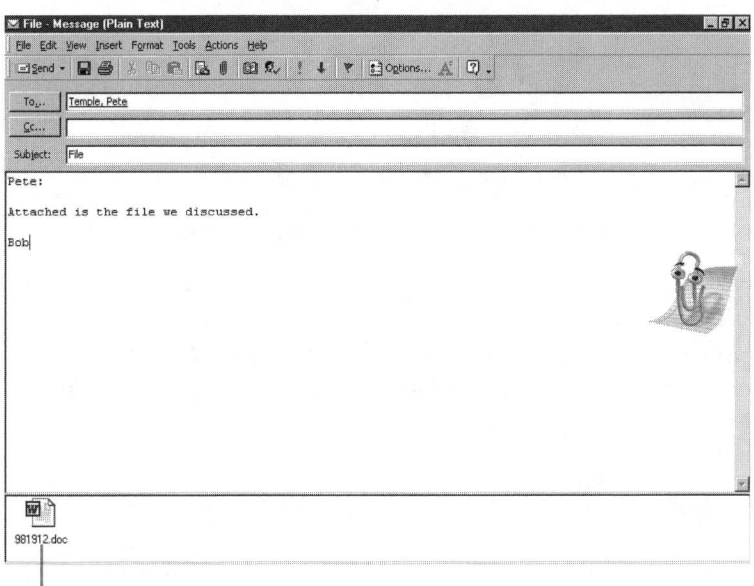

Attached Word file

The attachment appears at the bottom of the email window.

You're now ready to send your email with the file attached. Click the Send button to move it to the Outbox.

Size Matters

When you send a message out of Outlook that has a file attached, it takes quite a bit longer than when you send a regular email message. That's because of the file's size. The bigger the file, the longer it's going to take to send. Unfortunately, this also means that the bigger the file, the more likely you'll encounter some type of problem.

Here are a couple of tips for sending attached files:

- If you have more than one large file to send, you might want to send them as separate emails rather than all in one email.
- It's a good idea to have some type of compression program, such as WinZip, on your computer. Compression programs reduce the size of files or take multiple files and compact them into a single, smaller file. When you're using one of these programs, however, make sure that the recipient of the compressed file can decompress it.

How Will the Attachment Look to the Recipient?

That depends on which email program your recipient is using. If she uses Outlook 2000, it will appear the same way attached files appear to you (discussed later in this chapter). If she uses a different email program, it might appear differently. If your recipient is having trouble retrieving attachments you send in Outlook 2000, she should contact her system administrator or check the documentation for her email program.

In my line of work, writing and editing, I send and receive a lot of Word files—many of them by email.

Most normal-sized word processing files aren't going to cause any trouble when they're attached to an email. Large files, like a huge database, are more likely to cause problems.

Attaching Outlook Items

Exporting

Outlook does allow you to export its items, including the Calendar, out to other programs. For more information about exporting Outlook items, see Chapter 23, "Making Outlook Part of the Family."

You've already learned how to attach files created in other programs and send them via email using Outlook. You can also send Outlook items as attachments to email. This includes your contacts, journals, notes, tasks, and calendar. Remember, though, that it won't do much good to send your calendar to another person unless he's also using Outlook and can open and view it.

Attaching Outlook items is very similar to attaching a file created in another program. Open the new message window, and then fill in the To: field and the Subject: field as before. When you're ready to attach the Outlook item, open the Insert menu and select Item. This takes you back to the Insert Item window, but you'll be looking at the list of your Outlook folders and files, as you can see in the following figure.

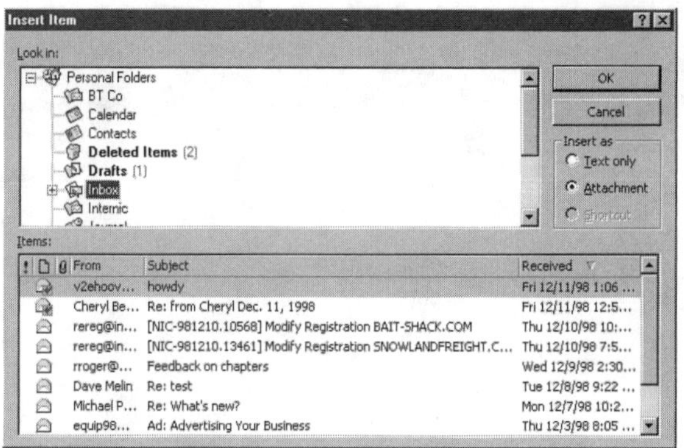

Choose the Outlook item you want to send.

Again, navigate to the file you want to send and select it by double-clicking it or highlighting it and clicking the OK button. The Outlook item will appear in its own window at the bottom of the message window, just like the attached files do. It's now ready to be sent.

I Got One!

One day you open your Inbox and there it is—your first attachment. Now what the heck are you going to do?

Well, you could run screaming for the exits, panicked at what someone might be sending you. Or, you could calmly open the email and save it. Hmmm. Tough call.

Handling incoming emails is every bit as easy as handling outgoing ones. An incoming email with an attachment will show up in your Inbox with the little paperclip icon next to it. When you open the email, the attached file appears in a separate window at the bottom of the message window, as you can see from the following figure.

Got the Sniffles?

These days, everybody should have virus protection software installed on their computers. This is especially true if you're going to be receiving files over the Internet. Some viruses can take effect immediately when you open the file. A good virus protection program will examine every file before it's opened. A little money spent now can go a long way toward avoiding major problems later. It's also a good idea to not open files at all unless you trust the source of the file.

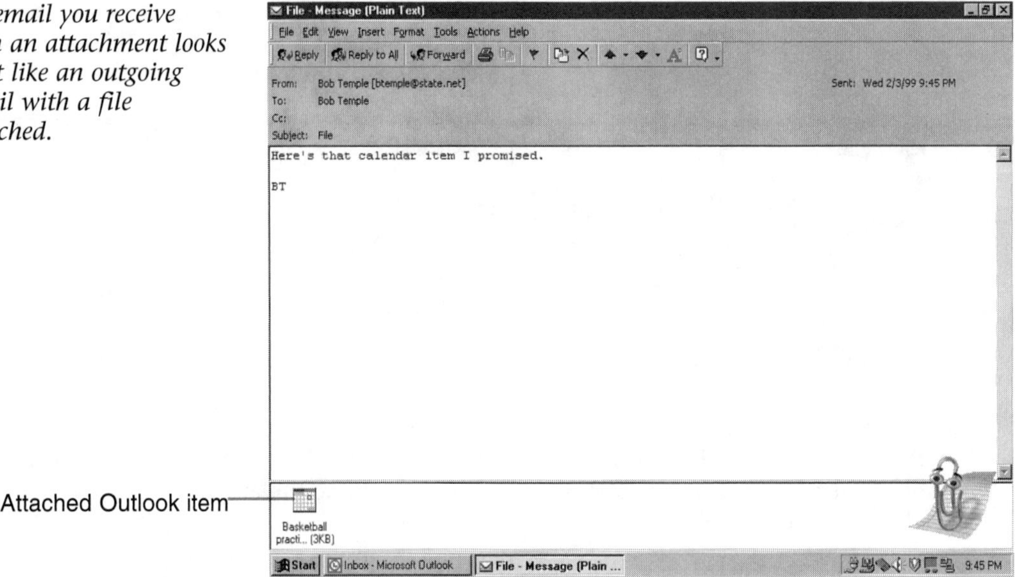

An email you receive with an attachment looks a lot like an outgoing email with a file attached.

Once the file has been received, it is saved on your computer whether you open it or not. However, it's saved only as a part of the email. To save it in a more permanent location (or to view it), double-click its icon at the bottom of the email window. You're presented with the Opening Mail Attachment window, as seen in the following figure. It includes a warning about viruses and gives you two options: Open the file, or save it to disk and open it later.

To work with an attachment without opening the email, you can right-click on the message in the Inbox list and then choose View Attachments. Or, if you're using the message preview pane in your view, you can click the paper clip icon and open the attachment.

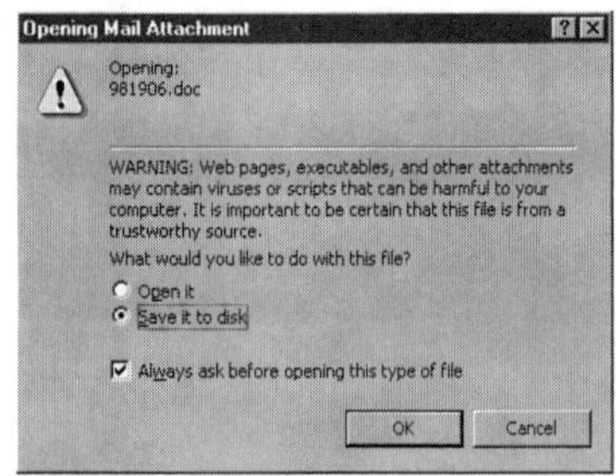

Using this window, you can open or save the file attachment.

To open the file, now or later, you'll need to have the program that the file was created in installed on your computer.

If you have the program installed, you can choose Open it. The program will launch and the file will be displayed. If you just want to save it and look at it later, you can choose Save it to disk, and save it on your hard disk or a removable disk, such as a floppy.

The Least You Need to Know

- In Outlook, you can attach any type of file to an email message. The file can be created in any program.
- Attaching a file to an email is a more efficient way of sending it to a recipient than any other method, including an overnight service.
- You must know where a file is located on your computer before you can send it to anyone.
- You can attach items from any of your Outlook folders to an email, including the Calendar, Contacts, Tasks,The Journal, Notes, and so on.
- The larger the file you attach, the longer it will take to send it and the more likely you will encounter problems. A file compression program will help speed the sending of attachments.
- If you're going to be receiving files by email, make sure to have a virus protection program installed on your computer.
- Double-clicking an attached file brings you to a screen from which you can decide whether to open or save the file.

Chapter 13

Just the Fax

In This Chapter

- Outlook gives you one less machine to buy
- Setting up WinFax Starter Edition
- Sending faxes
- Attaching documents to a fax
- Sending group faxes
- Receiving faxes
- Opening received faxes

You already know about the wonders of Outlook's email capabilities and the myriad ways it can simplify your life. Email has become a staple of everyday business for companies large and small. However, email could be said to be an enhancement of another communications revolution of the last decade: the fax machine.

Faxing came into the mainstream in the late '80s as a way to quickly communicate and send complete documents over phone lines without having to wait for regular mail. Email matched faxing in terms of speed, and then surpassed it. Email also added further benefits, like the lack of long-distance charges and the ability to reprint a document without it looking like it came out of a fax machine.

There's one thing email hasn't been able to do—replace the fax machine. Just as faxes were purported to be the death knell for "regular" mail, email was quickly deemed to be a death sentence for faxes. Yeah, and television was supposed to eliminate radio. History is littered with innovations that, instead of replacing their predecessors, only added another machine to your home or office.

One Less Machine to Buy

In recent years, manufacturers of printers, copiers, and fax machines have figured out a way to combine them all into one easy-to-use machine. It's rare when such a life-simplifying innovation actually works, but these machines appear to do the trick. Similarly, Microsoft's designers have figured out a way to keep your home less crowded (or office, or home office, for that matter).

As more people start and run home-based businesses, the need for these machines has risen sharply. Outlook offers full faxing capabilities—both sending and receiving—for Internet-only and corporate users alike. Now you can email your contacts, and fax them as well, without having to purchase additional fax software and use the same Internet connection for both.

But why would you want to fax someone when you can just email her? Well, as mainstream as email has become, not everybody has an email account. And, for whatever reason, some people prefer to work by fax rather than email (especially those with unreliable ISPs).

And faxing offers one distinct advantage over email. If I fax you a document, it will come out on your end looking like a fuzzy version of the original. However, if I email you the document, you might not be able to see it at all if you don't have the same program that I used to create it.

So, for those times when faxing is the best—or only—way to communicate with one of your contacts, Outlook offers a simple fax program for its users.

What Type Are You?

Depending upon the type of installation you did at the beginning of this whole process, you'll have slightly different software to use for faxing.

If you're on a network and you installed Outlook as a corporate user, you can use Microsoft Fax as your faxing software. If you're an Internet-only user of Outlook, you must use the WinFax Starter Edition to send and receive faxes.

Setting Up WinFax Starter Edition

Corporate Users Take Note

There are some differences between Microsoft Fax and WinFax. This chapter covers WinFax; Microsoft Fax is not covered in detail in this book. Corporate Outlook users who are using Microsoft Fax can follow the same steps as described here if they select New Mail Message when Internet-Only users are told to select New Fax. If you need to get serious about faxing—adding some features such as scheduling faxes, editing faxes, or sending and receiving faxes as binary attachments—Microsoft Fax is the way to go.

Your WinFax account is visible in the Accounts dialog box—the same one that houses your email account. You can view it at any time by clicking on Accounts from the Tools menu, but you probably shouldn't make changes to your WinFax account here.

The Account setup area is where Outlook automatically stores all the settings it needs to make the WinFax software run properly. You can make some choices on your own in the Options area for WinFax. To get there, choose Options from the Tools menu and then select the Fax tab. All your initial information should be visible, as shown in the following figure.

At the top of the window is your cover page information. This is the information that will be printed out on the cover page your recipient will get with the fax, so make sure it's correct.

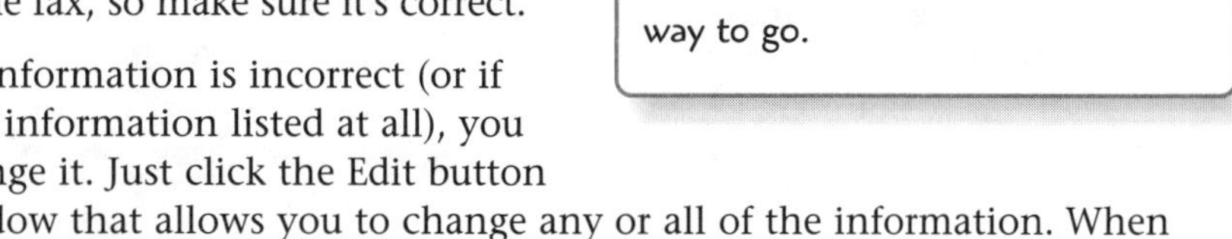

If any of that information is incorrect (or if there isn't any information listed at all), you can easily change it. Just click the Edit button to open a window that allows you to change any or all of the information. When you're done, click the OK button and the new information will appear in the window.

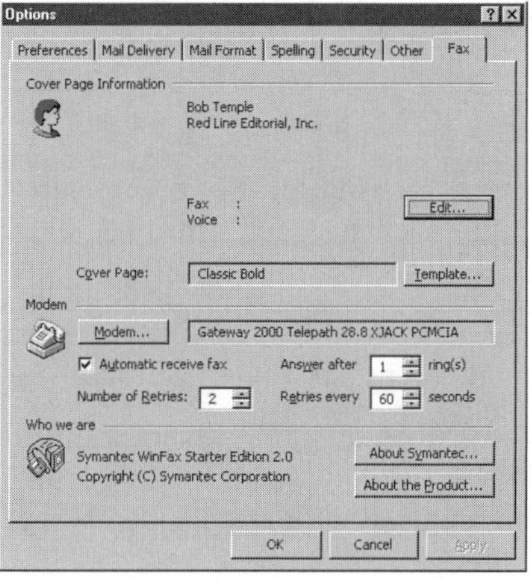

Make changes to your fax setup here.

Modem Trouble

If your modem's name doesn't appear with TAPI after it, then it is not configured to work with WinFax. To reconfigure it, highlight the modem and, while holding down the Shift key, select Properties. You will then get a prompt asking you to run the configuration now. Make sure your modem is turned on and you are not connected to the Internet, and click OK. Your modem will then be configured.

At the bottom of the Cover Page area is the Cover Page setup area. Click on the Template button, and then choose from five different templates to use as your cover page.

The Modem area is probably the most important part of the setup process. If this area shows an incorrect modem, or no modem at all, you won't be able to send or receive faxes in WinFax. Also, some modems don't support sending and receiving faxes. If that's the case with your modem, you'll need to upgrade it before you can use WinFax.

To make changes, click on the Modem button and a Modem Properties window will open. You can delete the current modem by highlighting it and pressing the Delete key on your keyboard, or by clicking the Remove button. To add a new modem, click the Add button and you will be walked through the process. Outlook will even attempt to detect your modem automatically.

Also in this area, you'll probably want to have the Automatic receive fax box checked if you expect to receive faxes when the computer is unattended. This tells Outlook to answer the phone automatically after a certain number of rings in order to receive an incoming fax. This way, you won't have to sit by the computer waiting for a fax. If you have this button checked all the time, however, you might get disconnected from your Internet Service Provider whenever a fax comes in.

The bottom two boxes in the Modem area refer to faxes you're sending. You can set the number of times Outlook should retry a number if it's busy, and how long it should wait between redialing attempts.

Sending One Off

Sending a fax from a traditional fax machine isn't terribly complicated. Typically, you stick the paper in the machine, punch in the phone number, and press the Start button.

Since there's no place to put a piece of paper into Outlook, it's a little bit different. However, Outlook's designers have made faxing extremely similar to sending email.

As usual, there are a number of different ways to start the process of sending an email with Outlook. The easiest is to pull down the New button's drop-down menu and select Fax Message from the list that appears. (Corporate mode users can open the Actions menu and select New Mail Message.)

The Fax window appears, which looks almost identical to the email window you're accustomed to. (See the following figure.)

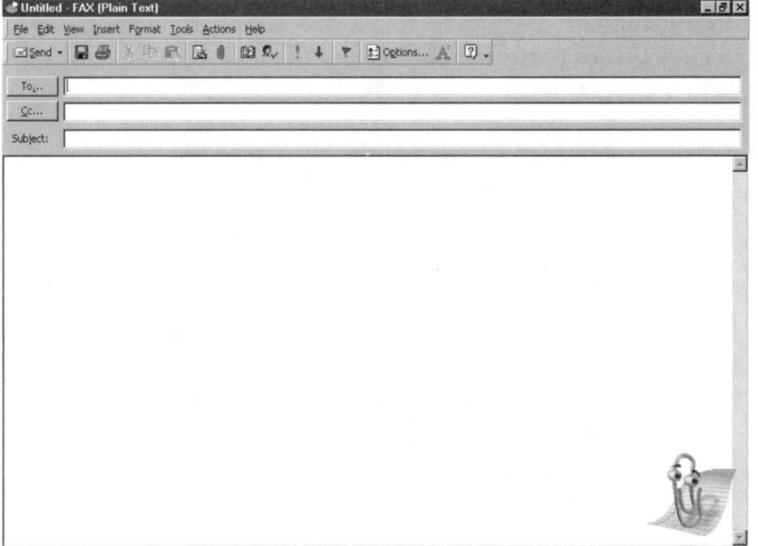

Use the Fax window to send a fax.

As you'll recall from our previous discussions of email, if you don't have your recipient entered in your contact list, you can simply type the person's email address in the To field.

This is one of the major differences between the email and fax forms in Outlook, even though they appear to be exactly the same. To send a fax, you *must* have the person's name and a fax number entered into your Contact database. If you don't have this information entered properly, you can't just enter the person's fax number into the To field. You'll receive an error message. Instead, you'll enter "fax@" followed by the number. So, if the person you're dialing has a fax number of 555-1234, you would enter "fax@5551234" in the To: field. Still, it's easier to have the information entered in your Contacts database.

There's One Other Way

If you want, you can enter the recipient's name in the To field even if he isn't in your Contact database. After you click the Send button, Outlook will ask you for the person's fax number. However, it's best to enter the name into the Contact database. That way, if you're sending the same fax to several people, you don't have to sit in front of your computer and enter the names one at a time as each fax number pops up on the screen.

So, if you're sending a fax to someone without a contact entry, click the To button. Then click the New Contact button and enter a name and fax number for the recipient, at the very least.

If you're sending a fax to someone in your Contact database, simply type her name in the To field. Or, you can click the To button and select her name from the list, as you see in the following figure.

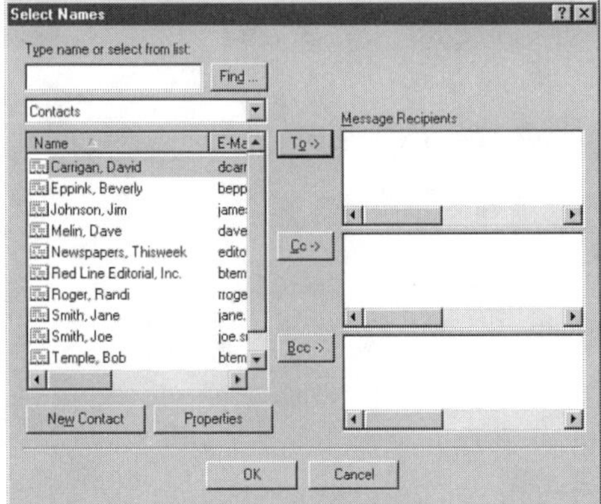

Select the recipient's name from this window.

Then enter a subject. The large open window can be used for the content of the fax, but is more often used to type a message that accompanies an attached document.

Attaching Documents

Unlike email, every time you send a fax to someone you'll probably attach a document. A fax is usually a previously created document, not a quick little note to a contact.

Attaching documents to a fax in Outlook is every bit as easy as attaching documents to an email. Simply click the little paper clip icon in the toolbar, and then navigate your way to the document you want to send. Once you've found it, highlight it and click the Insert button. An icon representing the attachment will appear in a separate window at the bottom of the fax window, just as with an attachment to email. The following figure shows the attachment as you will see it.

Now use the large window to type any notes you want to include with the document, and then click the Send button.

Unlike email, faxes are sent immediately in WinFax instead of going into the Outbox. If you've attached a document, you'll see a message indicating that Outlook is *rasterizing* the document. This means that it's being prepared to be sent as a fax. You'll see the document open in its original application. Depending upon the length of the document you're sending, this can take a little while.

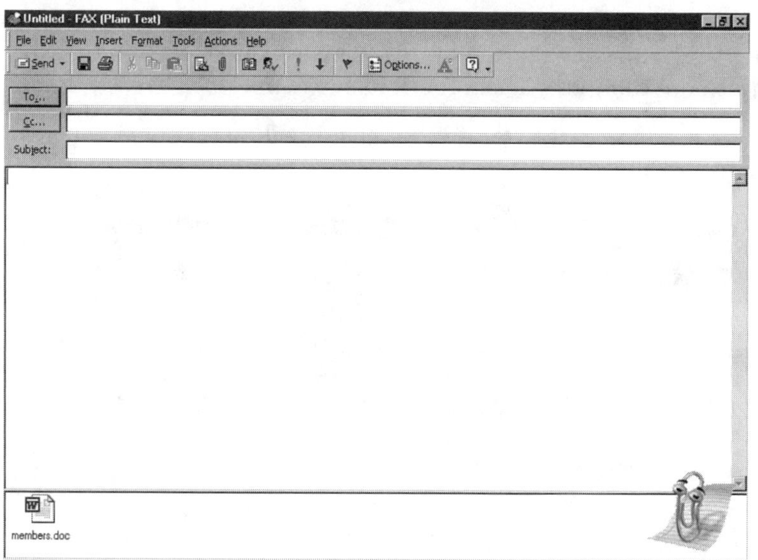

Attachments to faxes appear as icons at the bottom of the fax, just like attachments to email.

Finally, you're asked to verify the fax number for your recipient. This is your final chance to make sure the number is correct. Then click the Send button and your modem will dial the number. Once the fax has been sent, the modem will automatically hang up. If you've selected a Contact entry with a valid fax number, you won't get this verification message.

Sending Group Faxes

If you want to send the same fax to a number of people, you can do so easily in WinFax. Just click on the To button and select the names of all your intended recipients. Remember, if you don't have a fax number entered into a contact's entry, you can't send him a fax without sitting at the computer to enter the number as the fax is being sent.

You can send the message once you've selected all the names, but it will take some time because each number must be dialed individually.

Receiving and Opening Faxes

Receiving a fax in Outlook is easy if you've set up the parameters properly in the Options window. However, in order for Outlook to receive a fax, it must be active on your computer when the call arrives, and you must have the auto-answer option checked. If you don't have Outlook active, the call won't be answered.

When someone calls your fax number with Outlook active, it will pick up the line in the number of rings you specified in your settings.

Once the fax has been received it will appear in your Inbox, just like an email. In most cases, it will look a lot like an attached document in an email looks. If the sender used Outlook and didn't attach anything to the fax, the actual fax appears in the window.

To open the fax, just double-click on it in your Inbox list. It will open into a window, as you see in the following figure.

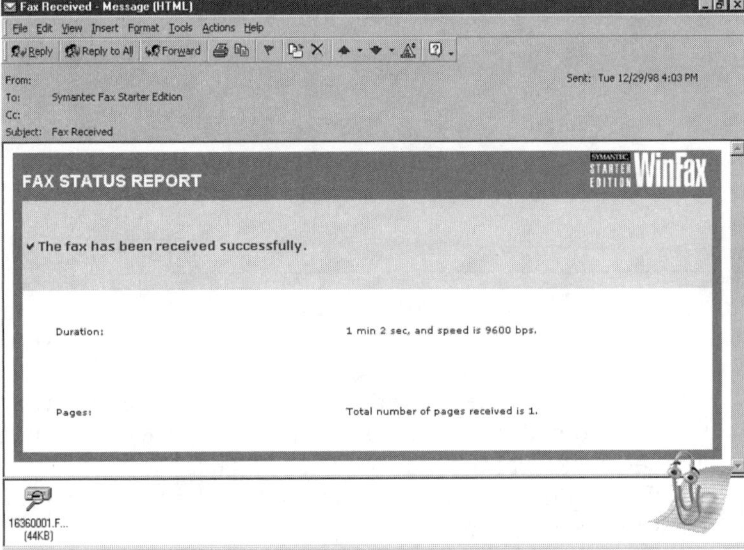

A received fax with an attachment appears like this.

The attachment appears just like an attachment to email, as an icon in a separate window at the bottom of the screen. Double-click on the attachment to open a dialog box that asks if you want to open the document or save it to disk.

What About Corporate Mode?

As stated earlier, if you've set up Outlook in Corporate mode, you'll use Microsoft Fax to send and receive faxes. Working with Microsoft Fax is very similar to working with WinFax. You'll have more options in certain areas, though, and you'll need to make some different choices in the setup process.

Before you start sending and receiving faxes in Corporate mode, you should check with your network administrator to make sure you can fax from your workstation. He or she can also help you configure Microsoft Fax in the way your company uses it.

The Least You Need to Know

- Using Outlook to send and receive faxes allows you to save money and space in your home/office because you won't have to buy a fax machine.
- You should make sure you have WinFax (or Microsoft Fax) configured properly before attempting to send a fax.
- Sending faxes is very similar to sending email in Outlook. In fact, the windows are almost identical.
- You can attach a document by clicking the paper clip icon in the toolbar and selecting the document.

Part 3

Let's Get Down to Business: Managing Contacts

Most people maintain an address book of some kind. Some of us even have separate address books for business and personal contacts. Outlook allows you to compile all of this information into one place, yet lets you divide it back out quickly whenever you want. In this part of the book, we'll cover Outlook's Contacts feature and the basics of how it works. Then we'll look at how to sort and organize your Contacts database. Finally, we'll look at some of Outlook's advanced features that make the Contacts feature really sing.

Chapter 14

Keeping in Contact

In This Chapter

- How contact lists work
- Why contact lists help
- Setting up a contact list
- How to enter a contact
- Revising and deleting contacts
- Viewing your contacts
- Getting in touch with a contact

You pick up the phone to call so-and-so, but you realize you don't have the number handy. Or you need to send off a quick letter to what's-her-name, but you can't find her business card. Or you'd love to send some jerk a nasty email, but you can't find the scrap of paper on which you wrote his address.

Any of these sound familiar?

In the previous section of the book we discussed email and faxing, two ways to communicate with the people you need to talk to from time to time. But how do you keep track of all these people?

Think about the many people you keep in touch with for one reason or another. At home, you've got your relatives, your friends, the people in the PTO, the teachers at school, perhaps a member of the clergy, your neighbors, the board of the youth athletic association, and so on. You probably have a written address book, maybe a holiday card list, and heaven knows how many directories for different organizations. At work, you've got the people in your department, the others in your office, a list of clients or vendors, maybe another office or two or division of your own company, etc. You've probably got the intraoffice directory and a Rolodex full of other business contacts.

It's time to get that all organized into a single program, and Outlook is the answer.

Why Use Outlook's Contacts?

Sure, it would be great to be able to compile all this information into one usable source, but you could do that with a notebook and a pencil. Outlook's Contacts program allows you to do so much more than just keep a list.

What if you could group your contacts and organize them into categories so that they were easy to sort? What if, when you needed to invite people to a party at your home, you could quickly create and print a list of those people? What if you could be automatically prompted a few days before your most important clients' birthdays? What if you could keep track of every communication you have with a contact so you could document when you requested supplies, when you delegated a task, and more?

In Outlook, there are dozens of different fields in which you can enter information. Although you'll probably never use all of them for all of your contacts, you'll find most of them to be very useful from time to time.

Once you have the information entered, Outlook can help you keep it organized as well.

There are many different ways to categorize and sort your contacts, and there are a number of ways to view them as well. Most commonly, they're viewed in the Address Cards mode, which makes them look like entries in a Rolodex. (See the following figure.) However, you can easily view the entire contents of your contact list any time you like.

You'll learn more about the different ways you can view your contact list later in this chapter. After all, you've got to create the list before you can worry about how to view it.

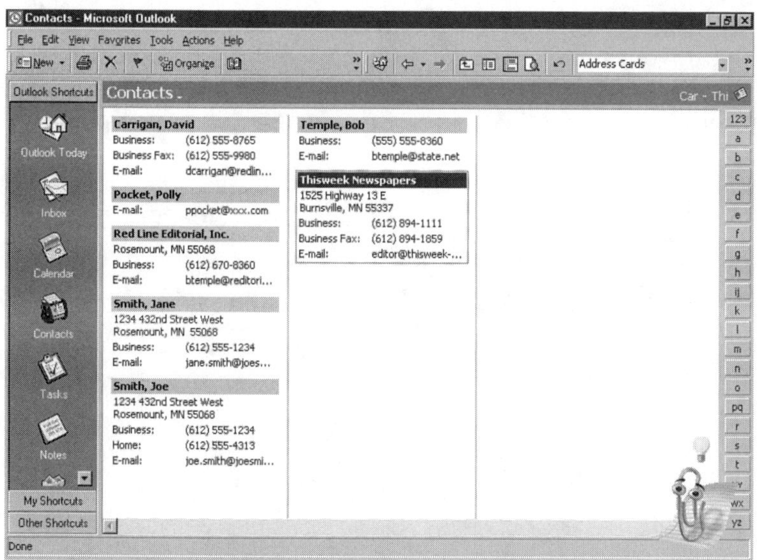

Contact lists are commonly viewed in Address Cards mode.

Entering a Contact

You may remember that in the previous chapters about email, you made a few listings in your Address Book, which is essentially a part of your contact list. All you entered was a name and an email address, because that's all you needed at the time.

Entering contacts is one of the first things you should do in Outlook. It takes precedence over the Calendar and the other areas of Outlook because so much of the rest of Outlook feeds off your contact list. You've already seen how contacts can help you with email, and you'll see more uses for contacts in this section and others.

Entering contacts is simple and can be as quick or as time-consuming as you like, depending on how much information you want to enter for each person on your list.

To begin, you can use the drop-down menu on the New button and select Contact. Or, if you are already at the Contacts screen, click the New button to open the Contact window.

As you can see, there are five different tabs for information about your contact. For now, let's concentrate on the General tab shown in the following figure.

Going down the left side of the General tab, you can enter your contact's basic information—name, job title, company, and address. You can navigate from field to field either by pressing the Tab key or by left-clicking in the next field.

Once you've entered the contact's name, it also appears in the File as: area, except with the last name first, a comma, and then the first name and initial. This indicates how Outlook will file the contact in its alphabetical listing. Note that the File as: box is also a drop-down menu. If you want the listing to be made with the first name first, open the drop-down menu and choose the manner in which you would like it to be displayed from the list. For example, you might not want the last name first if the contact you're entering is a company name, not an individual's name. You probably wouldn't want General Electric to be filed as "Electric, General" in your alphabetical listing.

Enter your contact information in this window.

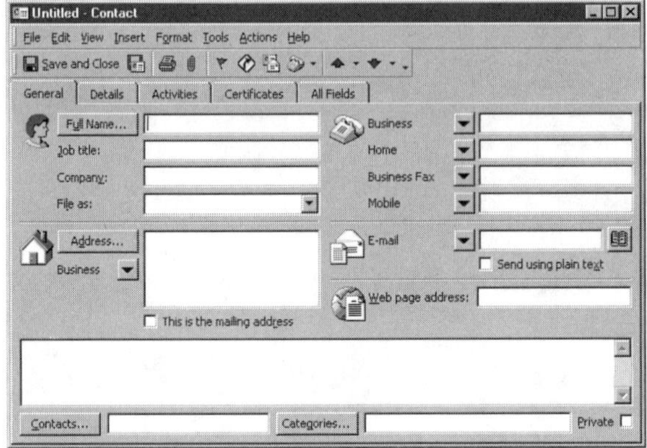

Changing the Contacts Form

You'll note that several of the fields have drop-down menus next to them. The reason for this is that you'll have different information for some people than for others. Think of it this way: Some of the people that you're in contact with have different types of contact information than other people. One of your contacts may have a pager and no fax, or a cell phone and a pager.

If you want to change one of those fields so you can enter different information, open the appropriate drop-down menu and click on the name of the field you would like to use. That field will be changed for this particular contact only, not for all of your contacts. (See the following figure.)

Both the Full Name and Address fields also have buttons you can click to add more options to the contact. For example, in the Full Name window (which is displayed after you click the Full Name button), you can add a prefix title (Mrs., Dr., Mr., and so on) and a suffix title (such as Jr.). The Address window allows you to enter address information in a more detailed form so that it can be displayed properly in Outlook's contact lists.

Usually, though, you can just type the information into the appropriate fields, and Outlook will handle it correctly. If, however, you enter information that Outlook doesn't know how to handle, Outlook will ask for clarification by opening one of these windows. For example, if you enter just a street address with no city or state, Outlook opens the Check Address window to prompt you to enter the complete information.

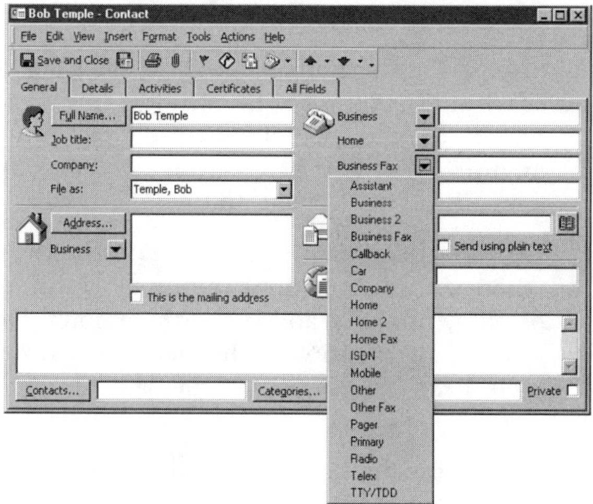

There are a number of different fields from which to choose.

At the bottom of the General tab is the Categories button. This allows you to choose some categories that apply to this particular contact, as you can see from the following figure.

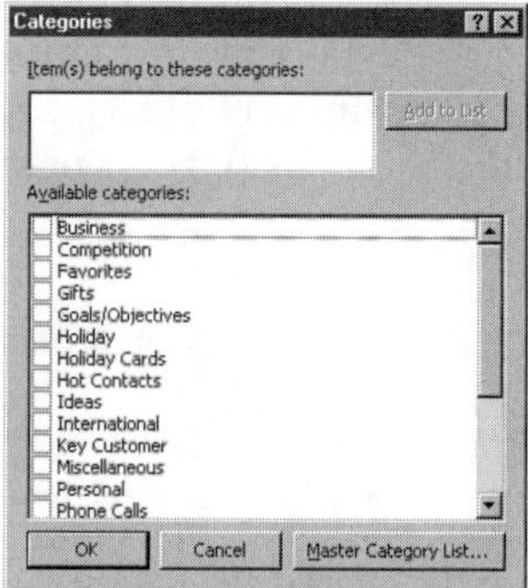

Select the categories that apply to the contact.

For example, if the contact is a person you send a holiday card to every year, click the Holiday Cards category. If he's an important client, click the Key Customer category (you can pick more than one category for each contact).

This is one of the most important fields in the Contact window because these categories will be used later to help you sort your list. A more lengthy discussion of categories can be found in Chapter 15, "Working with Contacts."

If you would like to link one contact with another on your list, click the Contacts button at the bottom-left corner of the main Contact window and double-click the name of the secondary contact.

Making Notes

Also on the General tab, you'll notice a big open space at the bottom of the window. This is a place for you to type notes about the contact. You can say anything you want here without worrying about it being displayed in your Address Cards view.

However, be aware that if you're on a network where you share Outlook information with coworkers, they might be able to see these notes. You might not want to mention in this field that the department head is a real pain in the backside.

Instead, use this field for constructive purposes. This is a good spot to enter things like the time of day a person prefers to be contacted or other pertinent information, like the dates the person is going on vacation.

Private Parts

If you do share Outlook information with others at work and you'd like to keep a contact or two private, you can do that as well. Just click the little Private box in the lower-right corner of the General tab to hide the contact from the others on your network.

Details, Details

On the Details tab you can enter... well... more detailed information. Across the top, you can enter additional information for your business contacts, such as their department or office names, their professions, and the names of their managers or assistants. (See the following figure.)

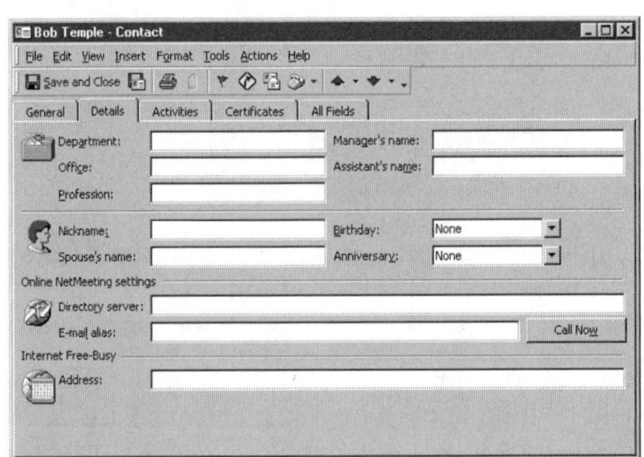

The Details tab offers a place for more information.

I've found the Profession field particularly useful. Let's say you called a plumber a while back and you entered his information into your contact list at that time. If you need to call him again two years later, you won't need to search for a long-lost receipt or business card someplace. You can simply open Outlook and conduct a search for a plumber. As long as you entered "Plumber" in the Profession field, that person's name will pop up.

In the middle of the Details tab you can enter a nickname and spouse's name, plus a birthday and/or anniversary date. Each of the latter two fields offers a month-by-month calendar where you can click the date.

Once these dates are entered, they will always pop up in your Outlook Calendar, year after year after year. You've just lost your excuse for forgetting those important dates!

Saving a Contact

When you're all done entering a contact's information, you have one final decision to make. You must save the contact, but you need to tell Outlook whether you want to enter another contact or be done with it for now.

Click the Save and Close button if you're done entering contacts for now. If you'd like to enter another one immediately, click the Save and New button, which is right next to the Save and Close button.

If you would like to enter a new contact from the same company, select New Contact from Same Company from the Actions menu.

Editing Your Contacts

There are lots of reasons why you might want to make changes to your contact list. People move, get new phone numbers, change departments, get married and change their names, and so on. Or maybe somebody who you thought was a friend turned out to be not much of one, and you'd like to delete him from your list. (Hey, it happens.)

Making changes or deleting contacts altogether is very simple, and as usual, there are about a thousand different ways to do it. We won't cover them all here—just the best ones.

No Need for White-Out

You can leave the White-Out in the desk drawer. (It would make an awful mess on your computer screen anyway.) Making changes to contacts is very simple.

You can change any contact information easily just by opening the window for that contact. To do this, just double-click anywhere on the contact, regardless of how it's displayed on your screen. This opens the full Contact window, where you can enter new information, delete old information, and make any changes you want on any of the tabs. (See the following figure.)

If you have the contacts displayed as address cards or detailed address cards, you can make changes right on the card. Simply click in the area of the card in which you'd like to make the change. The field will be surrounded by a dotted line and a cursor will appear inside it. You can then delete information and type new information.

You can edit a contact in the Address Cards view.

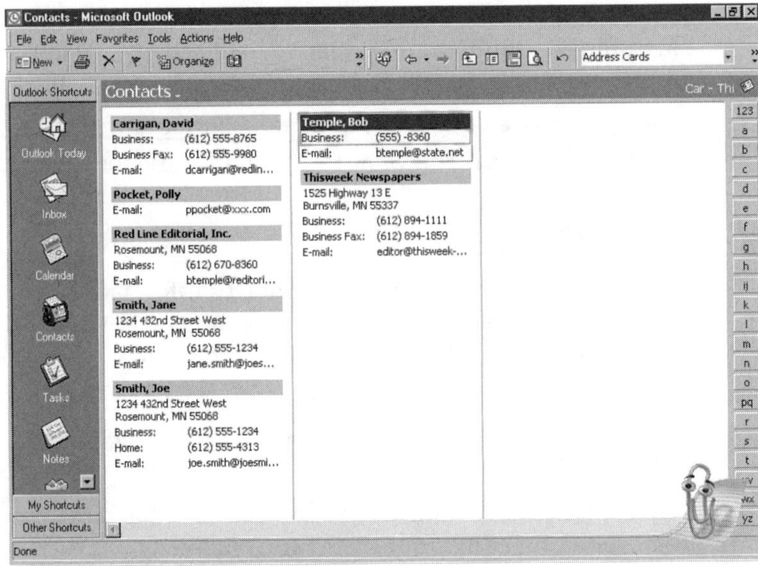

Editing a contact in the Address Cards view is limited, however, in that you can only make changes to the fields you can see. For example, if you wanted to add a second phone number for a contact, you would have to open the Contacts window to do it.

You're Out of My Life

If you've cut off communication with a contact, you should delete him from your contact list so he isn't consuming valuable space.

There are a number of ways to delete a contact, but the easiest is simply to highlight the contact in your View window and click the delete button on the toolbar (it looks like an "X"). You can also right-click on the contact and select Delete from the menu that appears.

Viewing Your Contacts

As with all of Outlook's folders, there are a number of different ways you can display information. You can change your view using the drop-down list from the Advanced toolbar.

Let's take a brief look at the different ways to view your contact list:

- **Address Cards** This is the default view for contacts. It displays a contact's name and address, all phone numbers from the General tab, and the email address. This is the most commonly used view for contacts.

- **Detailed Address Cards** The cards are laid out exactly as they are in the regular Address Cards view, but more information is displayed: the contact's job title and company name, Web site address, and the categories you have selected for him.
- **Phone List** This view lists the contacts in a table format and displays the full name, company name, and business telephone information first. You can sort the list quickly from any of the fields by clicking on the field header. The following figure shows a contact list in Phone List view.

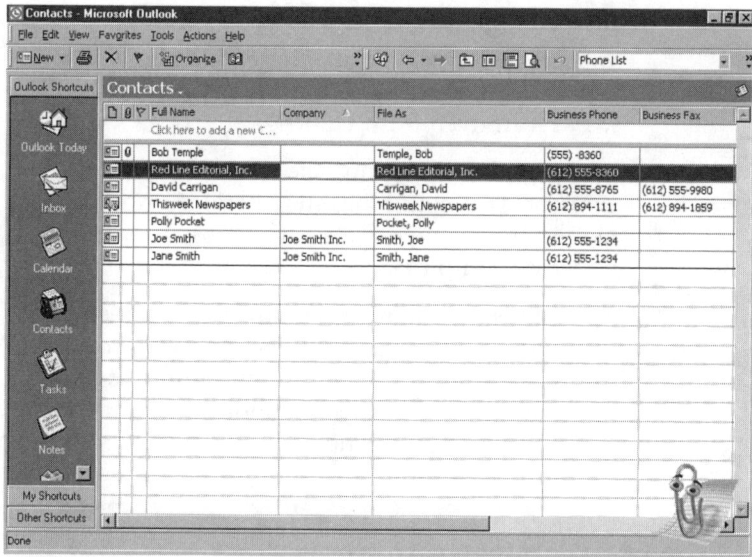

In Phone List view, you can quickly sort the list by clicking on a header.

- **By Category** If you have selected any categories for specific contacts, this groups them based on those categories.
- **By Company** Arranges the list based on the company name you entered for each.
- **By Location** If you've entered any country names or regions for your contacts, this view sorts them based on those entries.
- **By Follow-Up Flag** If you've entered any follow-up flags on emails for any of your contacts, they're sorted out in this view.

Getting in Touch

Back in the email section, you learned how to use the To: field to pull information from your contact list, making it easier to send email quickly.

Now, let's look at it from the other end of things. From Contacts, you can send an email, write a letter, and more. Before you can do any of this, however, you have to have the correct information entered for the contact. For example, Outlook can't help you send a letter to a contact unless you have a mailing address entered.

Emailing

Sending emails to contacts is simple. Just highlight the contact in your View window, open the Actions menu, and select New Message to Contact. Or, you can drag a contact to the Inbox icon. Either way, the email message window will open and the contact's name (or email address) will appear in the To: field. You're ready to go!

Other Options

Some of the other items on the Actions menu, such as New Meeting Request to Contact and New Task for Contact, are a little bit more advanced. These will be covered later in this book.

Message in a Bottle

You can also send a regular letter to a contact by using the Microsoft Word Letter Wizard, which works intuitively with Outlook.

From the Actions menu, select New Letter to Contact. This option has the Microsoft Word icon next to it. When you select it, Word opens and the Letter Wizard starts.

All you need to do now is follow the onscreen instructions. The purpose of creating a letter this way is that the recipient's mailing address is automatically entered in the appropriate place at the top of the letter, so there's no need to retype it.

The Least You Need to Know

- Contact lists are helpful for keeping all of your information about both your business and personal contacts in one place. You can also sort and group your contacts as needed.
- Entering a contact can be simple or complex, depending upon how much information you choose to enter.
- A contact can be edited from the View window or by opening the contact and making changes. In the View window, you can change only those fields you can see.
- There are a number of different ways to view your contacts. The most popular way to view them is in the Address Cards view because they appear as Rolodex entries.

Chapter 15

Working with Contacts

In This Chapter

- Creating a new Contacts list
- Adding contacts in new ways
- Adding new categories to contacts
- Using custom categories
- Organizing and manipulating contacts
- Finding a contact
- Sorting contacts
- Filtering contacts

So you've got a bunch of names, addresses, phone numbers, email addresses, Web site addresses, and more entered into your Contacts folder. What good is it to you?

Well, if all you're using it for is to look up someone's address to send them a letter or give them a call, it's not worth much more to you than that address book you've been carrying around for years.

For your contact list to really be useful to you, you need to learn to work with it in more complex ways. It's an odd little paradox, but it's true: By learning some of the more advanced features of the Contacts feature, you can actually make working with your list of contacts easier.

Before you start to get too worried, however, you can relax. The features covered in this chapter are not terribly complex—just a little more advanced than the features that we covered in the previous chapter.

Here, you'll learn how to manipulate your Contacts folder in a variety of ways. You'll learn how to make a new contact list and a couple of different ways to enter contacts. We'll cover sorting and filtering contacts and some of the more advanced types of information you can enter into your Contacts folder. We'll take a more in-depth look at categories and other ways to organize your contacts. By the time we're done here, you'll be ready to move on to the real advanced stuff!

A New Folder, Just for You

In the last chapter, you entered some contacts into the Contacts folder. Now, it's time to learn how to create a new Contacts folder.

Why would you want to do that? Well, there are any number of reasons why you might want to have separate Contacts folders. The most common is probably to keep business and personal contacts separate from one another.

But there are other reasons, too. You may want to have separate folders for different customers. Or maybe you want to separate your contacts by regions or countries.

As mentioned in the last chapter, these are functions you can perform by using a single folder. Later in this chapter, we'll discuss some ways to sort and filter your folder(s). But there are times when it simply works best to have completely separate folders. Trust me.

Creating a new Contacts folder is easy. In fact, you don't have to be working in Contacts to do it.

From the File menu, choose New and then select Folder. A Create New Folder window opens, as shown in the following figure.

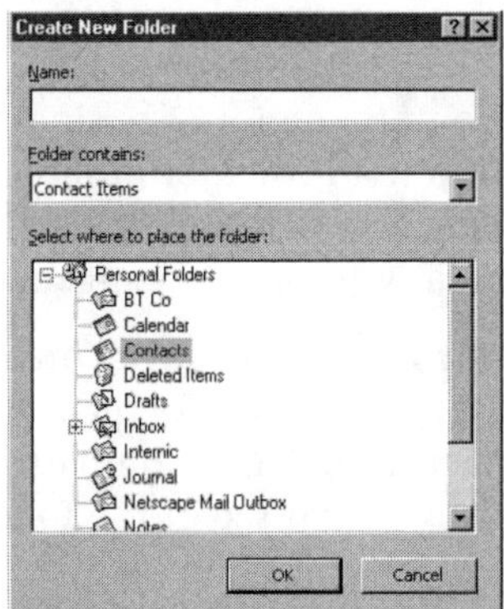

Creating a new Contacts folder is as simple as creating a new folder.

In the Name field, type a name for your new folder. If this folder is for personal contacts, for example, call it Personal. If it's for a specific group of people you deal with at work, name it accordingly.

I'm setting this up as a folder just for my clients, so I'm calling it Clients. Clever, huh? Now make sure that the Folder contains window shows Contact Items, and that the Contacts folder is designated as the place where the folder will be stored. Then click the OK button.

When you're asked if you want to create a shortcut in the Outlook Bar, click Yes.

To view the contents of this folder, click the My Shortcuts bar in the Outlook bar. Because you just created a shortcut, you should see your new folder listed there with an icon that looks like a little Rolodex. Click that icon to open the folder. It will be empty, of course, but this is where you need to start.

Now you're ready to enter a few contacts into your new folder. Take a few minutes to enter some. Remember, you begin to enter a new contact by clicking the New button in the upper-left corner of the Contacts folder.

Which Folder Do I Use Now?

If you want to use this new folder for the rest of the features covered in this chapter, you should enter several contacts into it now. If you'd rather just move ahead, go back to your regular Contacts folder for the rest of this chapter.

Speeding Up the Process

If you've created a Clients folder or you're entering a lot of business contacts into any of your Contacts folders, you'll probably find it a little monotonous. You probably have several contacts that all work for the same company. Wouldn't it be great if you could avoid reentering all of the same company information again and again?

Well, you can. To do this, open a contact for which you have entered company information by double-clicking it in whichever Contacts folder you like. From the contact's Actions menu, choose New Contact from Same Company. A new Contact window opens, but it isn't entirely blank, as you can see in the following figure.

Some fields are already filled in when you add a contact from the same company.

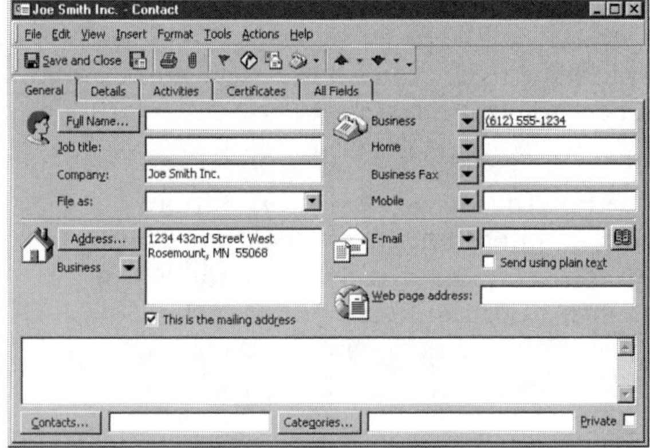

As you can see, the company name, address, and phone number have already been entered in the Contacts entry screen. If you had entered a Web page address for the previous contact, that field would be filled in as well.

The name and job title fields are blank, as are any other personal fields, such as the home phone number. You've saved the need to reenter all of the corporate information.

However, the business telephone number remains, so you'll have to change this information if the new contact has a different number (or extension). This function doesn't save you much time at all, however, if the new contact works for the same company but at a different address.

Quickie Phone Numbers

Here's a little shortcut that can save you a lot of time when you're entering contacts. When you enter a phone number, there's no need to put parentheses around the area code or dashes between the first three and last four digits. Just enter the nine digits all in a row, such as 6125551234, and Outlook will automatically reformat it to (612) 555-1234.

Categorizing

In the last chapter, we briefly discussed adding categories to your contacts. Let's take a minute to understand why adding categories is so important.

As you become more comfortable with Outlook, you'll want to be able to sort and group your contacts for specific projects. For example, say you're in charge of a fantasy football league. You might want to have a category set up just for those contacts. Or you might want a category just for clients who purchase a certain product from you.

The point is, there are many reasons to have categories set up for your contacts. Categories may seem like an unimportant little extra that Outlook offers. Once you've been using Outlook for a while, however, you'll learn that categories are among the outstanding features that make Outlook such a powerful and useful tool.

Outlook offers a full list of categories from which you can choose, but you can also create your own categories. Doing the latter allows you to customize the list to your liking. Any category you create can be added to any of your contacts.

And you don't have to choose just one category to add. For example, if one contact is on a committee with you at church and is also one of your clients, you can add both of those categories to the contact's entry in your Contacts folder. That way, when you sort by either of those categories, that person's name will come up.

Adding Categories

The best way to use categories is through the main Contacts window. You can add categories to contacts as you enter them, or you can go back into any contact at any time and add or remove categories from that entry.

To assign a category or two to a contact, just open the contact's window and click the Categories button at the bottom of the window. The Categories window opens, as shown in the following figure.

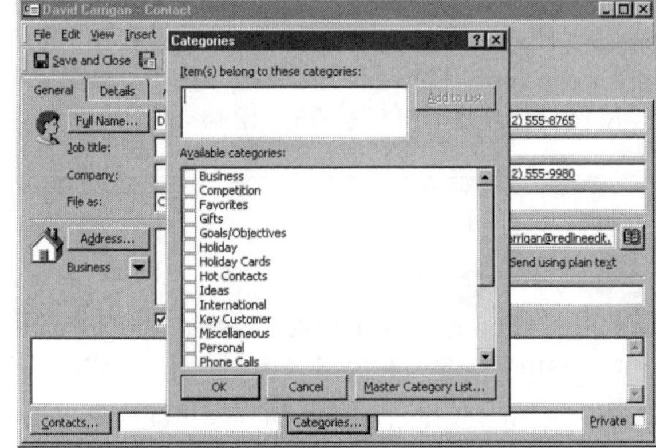

Add categories to your contacts from this window.

As you can see from the figure, you can type categories into the open field or you can click the category name in the Available Categories box. It's usually best to use the Categories list that is provided, because if you misspell a category when you type it in the Open field, it will be recorded incorrectly. For example, if you type "Busness" instead of "Business", Outlook will put that contact in a separate category called "Busness".

You can click as many or as few categories as you like for each contact.

Want to Get Really Tricky?

"Wait a minute," you might be saying. "You're telling me to add categories now, after I've already entered a bunch of contacts?" Well, yes, but you can go back and add them pretty quickly with a simple little trick.

For example, say you've got 25 contacts you've already entered, 15 of which could be categorized as key customers. In the Address Cards view, click one of those 15 contacts. Then hold down the Ctrl button and click all of the others. Once you have all 15 of them highlighted, open the Edit menu and choose Categories. Any categories you assign at this point will be applied to each of the highlighted contacts. If you want to assign the same category to every one of your contacts, you can click the first one in the list, and then hold down the Shift key and click the last one in the list. All of your contacts in the list will then be highlighted, and you can assign categories to all of them at that point.

Don't believe me? Give it a shot.

Making Your Own Categories

You can even create your own categories, a practice that is highly useful indeed. That way, you can create specific categories for various aspects of your business or personal life as you see fit. Assigning a contact to a generic Business category is probably a little too general.

From that Category window, click the Master Category List button. Not surprisingly, the Master Category List window opens. It looks like the one you see in the following figure.

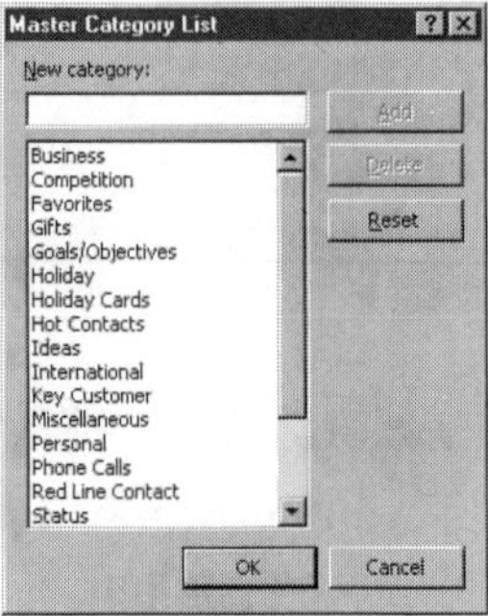

Create your own categories in this window.

The main window shows all the categories that currently exist. Type your category in the New category window. Note in the figure that the Add to List button is grayed out. Once you begin to type a category name, that button becomes activated.

Make your category name descriptive without being too long. It has to be specific enough that you'll remember to use it each time you need it.

What If It's Been Assigned?

If a category has been assigned to one or more contacts, it won't be permanently deleted from the Master Categories List until you've deleted the category from each and every contact that's using it. Until that's done, the category name appears in the Categories list along with a notation that it's "Not in Master Categories List."

Deleting Categories

As is usually the case with a Microsoft program, if you can add something to it, you can usually delete it as well. Such is the case with categories in Outlook. You can delete not only the categories you created on your own, but also the master categories that were originally installed as part of the program.

To do so, open the Categories window and click the Master Categories List, just as you did when you created Categories. Highlight any categories you want to delete, and then click the Delete button.

You won't get any kind of warning that the categories are about to be removed—they're just gone, quick as a hiccup. If you accidentally delete a category, heaven forbid, you can quickly put it back in (as you learned in the previous section).

Organizing Contacts

Right now, your folder probably takes up no more than a screen or two in Address Cards view (unless you imported a previously established Contacts folder from a previous version of Outlook). If so, you can easily find the contact information you're looking for by opening your Contacts folder. As your list expands, however, that's going to become more difficult. It's probably hard to believe now, but one day your Contacts folder will grow to dozens or even hundreds of entries.

That's the purpose of categories—they help you narrow your list a little so you can find what you're looking for more quickly without starting at the As and moving through the Zs. Heck, if you're looking for a specific person's telephone number, just click on the first letter of their last name from the list to the right of the Contacts screen. You're there.

It's not going to be that easy all the time, and the more contacts you have in your folder, the more difficult it can become. That's where the Find command comes into play.

Seek and Ye Shall Find

If you've been paying attention to the figures in Part 3 of the book, you've probably noticed that the contact list is made up of about 10 names. That's because it's fictional, and I didn't have time to fill it with 1,000 names. (Hey, I'm trying to write a book here.) It might seem a little silly to use a Find command on such a small list, but it works regardless of the size of the list.

The Find command is available only from the Address Cards view, so you should start by making sure your contacts are being displayed in that view.

From the Tools menu, select Find. The Find window opens above your contact list, as shown in the following figure.

In the Basic Find feature on the left side of the Find window, Outlook searches through the Name, Company, Address, and Category fields in this type of search.

If you would like to try a search now, type in the name of a city that you know appears in more than one address in your contact list. When you click the Find Now button, Outlook will display all of the contacts that met your search criteria.

You can search by a lot more than city, of course. You can search for a first, last, or middle name, any part of an address, any part of a company name, and any category. Even parts of words will work. For example, if I search my list for "ed", the result is four contacts. None of them have the first name "Ed", but instead have either the word "red" or the word "editorial."

You can search for specific information in this window.

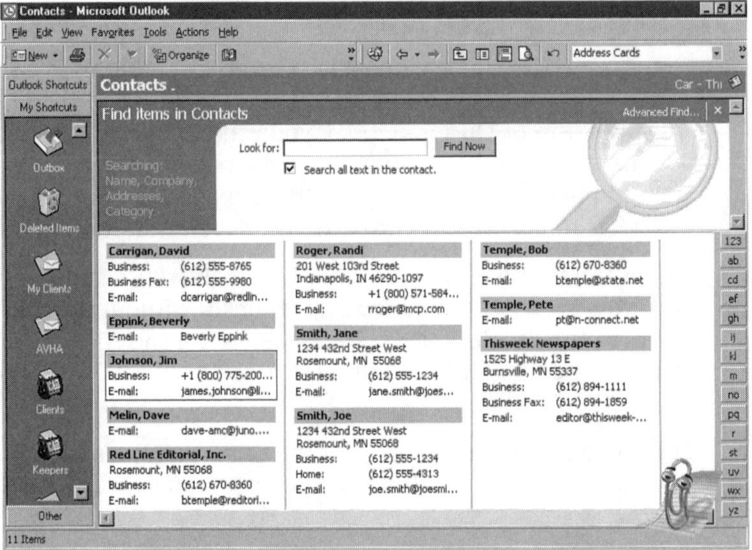

Removing a Find

Regardless of the kind of Find you do, removing it is easy. Simply click the little "X" in the upper-right corner of the Find window and you will again have the entire Contacts folder in your window. Be careful not to click the handwritten "X" that deletes Contacts from your folder!

Moving Up to the Advanced Class

If you'd like to conduct a more advanced search of your Contacts folder, you can use the Advanced Find feature.

Most often, this is used when the Find function hasn't narrowed the search enough—the result was too many contacts. Once you've done a Find and Outlook has displayed the results, you can click Go to Advanced Find from the Find window. (If you'd like to *begin* by doing an Advanced Find, you can select it from the Tools menu in any of the Outlook screens.)

In the Advanced Find window, shown in the following figure, you can select which fields Outlook should search, what type of item you're searching for, and more.

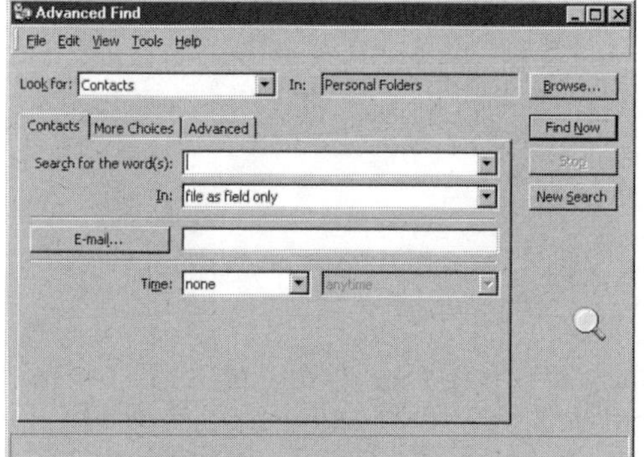

Advanced Find conducts a more detailed search.

Sorting and Filtering

You can also apply sorts and filters to your Contacts folder as a means of identifying a specific contact or group of contacts.

To better understand what these functions can do for you, let's take a look at exactly *how* they work.

A Sort, of Sorts

As you've probably noticed, your Contacts folder is sorted by the File As field, alphabetically. But you can arrange the contacts by any other field if you want. You can sort your contacts by anything from company name to Web page address to pager number.

To apply a sort, open the View menu while you're in Address Cards view, and then click Current View. Then select Customize Current View to open the View Summary dialog box. Click the Sort button and the Sort window will open. It should look like the following figure.

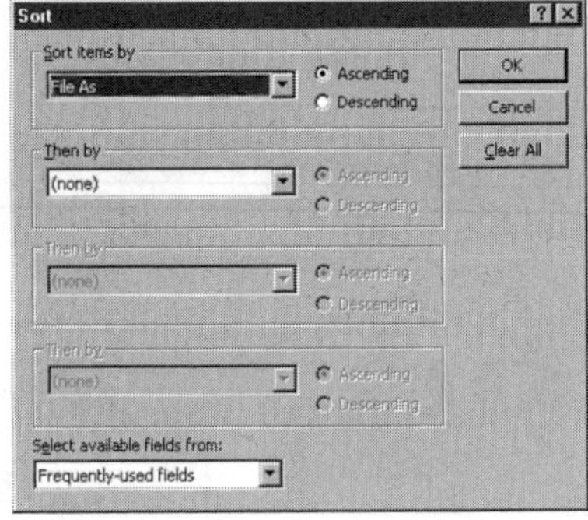

You can sort items by up to four different fields.

As you can see, you can sort contacts by up to four different fields. Go to the first drop-down list and choose the field you want the folder to be sorted by, and whether you want it to be sorted in ascending or descending order. You might want to choose secondary fields, in case there are several identical entries in the first field you've chosen. For example, if you sort the folder by company, and you have many contacts from the same company, you might also want to sort by a secondary field like File As.

When you're done, click the OK button and the folder will be sorted. To undo the sort, go back into the Sort window and click the Clear All button.

A Filter without Coffee

You can also filter contacts in Outlook. While a sort merely rearranges the contacts based on the fields you choose, a filter actually displays only those contacts that match your criteria, thus narrowing your list.

Filtering takes place in the View Summary window. To get back there, open the View menu, select Current View, and then select Customize Current View. You'll see that next to the Filter button is the word Off. This means you aren't currently applying a filter.

Click the Filter button and you'll get a window that looks like the following figure.

The Filter window looks a lot like the Advanced Find window. Again, you can search for words and tell Outlook the fields in which to look. You'll get a list of only those contacts that meet the search criteria you've applied.

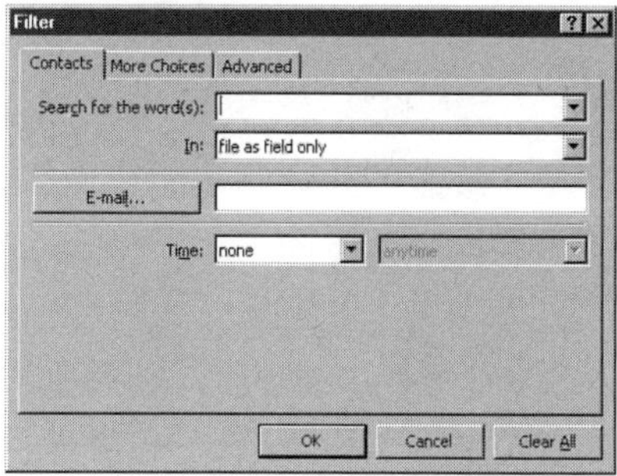

Applying a filter narrows the scope of your contact list.

One important thing to note—the contacts must *exactly* match the search words you enter, and you must enter whole words. For example, when you did a Find and searched for "ed", you got several contacts that had "ed" as *part* of a word. If you filter using the same criteria, the result will be no contacts at all because none of them in my folder contain the whole word "Ed".

Once your filter has been applied, you will see the words "Filter Applied" in the lower left-hand corner of your screen.

You can remove your filter by going back into the Filter window, clicking the Clear All button, and then clicking OK twice.

The Least You Need to Know

- You don't have to just work out of your Contacts folder. You can create new Contacts folders for different folders, if you want.
- You can reduce the time it takes to enter contacts who work for the same company by using the New Contact from Same Company command on the Actions menu.
- Categories are among the most important parts of the Contacts window because they help you sort out your folder as it grows larger.
- The Find and Advanced Find functions allow you to search through your folder quickly.
- Sorting allows you to display all of your contacts based on a list of fields that you specify.
- Filtering allows you to exclude those contacts that don't meet the criteria you apply. It helps you narrow your folder and locate only those contacts you want to see.

Chapter 16

Getting It Customized

In This Chapter

- Why you might want to customize the Contacts form
- Setting up a custom form
- Establishing a custom database
- Using the control toolbox
- Adding pages to your form
- Organizing the form by arranging tab order
- Publishing the form

In the last two chapters, you learned the basics—and a few advanced features—of Outlook's Contacts setup.

As you saw on the Contacts form, there are many, many fields where you can enter information about the people in your life, both business and personal. You might have been a little overwhelmed at the sheer volume of possible information you could record. But what if there was… even more?

Well, again, the program designers at Microsoft have thought of just about everything. Somewhere along the line, they figured out that the best way to make a program that's perfect for everyone is to make it customizable. You've seen this already in a number of areas. Most recently, you learned how you can create your own categories to add to the contacts in your database.

Well, you can go even further than that. Outlook lets you change the Contacts form itself. That's right, the General tab and all the others on the Contacts form can all be customized to suit your needs.

That's what this chapter is all about. Some of the concepts discussed here are more advanced than in the previous two contacts chapters (Chapter 14, "Keeping in Contact," and Chapter 15, "Working with Contacts"), but you're probably ready for that now.

What's the Point?

With all of those fields on Outlook's Contacts form, why bother messing with it? Well, there are a number of fields that you may *never* use. At the very least, you might want to delete them because they're just taking up space.

But over time, you'll probably find that there are additional fields you would like to add. Maybe you've been putting a certain type of information in the Notes field, and you realize it might be better to give it its own field.

Building a personal database and you don't need the Company field at all? Delete it. Would you rather have a field where you can put in the name of your contact's pets? Add one. Or maybe you've got a database of all of your clients and you'd like to add a field to indicate their gross expenditures with your firm in the last year. Whatever the reason, being able to customize the Contacts form is a handy tool.

You might not need to know how to customize your Contacts form right now, but someday you'll probably refer back to this chapter to learn how.

Some of the concepts involved in customizing the Contacts form are beyond the scope of this book. We'll just cover some of the most common ways to customize the form here.

Reproduce an Existing Database

Many businesses have existing databases for customers. By customizing the Contacts form in Outlook, you can actually re-create an existing database with all the same fields.

For example, a business could enter its customers into a customized contacts database, and assign categories to them. Then, the business could use the database to send out mailings to all customers or only those that fit in certain categories.

Some small businesses use the Contacts feature of Outlook to maintain their database of employees as well.

Setting It Up

It's time to get started setting up your own Contacts form. Before you do it, though, you may want to consider setting up a new database just for this form.

In the last chapter, you learned how to create a new contacts database. If you're going to customize the Contacts form for a particular set of contacts, you might want to group them in their own database. So begin by creating a new database for the records you will create using your custom form. To do this, open the File menu, choose Folder, then New Folder. Make sure you tell Outlook that the folder will contain contacts.

Once the folder is created, you need to open a blank version of your existing Contacts form by clicking the New button while you're in your newly created contacts database. On the new, blank form, open the Tools menu, select Forms, and then select Design This Form. A Design form opens, just like the one you see in the following figure.

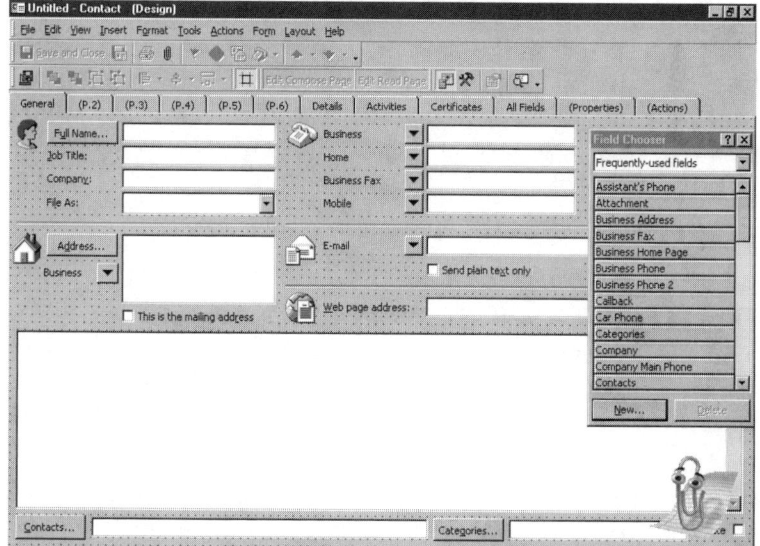

Use this window to redesign your Contacts form.

At first glance, it looks a lot like your existing Contacts form. There's a reason for that—it *is* the existing Contacts form, which you're about to redesign. However, you will notice some differences. First, there are little dots all over the form. These dots help ensure that all fields and boxes that are put on the form remain straight and properly aligned. You'll see how they work in a minute or two.

You'll also notice that all of the original tabs are still there, but they've been joined by seven new tabs with their names in parentheses. These tabs are additional pages, if you decide you would like to add some.

Tabbing

A *tab* gets its name from the old manila folder. On the Contacts form, and in many other areas of Outlook, pages are designed to look like a manila folder. In those cases, the name for each folder page appears on the tab, so these are called *tabs*.

At the right side of your screen, you should see the Field Chooser box. This includes all of the preset fields from which you can choose as you're building your own Contacts form. At the top is a drop-down list that allows you to choose between frequently used fields and any of a number of other field groups. This list includes one all-encompassing choice called All Contact fields.

We'll cover the Field Chooser a little later.

Quick-Change Artist

Earlier in this chapter, you learned about making basic changes to the Contacts form. The example used was a personal database in which there was no need to have a Company field, which was replaced with a field called Pets.

Let's take a quick look at how to make these basic changes.

A Click-Click Here, a Click-Click There

Everything that you see in the existing Contacts form can be deleted or moved. You can even change the shape of text boxes and the like. This even includes the icons that appear alongside some of the field names, like the face in profile next to the Full Name field.

To move or delete a field, first highlight it by clicking on it. For example, click on the word Company in the General tab. As you can see from the following figure, the field name is surrounded by a gray box with little white squares on it.

Highlight a field like this to delete or move it.

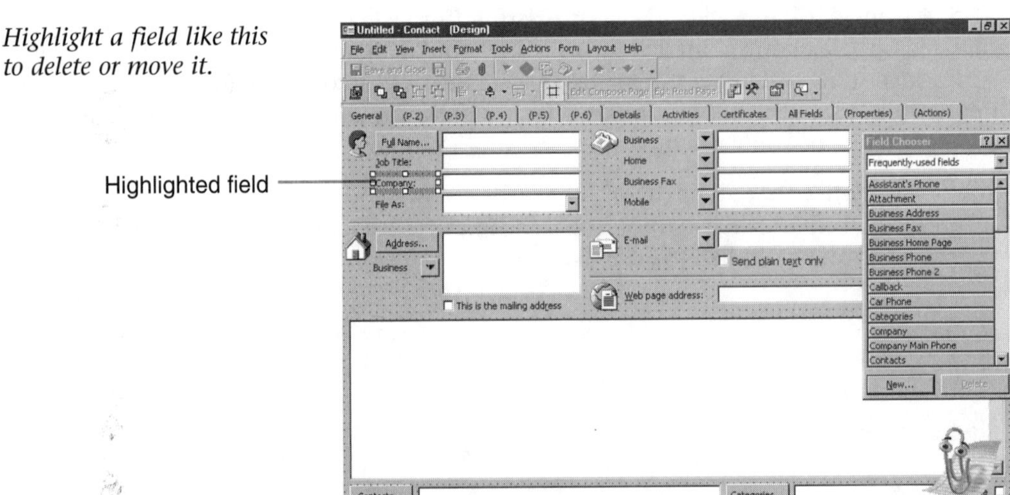

At this point, you have several options. But if you're going to do anything to this field, you should probably select the text box that goes with it by holding down the Shift key and clicking on it. Then, you can delete the field by simply pressing the Delete button on your computer. If you want to move it, you can click on either of the two selected fields and drag it to the place you want to go.

Before we get into adding a field in place of the Company field, let's work on resizing. Those white squares on all four corners of the highlighted field and on each side of the boxes can be used to resize it. This is best used for resizing a text box. Look again at your Contact Design form. That Notes field at the bottom of the General tab is awfully large, isn't it? Let's change that.

Click anywhere within the Notes box and it will be highlighted, with the white squares around it. Then grab any of the three squares at the top of the Notes area and drag this top border down about halfway. Then release. Your Contacts form should now look like the following figure.

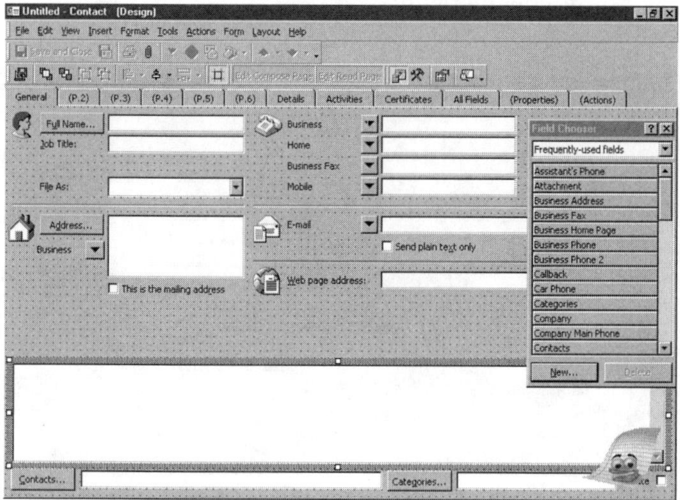

Your Contacts form with the Company field gone and the Notes field resized.

There. Now you've got a little room to add some fields.

Choosy Moms Choose the Field Chooser

Now it's time to add some fields. We've talked about creating a more personal form, so let's go ahead with that plan. Adding fields is easy when you use the Field Chooser, which should still be on the right side of your screen.

First, let's look at the personal fields that Outlook has to offer. Pull down the drop-down menu in the Field Chooser box and select Personal fields. A list of 10 fields appears.

Don't Overanalyze

This is just an example we're working on here. If you really created a personal-only Contacts form, you would probably remove other fields (like Business Fax and Job Title). We're just walking through the basics here so you can handle it as you see fit. That's the nature of a customizable form, after all.

To add a field from the Field Chooser, simply click on the name of the field you want to add in the Field Chooser window and drag it to the point where you want to insert it.

First, let's use the space you created by resizing the Notes window to add a few personal fields. Click on Children and drag it beneath the Address field. When you release it, it snaps to the nearest set of dots to keep the form straight. If it doesn't quite find the right spot, click anywhere on the gray-highlighted box (the cursor turns into a four-way arrow) and drag it to the right spot.

Now, add one more field beneath Children and two under the Web page address field on the right. Your form should look like the one in the following figure.

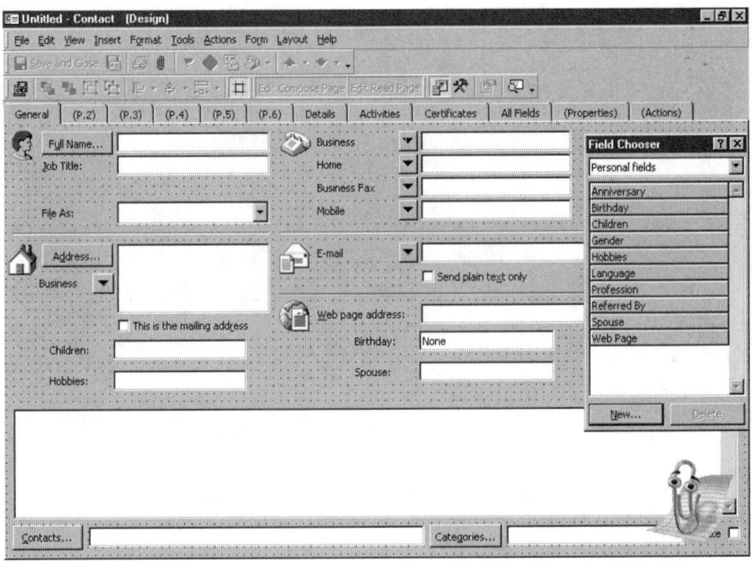

Four fields have been added above the Notes window.

Granted, you might want to rearrange the order of these fields, because the redesign doesn't flow terribly well. But you get the idea.

Also, you'll note that each of these fields comes with a text box already attached. If you think any of these text windows should be bigger, you can enlarge them in the same manner you used to reduce the Notes window.

A Field of Your Own

We've talked about adding a Pets field where the Company field used to be; you've probably noticed that Outlook doesn't offer you a Pets field.

At the bottom of the Field Chooser there's a New button. Click it to add a new field. You'll get a dialog box, in which you can enter a new field name. In our example, that would be "Pets," as you see in the following figure.

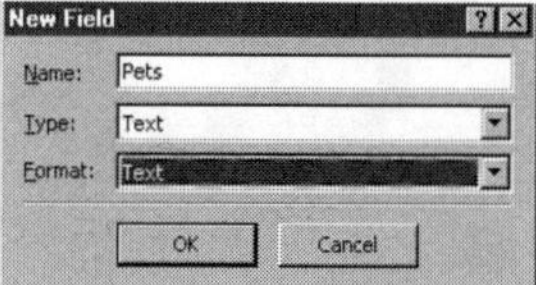

Add your own fields in this box.

Next, pick the type of information that will go into the field and the format for the field. In our example, both of these should be Text. Then click OK. As you can see, your new field falls into a User-defined fields in folder list. Now, click on Pets in the Field Chooser and drag it into the position where the Company field used to be.

What's Your Type?

When you created the Pets field, you had to choose a type. If you pull down the Type drop-down menu, you'll see there are a lot of choices. We don't have the space to cover them all here, but some of them can come in really handy. Depending on the type of information you want to include in a field, you might need to select a different type from the menu. If you do, you can then select the format for that information as well.

Using the Control Toolbox

The Control Toolbox offers a variety of ways to manipulate the form you're designing. Controls also allow you to insert special types of objects into the form, such as text boxes or different kinds of buttons.

To open it, click the Control Toolbox button on the toolbar at the top of the screen. The button looks like a hammer crossed over a wrench. The toolbox looks like the one in the following figure.

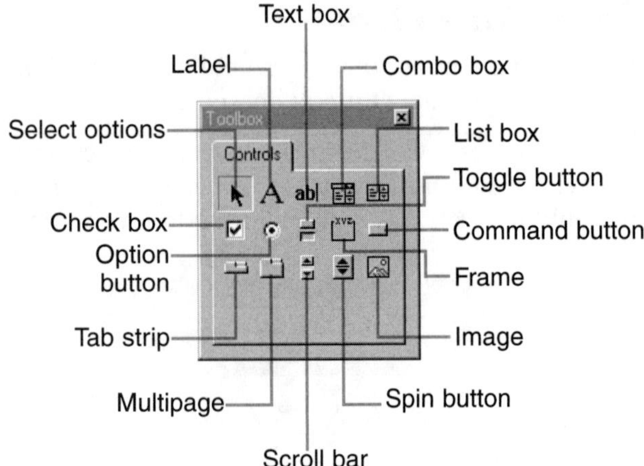

The Control Toolbox allows you to manipulate the form you're designing.

Each of the 15 controls performs a different function. To see the name of the control, point your cursor at a button in the Toolbox and leave it there until the name appears. Here are brief descriptions of these controls:

- *Select options* You didn't know it, but this control was the default control. This is the one that allowed you to select the fields and text boxes and delete them or move them around.
- *Label* Creates a label for a text box, or can be used for informational purposes on the form.
- *Text box* Creates an open text box that you can link to a field name or leave unlinked.
- *Combo box* Creates a box accompanied by a drop-down list.
- *List box* Creates a box with a list of choices.
- *Check box* Creates a small square box that you can place a check mark in.
- *Option box* Creates a radio button that, when grouped with others of its kind, allows you to select from a list of choices on the form. This is different from the list box because all the options would be visible, and more than one can be checked.
- *Toggle button* Like the check box, except that it's raised when inactive and depressed when active.
- *Frame* Allows you to place borders around objects, thus letting you divide the form into sections.
- *Command button* Executes a command, such as the Save and Close button. When it's clicked, it tells Outlook to perform a function.
- *Tab strip* Allows you to add tabs to a page.
- *Multipage* In essence, it creates a page within a page.

- *Scroll bar* Adds a scroll bar to a place in the form where there is more information than is currently visible.
- *Spin button* Allows incremental increases or decreases in a value. For example, when you print a page, there's a spin button next to the area where you choose the number of copies to print.
- *Image* Creates a frame in which you can put a picture or graphic.

Adding a Page (or More)

As you'll recall from earlier in this chapter, there are seven extra pages visible when you design a form. These are the seven forms in which the tab names are in parentheses. If you would like to create a new page for a form, you can do so with one of these pages. It's best to start with (P.2). These pages are visible, but aren't really added to your form until you name the page and tell Outlook to display it.

To begin, simply click the tab for the page you want to add. That will open a blank Contacts form page, to which you can add whatever fields you want to add.

Now you are ready to name the page, and tell Outlook to display it. Both of these functions are accomplished from the Form menu.

To name the page, select Rename Page. This opens a small dialog box into which you type the name you would like on the tab. Then click OK.

You'll see that this new name is still in parentheses. That's because you haven't told Outlook to display the page or added any fields. Unless you do one of these things, Outlook will only display the page in design mode, not when you want to actually enter contact information.

To display the page, open the Form menu and choose Display This Page. As you can see from the following figure, there are no parentheses on the Personal page, which is the name of the page I added.

Arranging Tab Order

This section isn't about setting the order of the pages. The pages are each opened by clicking a tab, as in a folder tab. This section is about your Tab key.

When you're entering information in the completed form, you're going to want the navigation of that form to be quick and easy. Anytime you enter something into a field, you click the Tab key to move to the next field. If clicking that Tab key moves you to a faraway spot, it will only frustrate you.

Let's go back to the General tab. Outlook lets you set the order in which the Tab key moves your cursor through the form. To do this, right-click on any blank spot in the form while you're in design mode. Then select Tab Order to display the current order, as you can see in the following figure.

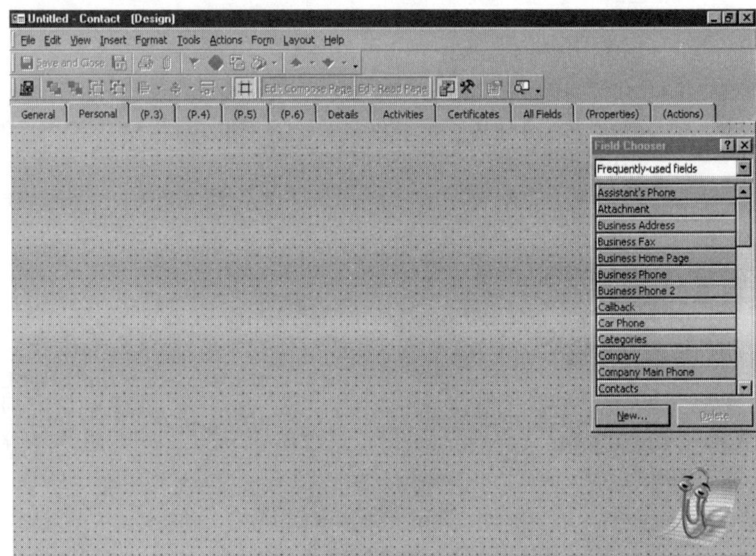

The new page is now called "Personal."

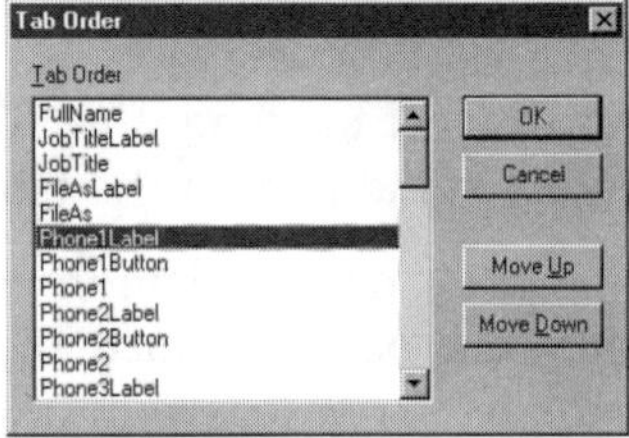

Set the tab order in this box.

Highlight any field and click the Move Up or Move Down button to change the order.

Publishing the Form

You aren't done designing the form until you've published it. Publishing the form allows you to use it as a Contacts form later on.

Once you've made all your changes to the form, you're ready to publish it. To do this, click the Publish Form button on the far left of the toolbar, or open the Tools menu, select Forms, and then select Publish Form As. You'll see the window shown in the following figure.

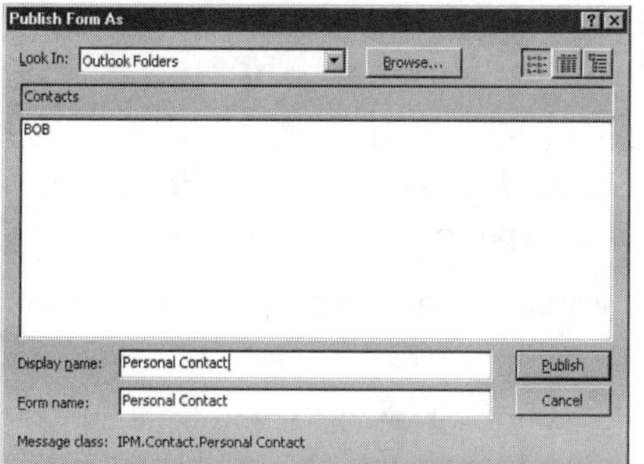

Publishing the form is the final step in the process.

Make sure the Look In window says Outlook Folders, and then type a name for the form. (Since we designed a form for personal contacts, I'm calling this my Personal Contact form, as you can see in the preceding figure.) When you type the name in the Display name field, it also appears in the Form name field. Click Publish.

After a moment you're returned to the Design screen, which you can now close. If you're asked to save the changes you've made, click No because you've already published the form.

So, how do you get back to this form again? Simple. Just open the File menu, choose New, and then select Choose Form. Put Outlook Folders in the Look In field and the name of your form will appear. Open it and you're on your way.

If you want to make your new form the default form for a particular Contacts database, you can. Right-click on the folder, then select Properties. You'll see a drop-down menu in which you can select the form to use "when posting to this folder."

The Least You Need to Know

- Customizing the Contacts form allows you to include all of the fields you want to include, and only the fields you want to include. It also allows you to create a special form for special types of contacts you may have.
- Setting up a custom form is very easy. The basic types of form editing can be done using drag-and-drop.
- The Control Toolbox contains controls that allow you to manipulate your form and add specific tools, like drop-down lists, scroll bars, and so on.
- Add pages to your form to ensure that you can include all of the information you want and have it set up the way you want it.
- You can arrange the order in which the cursor will move through the form when the Tab key is used.
- When you're done designing the form, you must publish it to be able to use it as a form later.

Part 4

Where's the Time Gone? Getting Organized

It's time to get organized, and Outlook has some good tools that can help. This section of the book covers the organizational side of Outlook 2000. We'll start with some background information on Outlook's Calendar, and then we'll put the Calendar to use. Then we'll look at how the Journal and Notes can help. Finally, we'll prioritize your to-do list by using Outlook's Tasks.

Chapter 17

More than Numbered Boxes on a Page

In This Chapter

- Why use Outlook's Calendar?
- Home uses for the Calendar
- Work uses for the Calendar
- Getting started with the Calendar
- An overview of the Calendar's features
- Calendar views

Early in the morning on Saturday, December 12, the phone rang at my home. I stumbled out of bed and ambled over to the phone. The voice on the other end asked me if I wanted to play golf. Not that unusual, really—depending on what part of the country you live in. Me? I live in the suburbs of Minneapolis-St. Paul, so someone asking me to play golf on December 12 is a little odd.

Sounds like fun, I thought. I looked outside at a beautiful, sunny morning. "What's the date today?," I asked. "The 12th?" My soon-to-be golf partner confirmed that, despite temperatures in the 50s, it was in fact December 12.

The temperature had been making a liar out of my calendar all fall. When I played golf on the day after Thanksgiving, it was a first for me in Minnesota. That I still had two weeks left to play golf was virtually unbelievable.

If it weren't for Outlook's Calendar, I never would have been able to convince myself that it was time to get my Christmas shopping done. After all, why shop for Christmas presents when it feels like Spring? With Outlook's Calendar greeting me each day with pre-holiday events, I couldn't help but keep my focus on the season.

(Okay, okay, so it wasn't *just* Outlook that kept me focused on the upcoming holidays. The three little people in my home do a pretty good job of that, too.)

In truth, Outlook's Calendar does a lot more than remind you what today's date is. After all, a decent watch can help you with that task. No, Outlook is a serious time-management tool that can help you organize your personal and business time while making sure you don't miss out on anything important.

In this chapter, we'll cover the basic features of Outlook's Calendar in a basic way. We'll look at setting appointments and recurring appointments, and we'll cover events and meetings.

The next chapter includes more in-depth coverage on these and other Calendar features.

Why Use Outlook's Calendar?

Why not?

Outlook's Calendar is the perfect tool for organizing your business and personal schedules. You can even create different schedules for different people in your household without having it all show up in the same place.

Around the House

It doesn't really matter where you are in life—single, just married with no kids, or married with young kids, teenagers, or college-age kids. Everybody seems to think they're busier now than they've ever been in their lives (unless, of course, you've recently retired).

In an average week—in addition to your 9-to-5 responsibilities—you probably have many things you need to remember. Little Jenny's dance lessons, Girl Scout meetings, piano lessons, basketball practices, and little Jimmy's karate classes. Add in a meeting or two at church for you and/or your spouse, and there are plenty of things you need to remember.

If your house is anything like mine, you probably have at least one calendar hanging on a wall in your kitchen. It's probably got dozens of appointments or events written on it, maybe even color-coded by kid. It's probably got eraser marks or scribbled-out appointments that have been changed or cancelled.

With Outlook, you can organize all of this into a single source that you can edit at will without creating a huge mess. And if you still want to put up a calendar on the wall at home, you can always print out a copy of your Outlook Calendar and stick it up there.

Going to Work

With these home uses in mind, you should have a pretty good idea of how the Calendar can be applied at work. But at work, it can go way beyond keeping track of all of your meetings, events, and other appointments.

If you're on a networked system using the Corporate version of Outlook, you can share your Calendar with others. You can even schedule a meeting and quickly learn if any of the attendees have other meetings scheduled for the time in question. Or you can give your assistant access to your Calendar so he knows when you have free time available.

In the rest of this chapter, and all of the next one, you'll learn about the features of Outlook's Calendar in detail. Once you've worked your way through these features, you'll have a better idea of exactly what Outlook's Calendar can do for you.

Start Me Up

Like so many other features of Outlook (and every other Microsoft program), there are a bunch of different ways to start the Calendar. As usual, we'll cover those that are most common or easiest to use.

The easiest way to start the Calendar is directly from the Outlook Shortcuts bar. One of the default shortcuts there is for the Calendar. Click it to launch the Calendar. You'll see a screen much like the one in the following figure.

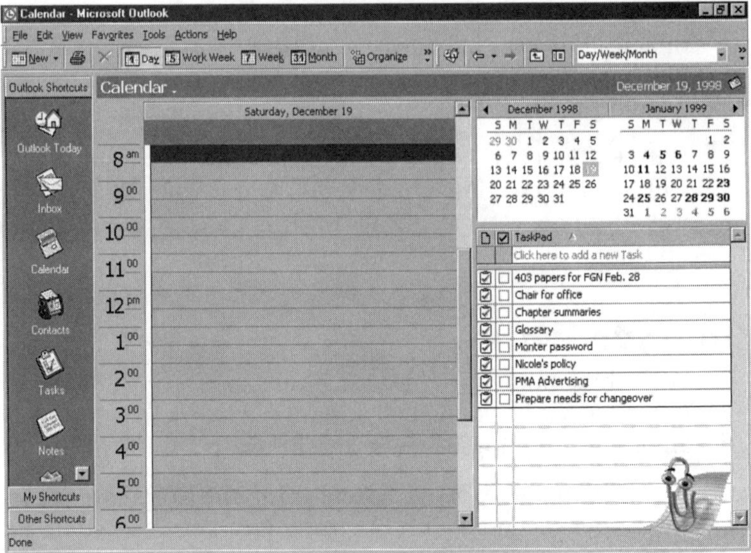

The default Calendar screen is a good place to start.

Working by Default

As you can see from the upper-right corner of the figure, the Calendar's default view is Day/Week/Month view. But unlike other modules of Outlook, the Calendar is usually left in this view. (We'll cover views later in this chapter.)

Month-in-View

If you select the Month view from the toolbar above the Calendar, it takes over the entire Calendar screen, not just the Appointment Calendar pane. Displaying an entire month would make each individual day pretty small if you still had to show the other panes.

Day/Week/Month view offers views within a view. That is, when you are in Day/Week/Month view, you can choose one of four different ways to display the Calendar on your screen.

Buttons on the toolbar allow you to determine whether your screen shows a single day, a five-day workweek, a seven-day period, or the full month.

Normally, Calendar's window has three panes. The largest, on the left, is for your Appointment Calendar. It shows whatever number of days you choose. For example, the preceding figure shows a one-day view. If you changed that to a five-day or seven-day view by clicking the appropriate button on the toolbar, it would still appear within this pane.

The upper-right pane shows the Date Navigator, which normally displays the current month and the next month. This can be changed by using the arrows above the months. This also allows you to change what is displayed in the Appointment Calendar pane. If you click a different date on the Date Navigator, it opens that date (or week, depending on how you have it displayed) in the Appointment Calendar area of your window.

The lower-right pane shows the TaskPad, into which you can enter the things you need to do. Tasks and task lists are covered in depth in Chapter 20, "Multitasking with Task Lists."

Setting Basic Stuff

In Calendar's default setup, the normal working hours of 8 a.m. to 5 p.m. are shown in yellow. The "off" hours are displayed in a grayed-out yellow. You can change these colors, as well as the beginning and ending time for your work day.

To do this, open the Tools menu and click Options. Then click the Calendar options button, and will open a window that looks like the following figure.

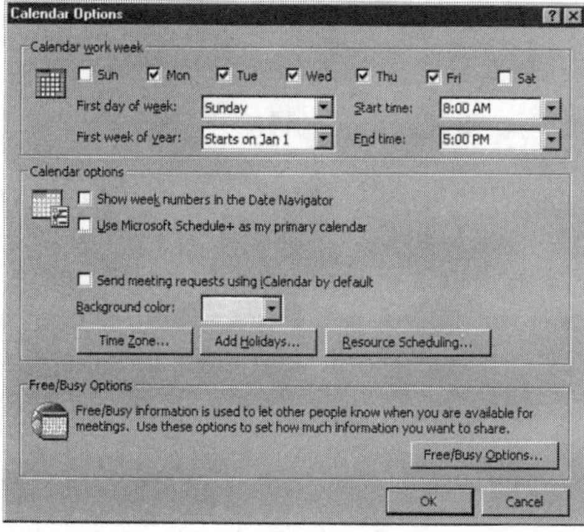

You can handle basic Calendar setup in this window.

In the middle of the screen, you can choose a different color for the background of your Calendar. There are 12 different color choices. Whichever color you choose, your "off" hours will be shown as a grayed-out version of the color. More importantly, though, Outlook allows you to set your normal working hours so they're automatically highlighted on your Calendar.

If you work nights, for example, you can change your beginning and ending hours. Or if you work on an odd schedule, such as Sunday through Thursday, you can set that as well. And you can make changes in this area whenever your work schedule changes.

A Quick Look at the Features

Depending on how you define the word *feature*, you could say that Outlook's Calendar has tons of them. For example, if you consider it a feature to be able to change your basic working hours, as shown in the preceding section, there are tons of similar features in the Outlook Calendar.

But really, there are only three basic features in Outlook's Calendar: appointments, recurring appointments, and events. These are features as defined by types of information you can add into the Calendar.

Don't Freak Out on Me

What about meetings, tasks, and the other stuff you can do in the Calendar mode? Although it's true that these are Calendar features, they're slightly different types of features. A task can be entered in Calendar. It can affect your Calendar (if it has a due date, for example). A meeting will result in an appointment on your Calendar. Before we can really look at these elements, we must learn about the basic stuff, such as appointments.

Let's take a brief look at appointments, recurring appointments, and events. They will be covered in greater detail in later chapters of this book, along with other features.

Appointments

Keeping track of your appointments is the basic goal of any calendar, be it a pocket calendar, a desktop planner, or scraps of paper on your desk.

Outlook allows you to keep track of your appointments, just like any other calendar. Then it goes well beyond that. It enables you to categorize your appointments by type (business, personal, or any other category you might want). It also allows you to make notes about your appointments, giving you a level of detail that is unavailable on any paper calendar.

To open the window where you'll enter a new appointment, click the New button while you're in the Calendar. You'll get a form that looks like the one in the following figure.

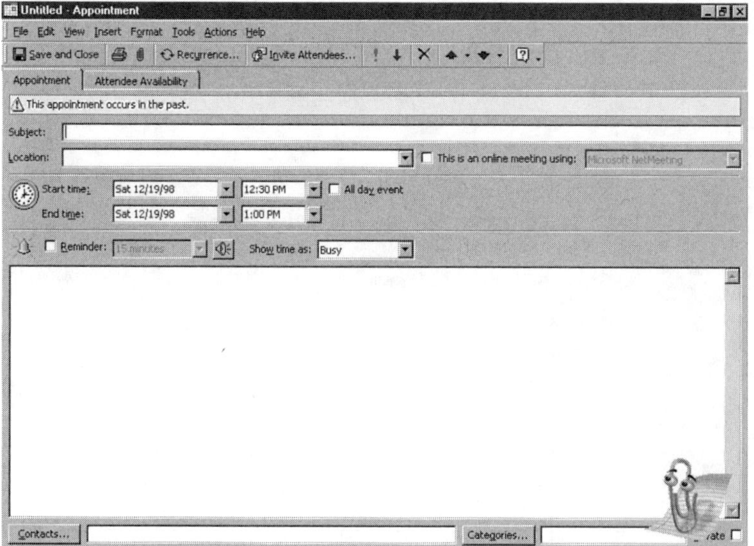

Enter appointment information into this form.

We'll get into more detail about appointments in the next chapter, but let's take a quick look at the Appointments screen.

You can enter a subject for the appointment and a beginning and ending time. But you can also use the large notes area at the bottom of the screen to enter anything else you like. For example, if it's an appointment with a customer you haven't previously visited, you might want to use this area to enter directions to the customer's office.

You can also tell Outlook to remind you in advance of the appointment, perhaps even with an audible warning of some sort. And you can set the amount of time before the appointment that your Outlook will remind you.

Events

What's the difference between an appointment and an event? That's a matter of definition. Outlook defines the difference thusly: An event is any occurrence that lasts at least 24 hours.

So a Rolling Stones concert may be an event to you, but to Outlook it's an appointment because it lasts only a few hours. Now, if you saw the Stones as part of an all-day festival, you would call *that* an event. And so would Outlook.

Designating something as an event is very simple in Outlook. Right next to the Start and End time fields in the New Appointment window, there's a little check box for All Day Event. When you click it, the time fields disappear and you can set a start date and end date for the event. When you display your Calendar, you'll see these dates covered by a banner, as in the following figure.

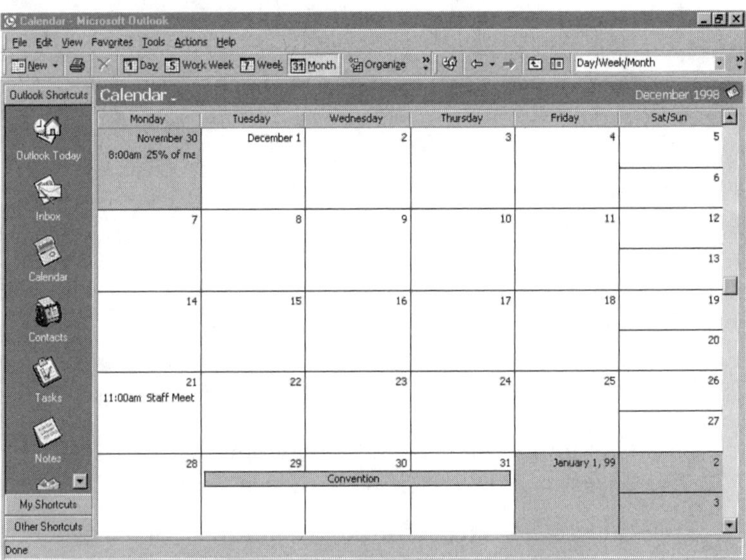

The three-day convention I planned to attend is blocked out for me.

In this figure, I entered a three-day convention that I need to attend at the end of the month. I displayed the Calendar in the Month view, and I can see those three days blocked out.

Recurring Appointments

This is one of the best features of Outlook's Calendar, and one that sets it far apart from any paper appointment calendar.

If you were using a traditional calendar and you had a weekly doctor's appointment, a monthly board meeting, or an annual event (like your anniversary), you'd have to enter it by hand every single time it occurred. But with Outlook's Calendar, any recurring event can be set quickly. You simply fill out one form and it's all set to go.

Near the top of the Appointment window is a button called Recurrence. Click that button to open a Recurrence window, shown in the following figure.

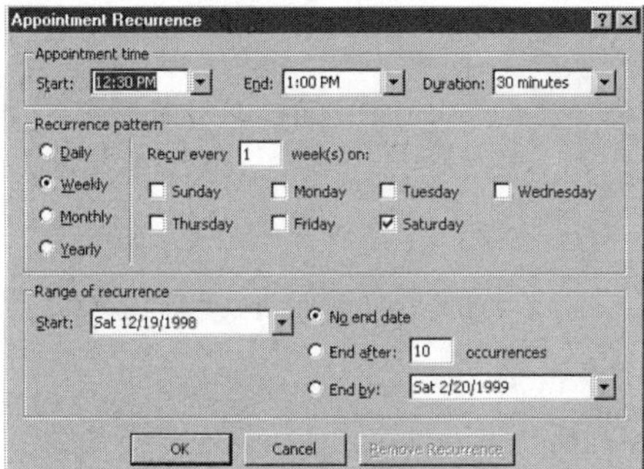

Set recurring appointments in this window.

There are three settings you must make in entering a recurring appointment:

- *Appointment time* Set the beginning and ending times for the appointment.
- *Recurrence pattern* Set whether it's daily, weekly, monthly, or annually. Depending on which of these patterns you choose, you can make further settings. For example, if you choose the monthly recurrence, you can set an appointment to happen on the third Saturday of each month.
- *Range of recurrence* You can set a start date for the appointment and the number of times it occurs. For example, if you have physical therapy for that tennis elbow every Monday for 10 weeks, set the start and end dates for the 10-week run here.

View Finder

Just as with the other modules of Outlook, you can set the view for the Calendar. Within the Day/Week/Month view, you can change how many days appear within your Appointment Calendar pane.

But there are other ways to view the Calendar as well:

- *Day/Week/Month* This is the default view we've already discussed, and it's by far the most common way to display your calendar.
- *Day/Week/Month with Auto Preview* Same as the Day/Week/Month view, except that the first few lines of the Notes section of your appointments are shown.
- *Active Appointments* Shows upcoming appointments in table form, sorted by the recurrence (and the rate of recurrence, if necessary). It looks like the following figure.

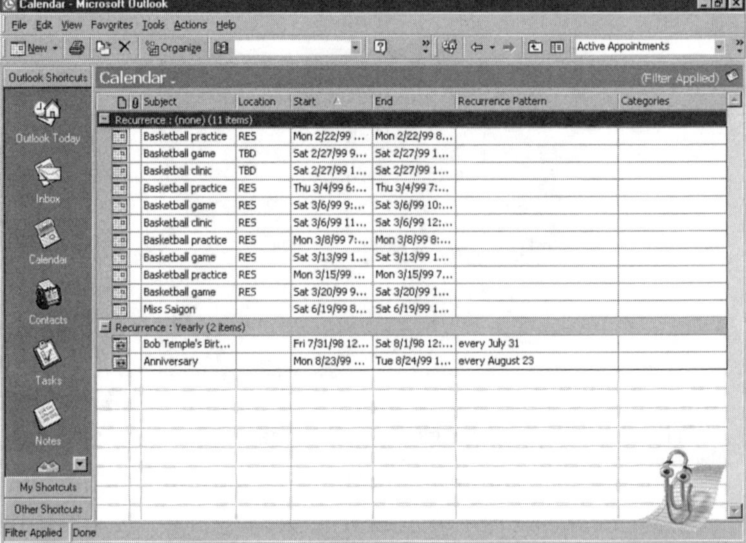

A list of active appointments, sorted by recurrence.

- *Events* Shows the events that you have coming up, also in table form. No appointments are shown.
- *Annual Events* Shows a table of only your annual events. This is great for getting a quick list of birthdays, anniversaries, and so on.
- *Recurring Appointments* Shows a table of any recurring appointments you have scheduled. No events are shown.
- *By Category* Sorts your appointments and events into a table by the category you've assigned to them, if any.

The Least You Need to Know

- Outlook's Calendar does everything a paper calendar can do and more.
- You can use Outlook's Calendar to organize your busy family schedule, your business appointments, or both.
- You can change the background color of the Outlook Calendar, and you can tell Outlook what your work and off-work hours are.
- You can easily enter appointments into Outlook and add a level of detail you couldn't possibly add on a paper calendar.
- With Outlook, recording recurring appointments is as easy as a couple of clicks.
- Blocking out a whole day or days is done by scheduling it as an event in Outlook.
- There are seven different ways to view the Outlook Calendar.

Chapter 18

Putting Calendar to Work

In This Chapter

- Adding an appointment
- Other ways to enter appointments
- Making changes to an appointment—rescheduling and canceling
- Deleting an appointment
- Planning an event
- Working with recurring events and appointments
- Deleting all occurrences of a recurring event
- Planning a meeting

In the previous chapter, we covered some of the basic features of Outlook's Calendar. You know how to open the Calendar, how to open the Appointment window, and how to change settings like background colors and working hours. You also know the basics of opening screens that will help you with recurring appointments, events, and so on.

In other words, we've scratched the surface of the Calendar, but we haven't really gotten into the nitty-gritty of what makes it such an effective organizational tool.

That's what this chapter is all about. We'll go beyond the surface stuff and dig into the Calendar's depths. We'll look at a couple of different ways to enter appointments and a couple of ways to manipulate an appointment once it's entered. You'll even learn how to delete an appointment or change its start and/or end times. You'll learn about the various options for setting recurring appointments, and you'll learn more about scheduling events. And finally, you'll learn how to use Outlook to schedule a meeting.

Adding an Appointment

Setting an appointment is a snap in Outlook, even if you're not in Calendar at the present time.

If you're in the Outlook Today window, for example, you can open the New button's drop-down menu, select New Appointment, and off you go. Or, if you're in the Calendar, you can just click the New button. The Appointment window opens, which looks like the following figure.

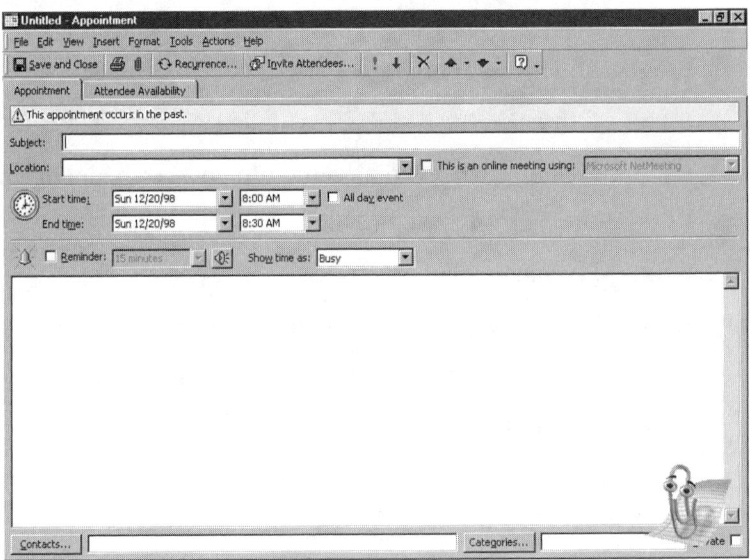

The Appointment window is where you enter information for a new appointment.

There are two tabs in the Appointment window—Appointment and Attendee Availability. The latter is for planning meetings by using Outlook, which is discussed later in this chapter. For now, let's concentrate on the Appointment tab.

Get to the Subject

The Subject line is the heart of the Appointment window. Whatever you enter here is what ends up on your Calendar view, along with the time of the appointment. Even though there's a lot of space for you to expound on the subject of the appointment, only a few words will appear on your Calendar when you view it. However, if you leave your mouse pointing at the subject in your Calendar view, the full subject line will appear.

If you write a subject such as "This is the weekly meeting I have with my staff," all that will show up on the monthly Calendar is "This is the…". You'll see a little bit more or less of it depending upon how many days you view, but still, it's best to keep the subject line brief. At the very least, you want to make sure that the first few words of the subject summarize the appointment enough to make sense to you when you view your monthly or weekly Calendar. So a better subject for this situation would be "Staff meeting".

Three Words: Location, Location, Location

The next line in the Appointment window is the Location field. Depending on the type of appointment you're entering, this field can be very useful or completely unnecessary.

For example, if you work in a large office building with many conference rooms, having a Location field will help you keep track of the sites for your various meetings. You can also keep track of the location for an offsite meeting by entering the building name or street address.

The best feature of this field is that as you use it, it becomes a drop-down menu that remembers the last seven locations you've entered, as you can see from the following figure.

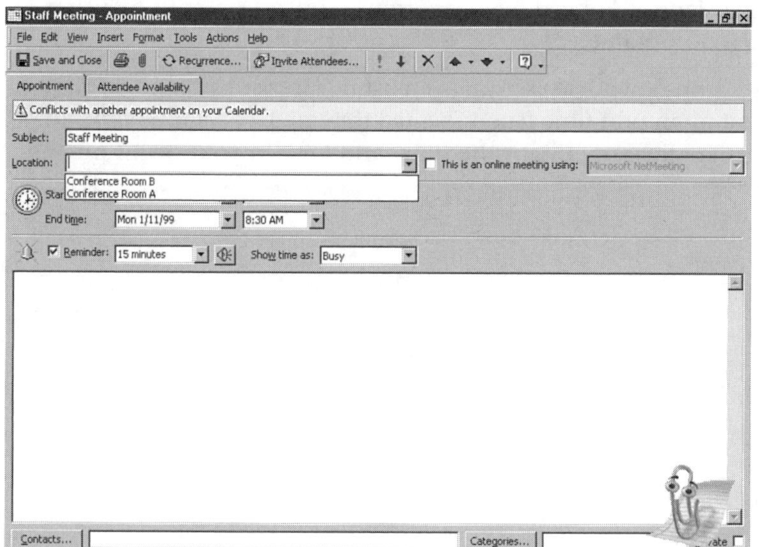

Use the Location drop-down menu to quickly select a location for an appointment.

In this figure, the drop-down menu shows the names of the last two meeting places. So instead of having to retype location information, you can pick one from the drop-down list.

When?

Next, it's time to enter the date and time for an appointment. Outlook automatically enters today's date in both date fields and schedules a half-hour increment from 8:00 a.m. to 8:30 a.m. in the time fields.

Back in Time

Notice that there's a warning message above the Subject line in the Appointment window. The message tells you that the event you're scheduling occurs in the past. Once you change the date and time fields, the warning will go away. Outlook has to default the date and time fields to something, and the result here is a temporary error message.

Each of these date and time fields is a drop-down menu. When you open a date field you get a one-month calendar, just as you see in the following figure.

The calendar opens to the current month, with today's date highlighted. To pick a date, just click it in the calendar. You can navigate from month to month by using the arrows next to the month name.

The time fields are also drop-down lists, set up in half-hour increments. If you have a meeting or appointment at an odd time (such as a tee time of 10:08 a.m.), you can just click in the appropriate field, highlight the time, and type in your own time settings.

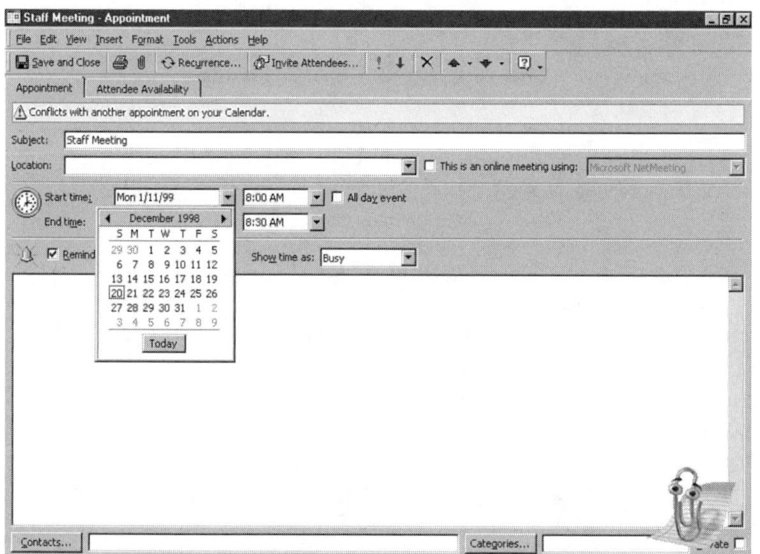

Use the drop-down calendar to pick a date.

Other Appointment Settings

There's even more to the Appointment window. Here are some quick summaries of the other things you can set:

- *Reminder* You can set an audible reminder to occur at a given interval before your appointment. The default is 15 minutes before the appointment time. There are several sounds from which to choose, and you can use your own sounds as well.
- *Show time as* You can tell Outlook to show the time period when you're in this appointment as Busy, Out of Office, Tentative, or Free. That's right, you can even schedule your free time by using Outlook's Calendar.
- *Notes* That big open box is for notes about this appointment: directions to the location, an outline for the meeting, or whatever you want.
- *Contacts* If there are people from one of your contact lists who are involved in this meeting, you might want to make note of that in this area.
- *Categories* Much like the way you used categories to help you sort your contacts, you can put your appointments into categories as well. This can help you determine at a glance what's business, what's personal, and so on.

Other Ways to Add Appointments

Depending upon where you are within Outlook, there are other ways to schedule appointments into your Calendar.

For example, if you're in the Calendar, you can double-click any half-hour segment and a New Appointment window will appear with that half-hour defaulted into the time slots.

Or let's say you've just made contact with a potential new client. You've called them up and arranged an appointment. You can go into the Contacts module and fill out the Contact form for the client to enter all of that information safely into Outlook. But you don't have to jump to the Calendar to schedule the appointment. While in Contacts, open the Actions menu and select New Appointment with Contact, as you see in the following figure.

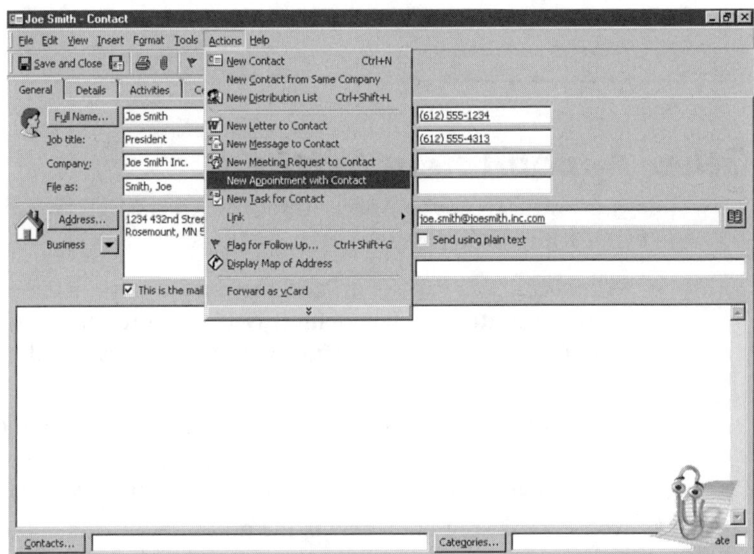

Scheduling an appointment from the Contacts module.

The Appointment window opens, and defaults drop into place for the date (today), time (next possible half-hour increment), and contacts (the name of the contact you were in).

Making Changes

Appointments are seldom set in concrete. The salesperson who's scheduled to come to your office at 1 p.m. may want to reschedule for 1:30, or maybe even a different day altogether. You may find it necessary to cancel that root canal for some reason. Your boss may call to tell you that the staff meeting has been moved from Conference Room B to Conference Room A.

There is a universal way to make any change you want to an appointment. You can double-click it in any Calendar view (daily, five-day, seven-day, or monthly), and the Appointment window will open back up. You can then change any of the information you've previously entered, or you can enter new information.

Certain types of changes must be made by going back to the original Appointments window. These include changing locations, categories, reminder times, and contacts. However, there are some shortcuts you can take.

Before you can make any changes to an appointment, you have to select it. The best way to do this is to view your Calendar in the daily view, go to the date on which the appointment occurs, and select it by clicking it once. When it's selected, the top, bottom, and left sides of the appointment are outlined in blue. Now making changes is easy. Your appointment will look like the one in the following figure.

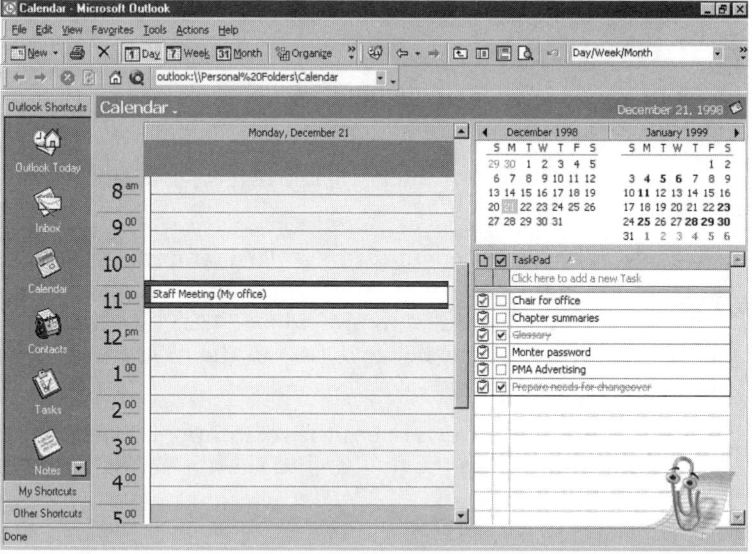

You can edit your appointments directly from the daily view.

When you view your Calendar in the daily view, you can see the subject of the appointment, followed by the location in parentheses. Once you click the Appointment to select it, however, the location disappears and a cursor appears next to the subject of the appointment.

Here's a quick look at some of the changes you can make:

- *Changing the subject* Once the cursor appears next to the subject of an appointment, you can delete letters or whole words and completely redefine the subject of the meeting.
- *Changing times* Once an appointment has been selected, your cursor will turn into an up-and-down arrow when you move it over either the beginning or ending time for an appointment. You can click the time and drag it either up or down the daily view. So if you want to block out two hours for your meeting instead of a half-hour, you can literally drag it out! If your meeting has moved from 11–11:30 to 3–3:30, grab the left side of the appointment and drag it to the new time.
- *Changing dates* If your meeting moves to a different date, you can grab the left side of the appointment in the daily view, drag it over to the monthly-view calendar, and drop it on the correct date. It will fall at the same time it was placed on the original date, unless you go in and change it.

Deleting an Appointment

So, you've decided to cancel that root canal after all, huh? Or maybe your salary review has been cancelled, heaven forbid?

Deleting an appointment is simple in Outlook's Calendar. The biggest problem is selecting which way to delete it.

From the daily view Calendar, you can do it a couple of ways. First, you must select the appointment by clicking its left edge. (Clicking in the subject area will place a cursor in that area, and any deleting you do will be to individual letters, not the entire appointment.) Once it's selected, click the delete button in the toolbar (the handwritten letter *X*) or press the Delete key.

You can also double-click the appointment, which opens the main Appointment window. Then, you can click the Delete button on the toolbar and the appointment will disappear.

Planning an Event

To heck with all these silly appointments. Let's plan an *event.*

According to Outlook, an event is anything that lasts 24 hours or more. So my brother's bachelor party won't qualify as an event (although it will be close), but the three-day convention I'll be attending does.

Scheduling an event is easy in Outlook's Calendar. Next to the start and end times is a check box called All day event. If you click it, the time periods disappear because Outlook assumes the event lasts all day.

And here's an optimistic little Outlook feature—it defaults to Free for all-day events. Unfortunately, I'll have to change that to Out of Office for my convention, as you can see in the following figure.

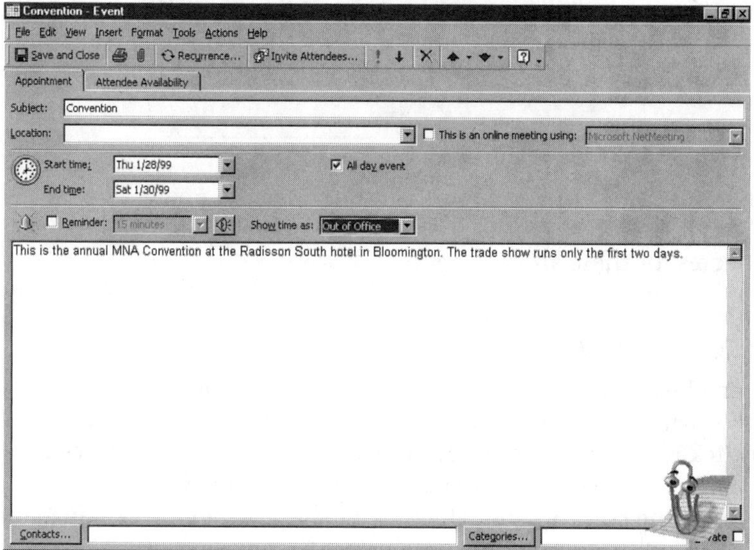

Schedule an event in the Appointments window by clicking the All day event button.

Once the event is scheduled, it appears on your Calendar (regardless of view) as a banner across the top of any day or days it affects.

Recurring Nightmares

Scheduling recurring appointments is far from a nightmare in Outlook. In fact, it's a piece of cake (birthday cake, that is).

As discussed in the previous chapter, you start the recurring appointments process by clicking the Recurrence button at the top of the Appointments window. That opens the Appointment Recurrence window, as you see in the following figure.

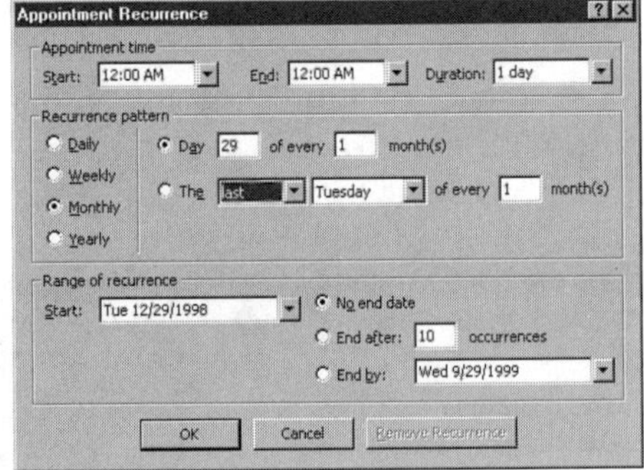

Schedule recurring appointments in this window.

You can get as fancy as you want in this window. For example, if you have a board meeting on the third Tuesday of every month, you can schedule it here. You can also set start dates and end dates for these appointments.

Scheduling Annual Events

Let's say you want to schedule an annual all-day event, such as my birthday. First, open a new Appointment window and enter the pertinent information—subject, date, and so on. Then click the All day event button. Finally, click the Recurrence button. Then set it up as yearly event with no end date (so as not to foretell the date of my demise), and then enter the correct date (which I will *not* provide) in the Range of Recurrence area. Click OK, and then save your appointment.

Another way to remember someone's birthday is to enter it into their entry in your Contacts folder. That will make an annual entry into your calendar automatically.

Working with Recurring Appointments

You can edit and delete recurring appointments just like regular appointments. However, you have to be careful that the changes you make to a recurring appointment are made to all of the recurrences, if that's what you want.

To edit or delete a recurring appointment, double-click the next occurrence of it in the daily Calendar. Your Personal Assistant interrupts to ask if you want to open only this occurrence of the appointment or the entire series. If you want to make changes to all occurrences of this recurring appointment or event, click Open the Series. If you're only changing this occurrence, click the This Occurrence button.

Take a Peek If You Don't Trust Outlook

Once you've made the change(s) you want, move ahead to the next occurrence to see if Outlook has handled things as you desire. For example, if your weekly staff meeting on Mondays at 10 a.m. has been moved to 11 a.m. for this week only, you'll want to make sure that Outlook hasn't made the change to the entire series.

Planning a Meeting

If you're a corporate user of Outlook and your Calendars are all networked together, there's a meeting planner function that allows you to schedule a meeting and find out in advance if the invitees are available to attend. To be able to use it, however, your company has to be using networking software like Microsoft's Exchange Server. This way, the calendars of various employees can interact with each other.

Even if you're not a networked user of Outlook, you can use it to help schedule a meeting.

Inviting Others

You can invite others to a meeting you're planning by sending them an email right from the Calendar. This is one of the marvelous ways that all of Outlook's features come together, making a chore like planning a meeting virtually effortless.

First, open your Calendar and schedule the time and place for the meeting. Then click the Invite Attendees button at the top of the window. A To: field appears at the top of your Appointment window, as you can see in the following figure. If you're inviting people who are on your contact list, you can click the To: button and select their names (or the Distribution Lists to which they belong), or you can just type in their names. If they don't appear on your contact list, you'll have to type in their email addresses.

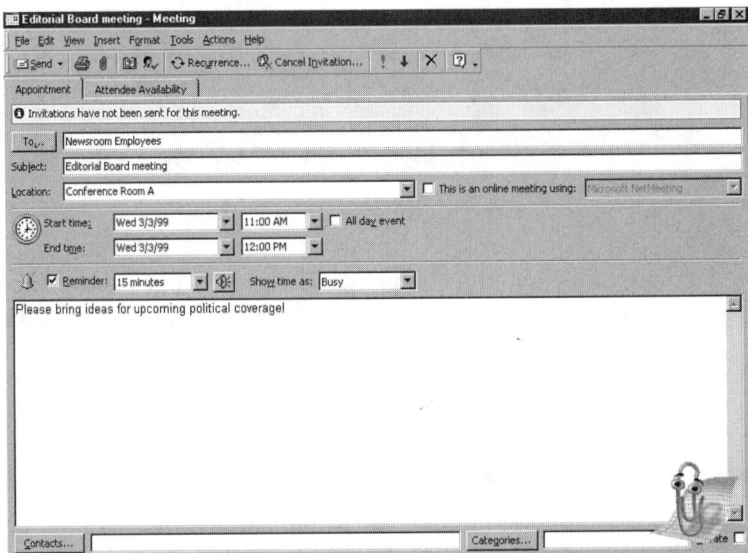

Inviting people to your meeting is easy in Outlook.

Once all the names have been entered in the To: field, click the Send button. The meeting announcement will be sent to the recipients as an email message. Once they've received it, they can handle it just as they would any other email. They can reply to your message, delete it, forward it, save it, and so on. But no matter how important you are, sending this invitation won't automatically schedule time on anyone's calendar.

Attendee Availability

It's time to look at that other tab in the Appointment window. You have to be networked with other Outlook users for this feature to work.

When you're trying to schedule a meeting with others on your network, click the Attendee Availability tab to get a screen like the one in the following figure.

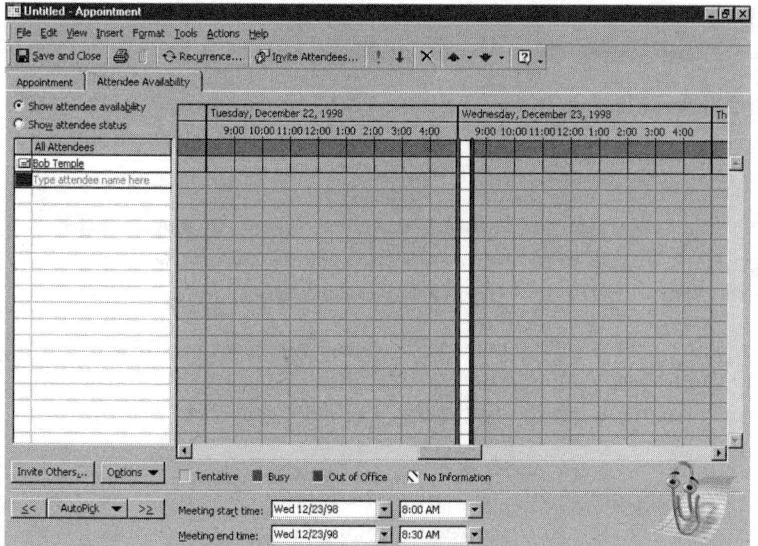

You can check the availability of possible meeting attendees here.

Type in the names of the people you want to attend the meeting, and you'll be able to see if they're free or busy in this screen. (There may be factors that limit your ability to use this feature. Check with your system administrator for specifics.)

The Least You Need to Know

- There are lots of different ways to open the Appointments window and schedule a new appointment. One shortcut is to double-click the appointment time to open an Appointment window.
- Editing and deleting appointments can be done in a variety of ways. Certain types of changes must be made in the main Appointments window, but things like the meeting subject and the start and end times can be changed from the daily calendar.
- Day-long appointments are called *events* in Outlook. You can schedule them in the main Appointments window by clicking the All day event button.
- Recurring events and appointments are easily scheduled in a special window. You can then edit and/or delete these recurring appointments individually or by making changes to the entire series.
- The Appointment window offers a couple of different ways to help you schedule a meeting. You can invite attendees through an email. Or, if you're networked with other Outlook users, you can check that they're available before scheduling the meeting.

Chapter 19

The Long and Short of It: The Journal and Notes

In This Chapter

- The purpose of notes
- Creating, editing, and deleting notes
- Setting note options
- Viewing notes
- The purpose of keeping a journal
- Why the Journal might not be necessary
- Automatic journal entries
- Manual journal entries

I arrived at my office this morning, a Monday, and found them piled neatly next to the phone on my desk: notes. There were no fewer than eight of them. Some were the ever-present "sticky" yellow kind, and many were just on scratch paper or the backs of envelopes.

They were full of little things I needed to do, stuff I needed to remember, reminders of upcoming things, and so on—all left over from last week, just waiting to drag down a Monday morning. I needed to call so-and-so back. I needed to run so-and-so's raise down to payroll. I needed to print out and file some things. And with so-and-so on vacation, I needed to handle some of her duties.

Some of these could be considered tasks and might be best handled by using Outlook's task list, which is covered in the next chapter. But you could also use Outlook's Notes module to help you remember some of these short-term projects that need to get done.

Better yet, notes are a great way to quickly jot down anything you want—an idea, a task, a reminder. They give you a place to hold those thoughts until you can transfer them into a more functional part of Outlook—an email, a task list, an appointment.

Outlook also offers a Journal function that allows you to keep track of all kinds of things, including your email, Office documents, and more. It gives you the ability to keep track of all contact you have with a particular person and is very useful for record keeping.

These two modules are among the simplest and most easily understood functions of Outlook. That's why they're covered together in one chapter, while other modules get multiple chapters to explain their various functions. But they're also valuable, especially notes. Therefore, it's important to take a few minutes to learn about them.

The Purpose of Notes

That little yellow piece of paper, a couple of inches square, can only do so much. The same is true for Outlook's Notes feature, although physical size is not an issue.

Outlook's Notes can do a lot of things and can fill a serious need for some people—especially scratch-paper consumers like me. But there are things that Notes absolutely cannot do.

For example, you can't email an Outlook note to someone. However, you can cut and paste the message from a note into an email and send that, or drag and drop the note onto the Inbox icon. You can't program a note to remind you 15 minutes before something you need to do (but you can cut and paste the information into an appointment subject, which can remind you).

Get the idea?

So, when you're on the phone with that important client and you remember that you need to send a thank-you for the order, you can type that quickly into a note. Then later you can follow up on that little note by either having the note remind you or by converting it into a task list entry or another Outlook function. You can simply drag and drop the note onto the appropriate icon and the content of the note becomes the content of the item you dropped it on.

Make a Note of It

Ever call a phone number that has been changed? You get that annoying recorded voice that tells you the old number is "no longer in service." She then tells you the new number and chastises you with "Please make a note of it."

In other words, "Listen, idiot. Write this number down, cuz I don't want to have to help you again."

Well, Outlook is much nicer than that. In Outlook, you can make a note of anything you want, and nobody's going to sass you about it.

Creating Notes

Guess what? There are a bunch of different ways to create a new note. Surprised? You shouldn't be. There are a bunch of ways to do just about *everything* in Outlook.

Assuming you're in Outlook, you can create a new note at any time. Simply open the pull-down menu that's part of the New button and choose Note. You also can click the Notes button in the Outlook Shortcuts bar, and then just click the New button. If you're not in Outlook and you have the full Office suite installed, you can click the New Note button from the Microsoft Office Shortcuts bar.

Regardless of the method you choose, a new Notes window opens. It will look like the one in the following figure.

This Note window isn't some fancy form you'll be using to create a new note. It's the actual note itself. As you can see, there's a cursor blinking in the note, just waiting for you to get off your duff and type something. Go ahead and type in whatever you want to note (pardon the pun). Unless you need to file this note somewhere for some reason, there's no need to save it. A note is automatically saved as it is until you tell Outlook to do something else with it.

Use the Notes window to type your note.

So, for example, even if you close Outlook completely, the note will stay active on your computer's desktop. An example appears in the following figure.

Notes stay active even after Outlook closes.

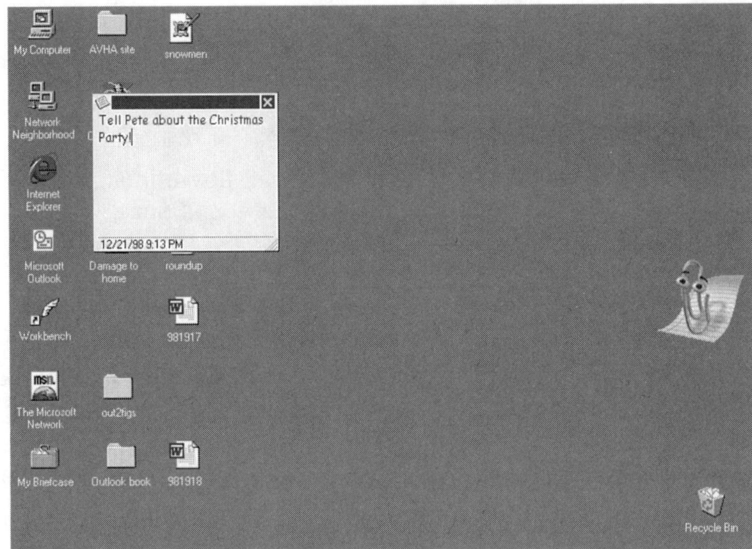

Closing Notes

If you want to keep the note but don't want it mucking up your desktop, you can close it. Just click the "X" in the upper-right corner of the note.

However, it is not deleted at this point. It still exists in your Notes folder—remember, you didn't need to "save" the note for it to remain within Outlook. If you go back into Outlook and click the Notes button in the Outlook Shortcuts bar, the note will appear as a Notes icon in the window, as you see in the following figure.

If you want to reopen the note, all you have to do is double-click on its icon in the Notes folder.

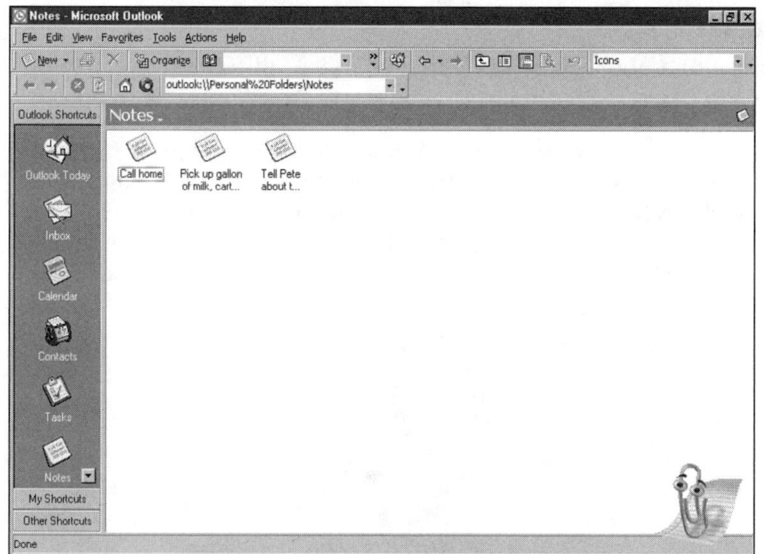

Notes remain in the Notes folder until you delete them.

Editing and Deleting Notes

Editing notes couldn't be much easier.

When it's time to edit them, there aren't many complicated functions to perform.

A note must be open to be edited. Then, you use the normal editing functions: highlight text and use the Delete or Backspace key to delete text; click at a point of entry with your cursor and type in additions; and so on.

Deleting a note is pretty simple, too. If the note is open, you can delete it by clicking on the little yellow Notes icon in the upper-left corner of the note (this opens a pull-down menu) and selecting Delete.

If the note isn't open, highlight its icon in the Notes folder. Then click the Delete button in the toolbar or press the Delete key on your keyboard. Either will get the job done.

Setting Note Options

As noted earlier, notes are a pretty simple component of Outlook, and there aren't many options. It's kind of nice to have a simple one for a change, isn't it?

However, you can alter the appearance of your notes. You can also assign them to categories or contacts.

More than Meets the Eye

Changing the appearance of a note can be done in a couple of different ways. As you have probably seen, the default color of notes is yellow and they appear as small squares, all in the same font.

You can change the default settings for notes. Any future notes you create will have these settings. Enter the Notes folder, open the Tools menu, and click Options. When the Options window opens, click on Note Options. The Notes Options window opens, as shown in the following figure.

You can change the default appearance of notes.

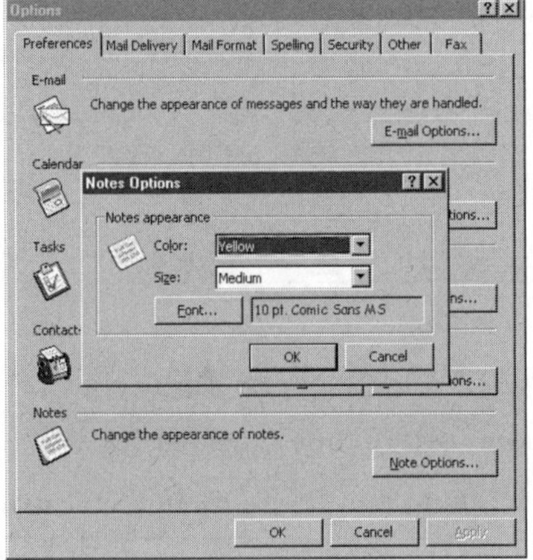

Here, you can select one of five different colors for your notes, decide from three different sizes, and pick from any font you have installed on your system. These values will be in effect for all future notes you create.

If you want to change the color of just one note, open it and click the little Notes icon in the upper-left corner. Then, select Color from the drop-down menu and choose the color you would like. This will change only the color of the note you currently have open.

Categorizing Notes

Also on the Notes drop-down menu is Categories. You can use this to assign categories to your notes. Generally this is necessary only if you have a bunch of notes. Then, you can sort them by category to keep them organized.

If you want to assign a note to a category, you must first open it. Then, choose Categories from the drop-down menu beneath the Notes icon. The Categories window opens (as in the other modules), and you can check the box for each appropriate category.

After you click OK, you return to the note, but the category name does not appear. The only time you'll see the category listed is when you view your notes in a list. There'll be more on viewing notes later in this chapter.

Making Contact

Also on the drop-down menu under the Notes icon, you can assign a contact person or two to the note. This is so that when you open a contact and click the Activities tab, the note will appear along with the various emails and other items you've associated with this person.

To add a contact to your note, click Contact from the drop-down menu in an open note. Then, select the name of the contact you would like to add, and the person's name will be linked to the note. Contact names aren't visible in any view of Notes.

Viewing Notes

As with the other Outlook modules, there are several different ways to view notes. However, the Notes module isn't as full-featured as other Outlook modules, so there are only five.

Here are brief descriptions of these views:

- *Icons* This is the default view for notes. When you open the Notes folder, you see a little colored icon for each note, and the first two lines of each note appear beneath it.
- *Notes List* This is a notes version of the Auto Preview view that can be found in other modules of Outlook. It sorts the notes by subject and shows most of each note (if not all), plus the date and time it was created and the category it belongs to.
- *Last Seven Days* Notes are shown in the Notes List view, but only those created in the previous seven days are shown.
- *By Category* Notes are listed in table form and grouped by category, so you can quickly see how many personal notes you have created, for example.
- *By Color* Some people color-code their notes to help organize them. This view shows the notes in table form, grouped by color.

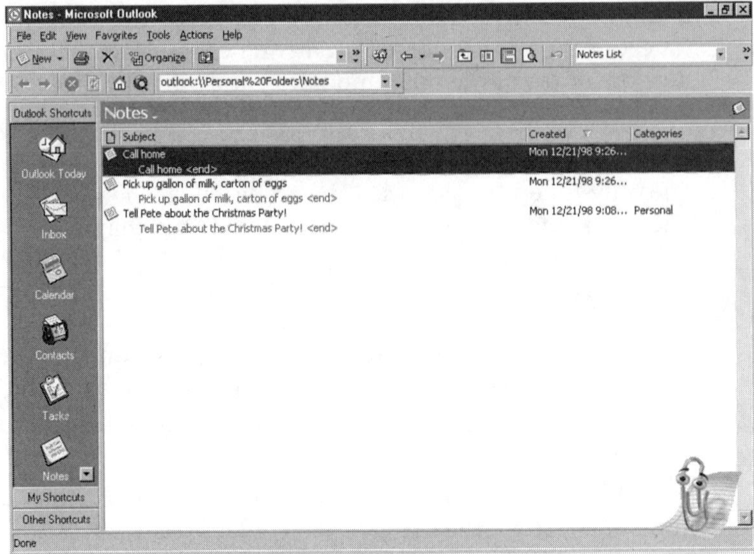

Notes viewed in the Notes List view.

The Purpose of Keeping a Journal

Some people see the Journal folder in the My Shortcuts bar, the one with the icon that looks like an open book, and think that it's a place for them to record their innermost thoughts. Not true.

This isn't a journal in the diary sense of the word. This is more of an accounting journal. That is, it makes a record of various things that occur between you and your contacts. For example, if there's a particular contact that you want to keep records for, you can keep a journal of any email, meeting information, or task information for that person.

This is useful if you're in a position to delegate tasks to other people in your office. It helps you keep track of various communications you have with these people and documents the progress of the assigned duties. (Tasks are covered in detail in the next chapter.) In fact, several of the views for journals appear as timelines in Outlook.

Perhaps the most useful feature of the Journal module is that it can record a communication that no other Outlook module can—a phone call.

Why Journals Might Not Be Necessary

The Journal is probably the least-used module of Outlook, and with good reason. Journals are somewhat redundant with Outlook's Contacts feature.

The Contacts module automatically records any Outlook communication that you have with a contact. For example, if you've assigned a task to a contact, sent or received email from the contact, arranged an appointment with the contact, or done anything else related to Outlook, it's already recorded in that contact's file.

To see this in action, open any contact that you've interacted with in Outlook. Then, click the Activities tab. There will be a pause while Outlook searches for your activities with this contact. Once it finds them, they begin to appear in the window, as you see in the following figure.

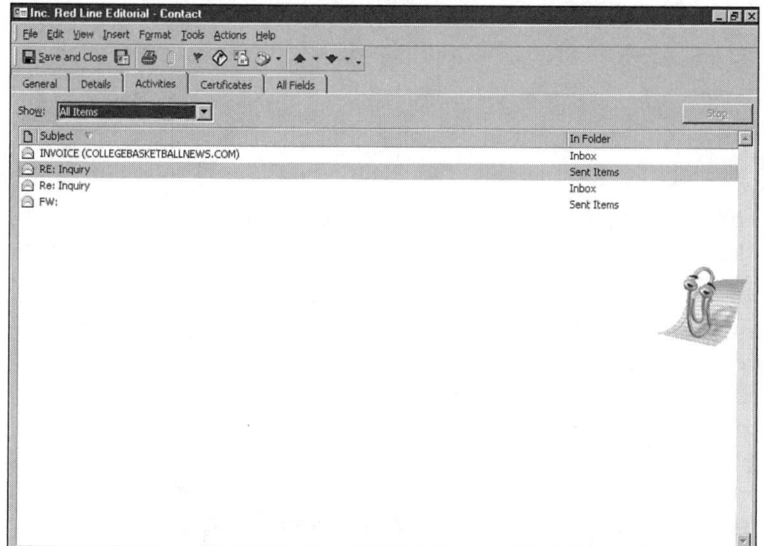

The Activities tab in Contacts acts as a journal.

The Journal does go beyond this in a few ways, however.

Automatic Journal Entries

If you would like to track your communications and files that relate to certain contacts, click the Journal icon in the My Shortcuts bar. The first time you do this, your Personal Assistant will ask if you want to start the journal. When you do, you'll be presented with the Journal Options window, as shown in the following figure.

Make your automatic journal settings here.

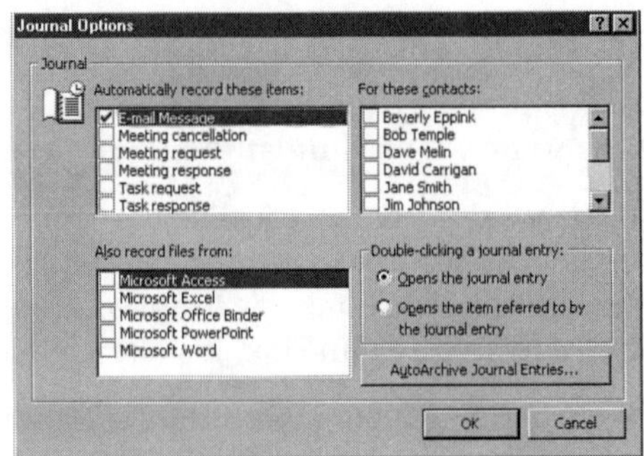

In this window, you tell Outlook what types of information you want it to automatically record and for which contacts it should be recorded. You can also tell it to record files from certain Office programs.

Once you've made these settings known to Outlook, it will begin to make the notations for you.

Manual Journal Entries

Making journal entries by hand is particularly useful for people who need to keep track of the length of phone conversations. People who bill for this phone time, such as lawyers, can use this feature to their advantage.

To make a manual journal entry, click the New button while in the Journal folder or choose Journal Entry from the New button's drop-down menu (if in another module). If you are in the Contacts folder with a contact open, open the Actions menu and select New Journal Entry for Contact. The Journal Entry window opens, as you can see in the following figure.

Make a manual entry in this window.

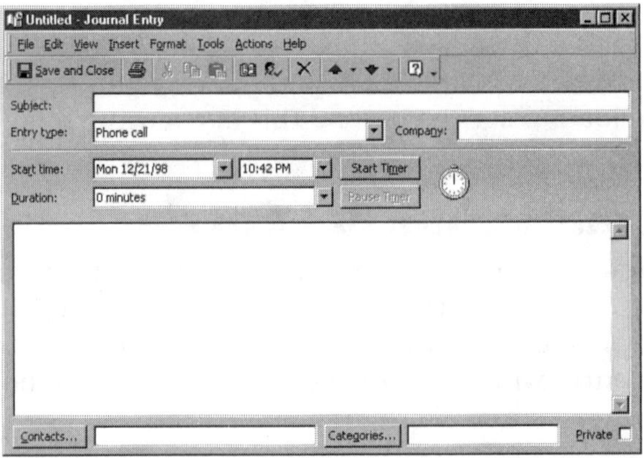

You can enter a subject and the type of entry it is. Outlook defaults to Phone Call because this is the most common use of manual entry.

The Start time field defaults to whatever the current time of day is. So if you open this window at the start of a phone call, you'll be all set to go. Once the call is connected, click Start Timer and Outlook will count out the length of the call until you hit the Pause Timer button.

You can use the large notes area to make notations during the phone call, and you can assign contacts or categories to it.

When you're done, click the Save and Close button, or print the whole thing out and pass it on to your billing department.

The Least You Need to Know

- Outlook's Notes module is useful for jotting down quick thoughts, tasks, reminders, and so on. You can use them to make quick notations that you can later transfer to a different Outlook module.
- Notes remain on your screen even after you exit Outlook. You don't even have to save them. You can delete and edit them quickly.
- You can change the appearance of your notes, and you can view them in one of five different formats.
- Outlook's Journal module helps you keep track of communications you have with your contacts. You can make automatic entries or manual entries.
- Some of the Journal module's functions are already handled by the Activities tab of the Contacts module.
- Manual journal entries are particularly useful for people who have to track the time they spend on the phone with clients. You can time a phone call and make notes in the same window.

Chapter 20

Multitasking with Task Lists

In This Chapter

- What is a task?
- How task lists can help
- Opening the Task screen
- Entering a task
- Using automatic tasks
- Editing, delegating, and deleting tasks
- Changing tasks' appearance
- Viewing tasks

There's a comic strip that my mom had stuck to her refrigerator for quite a while. It depicted a man walking down into his basement and thinking, "The mop, the mop, the mop…" The next panel, showed him walking up those same steps with the mop. The caption said, "He'll remember the mop, but he'll forget the bucket, the bucket, the bucket…"

I think most of us have been there at one point or another. Have you ever gone into a room to get something or other, only to forget what it was? Well, Outlook's Tasks feature can help you keep track of all the things, both little and big, that you have to accomplish on any given day.

Even better, Outlook can help you manage longer-term projects, delegate some or all of certain tasks, remember recurring tasks, and prioritize.

What Is a Task?

This question shouldn't be all that hard to answer, but what we're getting at here is what *Outlook* sees as a task.

It would be easy to define a task as "anything that you need to get done." That's true. Most of us have lots of things we need to do in any given day. Some of them are everyday chores, like feeding the dog or taking out the garbage, that you really don't need to remember by using an Outlook task list. On the other hand, task lists aren't just for major, long-term projects (although they are wonderful for those).

For Outlook's purposes, tasks are anything that you need to get done that, before Outlook, you might have put on your to-do list. Personal items like remembering to get your wife some flowers for your anniversary and business tasks like ordering supplies or touching base with a contact all belong on your task list.

Many of us have become to-do list junkies. I usually carry at least one in my pocket—sometimes two. There's the list of business tasks that I need to do during the day, and the list of errands I need to run on the way home. Some days I'll get home from work, empty my pockets, and find a list of things I hadn't done because I forgot about the list. Obviously, I need a list to tell me where I keep my lists.

Outlook simplifies all that.

How Task Lists Can Help

Outlook's task lists help in a number of ways. First, they force you to list on your computer all the important things you need to get done.

For some people, that alone is enough. Once you've been forced to think about something long enough to write it down, you're more likely to remember to do it.

With Outlook, you can invest a lot of time in your tasks or not much at all. It can be as simple as typing in the to-do item, just like writing it on a piece of paper. Or you can go into great detail, listing due dates, progress reports, assigning categories and contacts to the item, and so on. Unlike those scraps of paper you have all over the place, Outlook compiles all this in one location and, better yet, reminds you when due dates are approaching.

Your tasks even appear in Outlook Today, which is your default startup page in Outlook. That way, you're presented with your list first thing in the morning, as shown in the following figure.

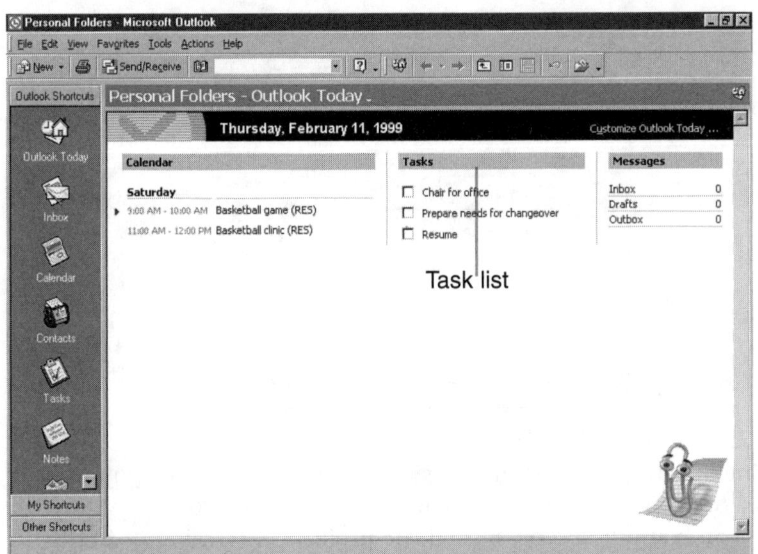

Your tasks appear on the Outlook Today screen.

And your tasks also appear in that lower-right panel of the daily view calendar so you can see them as you're going over your daily appointments.

In these and other ways, Outlook keeps your tasks in plain view, rather than you stuffing them in your pocket or shuffling them under the many other papers on your desk.

Outlook can also help you prioritize your tasks so you can schedule your time and do a better job of meeting deadlines and delegating.

Opening the Task Screen

The New Task window can be opened in a couple of different ways. Better yet, if you just want to quickly enter a task, you don't even have to open the Task screen at all.

To open the New Task window, just click on the New button's drop-down menu from anywhere in Outlook. Then select Task from the list. Or, you can click on the Tasks button in the Outlook Shortcuts bar and click the New button.

Entering a Task in the New Task Window

This is the full-featured way to enter a task into Outlook. It's only necessary if you have a detailed or long-term task to complete.

Just like email and the Calendar, you're presented with an open subject line (see the following figure). This is the summary of the task, and it will appear on every list of tasks you see in Outlook. Therefore, it should sum up the project as succinctly as possible.

Enter task information in the Task screen.

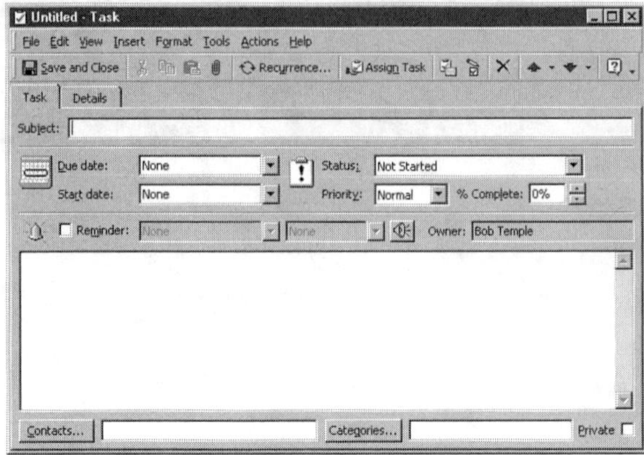

Beneath the Subject line are the date and progress fields. On the left side, you can select a Due Date and a Start Date for the task. The right side helps you keep track of the project's schedule. For example, if you started the project on the first of the month and it's due on the 30th, you can check it on the 15th to see if you're halfway done.

Both of these fields contain drop-down calendars from which you can click on a date that will automatically appear in the field.

On the right side of the window are three more fields that can be helpful to you:

- *Status* Here you can select from five choices: Not Started, In Progress, Completed, Waiting on Someone Else, or Deferred. In some views of tasks, you can sort your list based on these choices.
- *Priority* Select from three choices: High, Normal, and Low. Again, in some views you can sort your tasks based on these choices.
- *% Complete* Helps you keep track of your own progress or that of others.

Networked User Advantage

Some of these fields may seem a little silly to you. Why do you need to tell yourself how far along you are on a task? Don't you already know? Well, some of these features aren't just for you. If you're on a network or you communicate through email with another Outlook user, you can delegate a task to her and she can use the Task form to report her progress to you.

Just as with contacts, the large window at the bottom of the Task form is for entering any notes you may have about the task. For example, one of my tasks might be to finish my Christmas shopping. In the notes area, I can keep a list of the people I want to buy presents for, and even note what I want to get them. Then, as I complete each portion of that list, I can go back in and delete the name and present for each person.

The Owner field, also on the Task tab, cannot be changed manually. However, it changes automatically if you assign the task to another person.

Sweat the Details

The Details tab offers added features for your tasks. Click it to see a window like the one in the following figure.

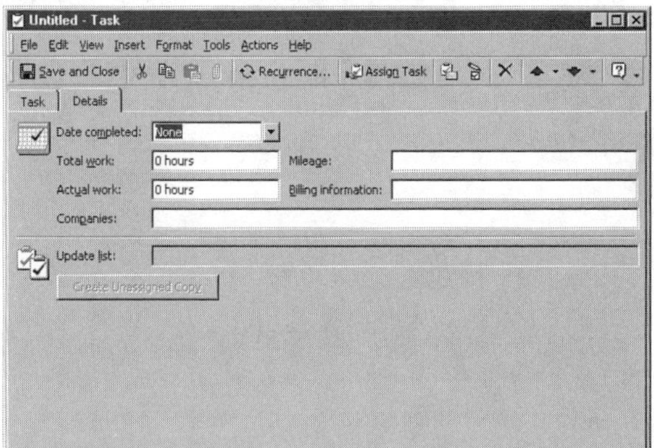

Track other information on the Details tab.

Here, you can track information that will be particularly valuable to people in certain walks of life. For example, if your task has something to do with a client—that is, if it's billable—you can use this tab to track some expenses.

First, select the date the task was completed. Then you can enter the total hours you worked on it (both total and actual), the mileage, and other billing information. Later, you can print this information and pass it on to your billing department.

Email It!

You can even email that task down to the billing department (or anywhere else) if you want. Just open a new email and send it as an attachment by opening the Insert menu and selecting Item. Then, find the task in the folder list, highlight it, and click OK. It will be attached to the email.

A Simple Plan

What if you've got a quick little task that you don't need to go into great detail about? For example, let's say your spouse calls and asks you to pick up little Johnny and Janey from their basketball practices on your way home from work. You'd hate to forget to do that one, but you also don't need to record your innermost thoughts about the task. Nor do you need to formulate dramatic plans about how to achieve the objective of the task. All you want is a simple reminder: "Pick up kids after practice."

Easy. You don't have to go into the Task form in order to enter a task. You can do it right from the Task folder.

To open the Task folder, click on the Tasks icon in the Outlook Shortcuts toolbar. Your tasks will be displayed in whatever view you've have chosen. (Views are covered later in this chapter.) However, at the top of the Tasks screen is a box with grayed-out text that says "Click here to add a new Task," as shown in the following figure.

You can add a task directly from the Tasks folder.

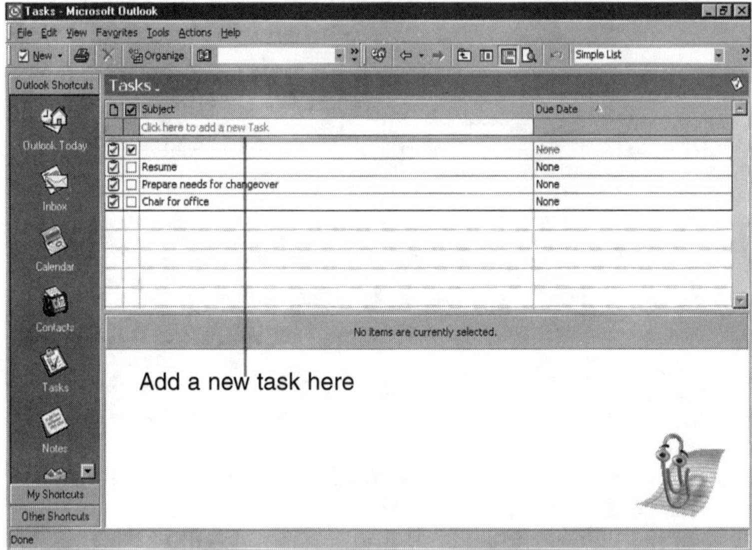

Click there and type in the subject for your task. In this case it would be, "Pick up kids after practice." Depending on which view you're in, you can add more information just by pressing the right-arrow key on your keyboard to move into the next field. In the Simple List View, which is the default, you can enter only a subject and a due date. In other views, you can enter more detailed information.

When you're done entering information, press Enter and the task will appear in your task list.

Automation Revolutionizes the Industry

Let's bring it all together here. Suppose that your boss sends you an email telling you there will be a meeting Monday at 9 a.m., at which he would like you to present your Vancouver proposal. In the email, your boss spells out the elements that need to be present for the presentation: an audio-visual component and a written proposal.

How can Outlook help you handle all of this? Well, you've already used Outlook to receive the email, but now you have two other things to manage: You need to add the meeting to your calendar, and the proposal needs to be finished by Monday at 9 a.m., which sounds like a task.

Off you go! You know from previous chapters how to make that appointment quickly in your calendar. How do you quickly make it a task without having to type in all the details?

There are a couple of different ways to automatically create a task from another Outlook item.

From the Inbox

In this example, you have an email that pretty much tells you what you have to do. Wouldn't it be nice to add that to your task list without having to write a note to yourself akin to, "See boss's email in the Inbox for specific details"?

Why not make the email part of the task? This feature (and the many others like it) is one of the reasons Outlook will soon become one of your favorite programs. It makes coordinating your busy life so much easier.

You can take any email you receive that includes some kind of task and make it a part of your task list in seconds. From the Inbox, just click on the message, drag it, and drop it on the Tasks icon in the Outlook Shortcuts bar. Immediately, a Task form opens, like the one in the following figure.

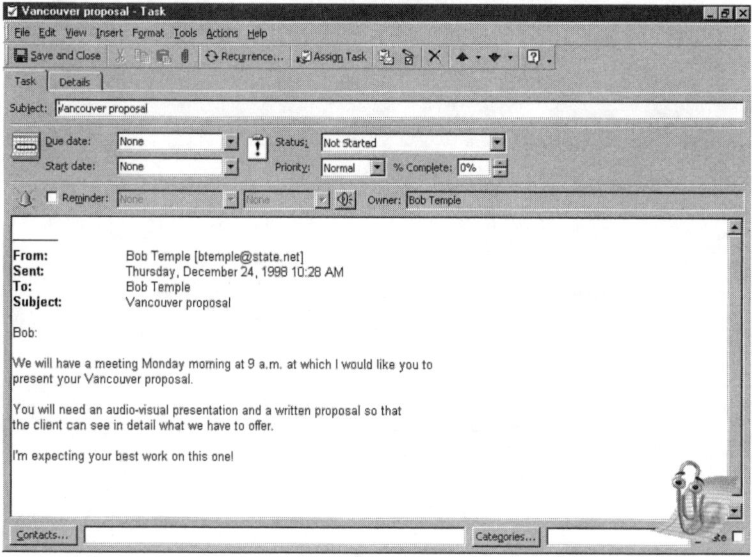

Dragging an email onto the Tasks icon turns it into a task automatically.

As you can see, the subject of the email becomes the subject of the task, and the text of the email message falls into the notes area so you don't have to retype it. You can then click in the notes area and delete any superfluous information. You can then delete the email from the Inbox, since you no longer need it. Fill in any other parts of the Task form you want to fill in, and you're ready to go!

From the Calendar

To see how to create a task from your calendar, let's start over and take a look at this whole Vancouver proposal in a different way. Let's say you've created an appointment on your calendar for the meeting on Monday at 9 a.m. You've already filled out the Calendar form for the appointment, but you should really make a note in your task list that you'll need to have the presentation ready in time for the meeting.

In the Calendar view, you have a TaskPad in the lower-right corner. To make a calendar entry into a task, just highlight the calendar entry and drag it either onto the Tasks icon in the Outlook Shortcuts bar or directly onto your TaskPad.

Again, the Task form opens. The calendar entry falls into the notes area, and the date information is added to the task automatically. Also note in the following figure that a reminder has been added automatically for one hour prior to the meeting. That's because I had a reminder set up for this appointment in the calendar. The Tasks reminder built in some extra time for me, though—my calendar reminder is set at 15 minutes.

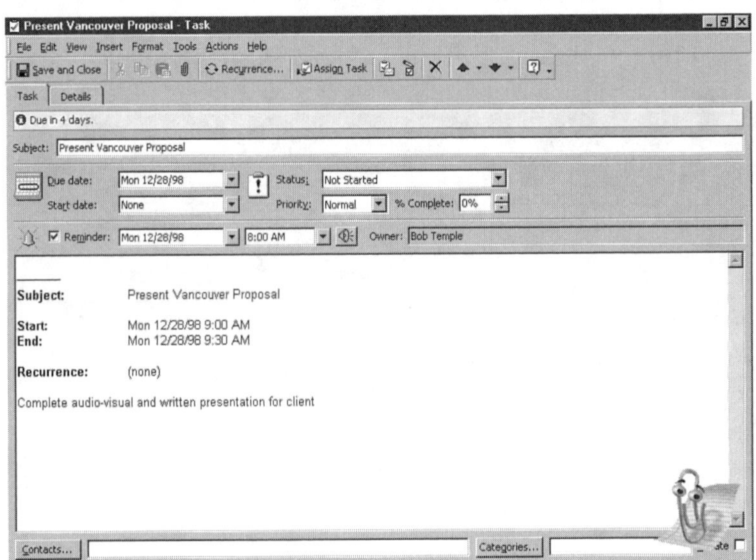

Creating a task from a calendar entry couldn't be much easier.

Working with Tasks

There's a lot you can do with a task once you've entered it. You can edit it, assign it to someone else, or delete it once it's completed.

Editing Tasks

As you learned earlier, Outlook never lets you get too far away from your task list. It's visible in Outlook Today, it's waiting for you there by your calendar, and, of course, you can open the Tasks folder if you *really* want to take a good look.

The good news is that you can open any task from any of these places. There are two ways to edit a task: You can open the Task form for it, or, if you're in the Tasks folder, you can edit right from your list.

If you have detailed changes to make to the task, such as updating its progress or changing the notes field, you must open the larger Task form. You can do this from anywhere that you can see your tasks. For example, if you're in Outlook Today and you want to edit a task, simply double-click on it and the form will open. You can then make any change you want to make to the task, save it, and it will be changed.

If you just want to change the subject of a message or the due date, you can do it right from the list in the Tasks folder. Just open your Tasks folder by clicking on the Tasks icon in the Outlook Shortcuts bar, single-click on the specific field you want to edit, and delete text or add whatever you want.

Delegating Tasks

Outlook makes delegating tasks easy, which is nice because everybody loves to delegate. You can delegate a task you've already created and saved, or a new one. Heck, why not delegate them all?

Delegating occurs on the Tasks form. Once the task has been delegated, you can keep track of it or completely forget about it.

On the Task form, click the Assign Task button. This opens a window that is a cross between an email and a task. Actually, it's both, as you can see in the following figure. It will send an email that officially assigns the task to another person.

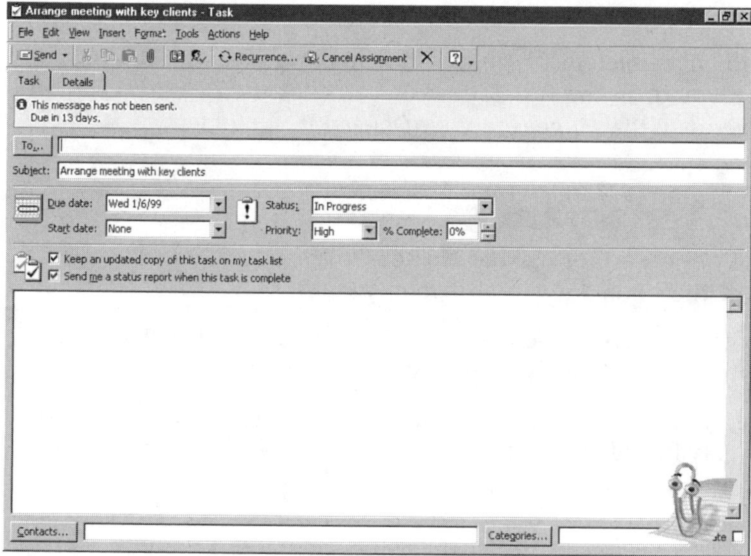

Assigning tasks to another person is accomplished by sending this form.

Keep 'em Checked

Keep these two boxes checked unless it's absolutely unnecessary for you to know the outcome of the task. For example, if your boss assigned the task and you're delegating some or all of it, you'll definitely need to know its status because you're accountable for it. However, if the task is being transferred to a different department and you're no longer responsible for it, it's okay to uncheck these boxes. (This applies whether you're in corporate mode or Internet-only mode.)

The To: field is where you designate which poor sap is going to have to do your dirty work for you. You can enter a contact's name (or click the To: button to choose a contact), or you can type in the email address if the contact isn't in your contacts database. Fill out the rest of the form as you see fit, click the Send button, and it's no longer your concern.

But wait! What if you're still ultimately responsible for the task? That's where those two little check boxes come into play. The first one keeps an updated copy of this task on your task list so that it's never completely out of your mind. The second one automatically sends an email back to you when the task has been completed, so that you can rest easy.

Deleting Tasks

When a task is complete, you can check the box next to the task in any area in which the task is visible. It will become grayed out with a line through it, but it won't disappear. This gives you the opportunity to sit and admire all the wonderful work you've done.

That may be okay for a day or so, but all those completed tasks can really bog down a task list. So let's delete them.

Deleting couldn't get much simpler. Just highlight the task and press the Delete key on your keyboard. Or, if you open the Task form, you can click the Delete button on the toolbar. Once you've done that, it goes to your Deleted Items folder.

Changing Tasks' Appearance

There aren't a whole lot of options for making changes to the appearance of your task lists, but you can change the colors for various circumstances.

To set these options, open the Tasks folder, open the Tools menu, and click Options. Then click the Task Options button and you'll see your two options.

When a task is overdue, it becomes red in your task lists by default. When a task is completed, it becomes gray by default. You can change these colors in this window.

Viewing Your Task List

As you've learned, your task lists are viewable from several different locations in Outlook. For example, you can change the way they appear in Outlook Today.

In this section, we'll talk about the different ways to view your task list in the Tasks folder. Here are your options:

- *Simple List* Displays the list, sorted by the field you specify and showing only the subject and due date. In the bottom window, you see the contents of the notes field for whichever task is highlighted.
- *Detailed List* Additional fields are displayed, including Importance, Status, % Completed, and Categories. The notes window does not appear, however.
- *Active Tasks* Same as Detailed List, except you cannot add a new task from this view.
- *Next Seven Days* Shows the active tasks that must be completed in the next week.
- *Overdue Tasks* Shows the same fields as Active Tasks, but only displays those tasks that are past their due date.
- *By Category* If you've assigned categories to your tasks, this view groups them based on these categories.
- *Assignment* Shows tasks you have delegated, their progress, and who their new owners are.
- *By Person Responsible* Groups all tasks based on the owner of each task.
- *Completed Tasks* Shows you the list of all the wonderful things you've accomplished (until you delete them, that is).
- *Task Timeline* This is the one time that I like the timeline view in an Outlook module. It shows you your tasks on a timeline based on when they're due, as you can see in the following figure.

The Task Timeline view shows your tasks by their due dates.

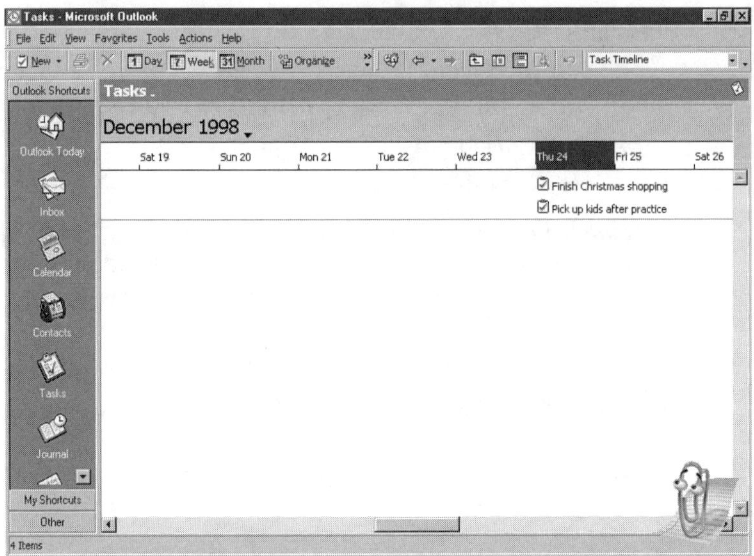

The Least You Need to Know

- A task is anything that you need to get done, whether it's a long-term project or a simple chore.
- Outlook's task lists help you keep track of your tasks, prioritize them, organize them, and see them through to completion.
- You can enter a task in detail by using the Task form, or quickly by adding it from the Task folder.
- You can automatically enter a task by dragging an email or a calendar item onto the Tasks icon or the TaskPad.
- You can delegate tasks to others by using the Assign Task command, which sends an email to the assignee. You can keep track of these delegated tasks automatically.

Part 5

Leftovers Again? Outlook's Other Features

This section covers topics that just don't fit well into any other area. Either that, or they fit into every *area. For example, printing Outlook items and backing up Outlook are covered here. Then, we'll look at using Outlook Express to surf through the Internet's many newsgroups. Finally, we'll bring it all together by looking at how Outlook interacts with other Office applications.*

Chapter 21

Hard Copy

In This Chapter

- Picking a print style
- Special styles for the Calendar
- Special styles for contacts
- Taking a look before you print
- Printing it out
- Finding your file folders
- Archiving manually and with AutoArchive
- Exporting your files
- Backing up your files

This chapter covers two topics that might seem to be unrelated printing and backing up. True, they aren't usually grouped together, and they aren't considered part of a common module of Outlook. Let's take a minute, though, and see how they're linked.

Backing up your files is all about making sure you don't lose data. In today's computerized world, a daily (or weekly, or monthly) backup is commonplace. After all, there's no worse feeling than showing up for work on the morning of an important meeting to find that the notes for your presentation were accidentally deleted from your laptop.

If an important file is lost, there are two ways you can save yourself. You can restore the file from a backup copy (*if* you made one), or you can use a printed-out version of the data to get you through (*if* you printed one out).

Of course, printouts aren't only used for backing up documents. Many Outlook users print out their contact list into a directory they can easily carry around with them. Or, they print out their daily calendar every morning so they can refer to it when they're away from the computer. Perhaps even more common, people will print out their task lists to carry around with them.

Another way to take it with you—or more accurately, to take it *home* with you—is to transfer your Outlook files from your work computer to your home computer. That's a form of exporting, which is a form of backing up your files, which is covered in this chapter.

What's Your Style?

Outlook offers a variety of printing styles from which to choose. The available options depend greatly on the module of Outlook from which you're printing. For example, the styles available to you in Calendar are different than the ones that are available to you in Contacts.

Too Many Options

There are as many different printing options as there are printers on the market. Some people will be able to print to different paper sizes than others, and it would be impossible to cover all of the options that *might* be available to you in this book. So unless otherwise noted, the options discussed in this chapter refer to 8 1/2 by 11-inch paper. If you can use larger or smaller paper, you will have more page setup considerations than are covered here.

Outlook's built-in print styles are more than enough for the average Outlook user. However, you can alter those styles as you see fit, or create your own print styles.

Print styles are selected during the printing process. To make your choice, the item(s) you would like Outlook to print must be open on your screen. Then, open the File menu and select Print. You will see a window like the one in the following figure.

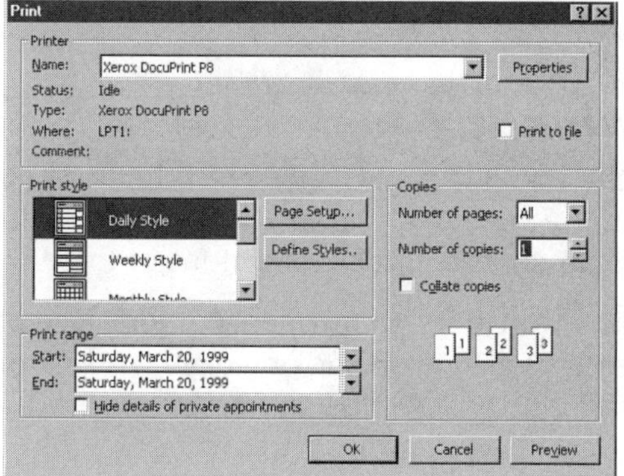

The Print window as seen in the Calendar.

The Print style area in the middle of this window is where you make your selection. This figure was created in the Calendar, so the options you see on your screen might be slightly different.

You can also select a print style from the File menu by selecting Page Setup and then whichever print style you would like from the list that appears.

The Basic Styles—Table and Memo

Two styles are available in most modules of Outlook—Table and Memo.

The Memo style is the most straightforward and widely available of the print styles. It displays the item as a text file with a header at the top of the sheet. The appearance will vary slightly between modules, but not much. The Memo style is available throughout most of Outlook. The Inbox, Contacts, Tasks, Journal and Notes all use it. Only the Calendar does not support the memo style in all of its views. To use the memo style in Calendar, you must have an entry selected (more on special Calendar styles later in this chapter).

The Table style is also pretty straightforward. In most cases, the table will look very much like the Table view of whichever module you're in. For example, when you view your Inbox in the Messages view, it displays the list as a table—columns and rows. When you print that list in Table style, it prints almost exactly as it appears on your screen.

Table style is available in the three modules that are easiest to break into a table—Tasks, Contacts, and Inbox. It is also supported in certain views of Notes and Journal.

Special Styles for the Calendar

Because of its unique attributes, the Calendar offers neither of the basic printing styles unless you move away from the Day/Week/Month views. Instead, it offers five styles of its own from which you can choose. Brief descriptions of these styles follow:

- *Daily style* Displays one day's worth of appointments on one side of the page, divided into half-hour increments as it is on the one-day view on your screen. The current month and next month are printed as part of the header. On the right side of the page is the TaskPad and a Notes area.
- *Weekly style* Displays one week's worth of appointments, with the five-day work week getting large boxes and the two weekend days getting half-boxes. Again, the current and next month are displayed at the top of the page as part of the header.
- *Monthly style* Shows a complete month on the page, just like a typical wall calendar. The first five boxes are the weekdays, and the two weekend days share a box on the far-right side of the page. The page is printed in landscape orientation.
- *Tri-fold style* The page is divided into thirds and printed in landscape orientation. The left side of the page is a daily calendar, divided into half-hour increments. The center of the page is your TaskPad. The right side of the page is a weeklong view of your Calendar.
- *Calendar Details style* Displays the Calendar items you have showing on your screen, in a list format. Along with the subject of each appointment are its complete details, including anything you might have entered in the notes area of the Calendar form.

Special Styles for Contacts

As mentioned earlier, you can print your contacts in Memo style. But there are also special styles you can use to print contacts. Here are some brief descriptions of these styles:

- *Card style* Prints the contact list just as you see it on your screen when you display the contacts in Address Cards view. You get headings for each letter of the alphabet for which you have contacts listed, and each contact includes the name, address, phone numbers, and email address. They're printed in a two-column format.
- *Small Booklet style* Prints the contact list in a one-column format designed to be placed into a small booklet, with eight pages per 8 1/2 by 11 sheet. You're asked if your printer supports double-sided printing, because this style is best used to print two-sided documents.
- *Medium Booklet style* Same as the Small Booklet style, except that the setup is for four pages per 8 1/2 by 11 sheet.
- *Phone Directory style* Prints like a telephone directory, with the contact's name, a series of dots, and then the phone number. Printed in a one-column format.

Let's Take a Look, Shall We?

Whenever you print an item in a new way for the first time, it's a good idea to get a preview of it on your screen before you go wasting paper on a mistaken idea.

If you have experience working with computers, you've probably used the Print Preview function that is available on tons of different programs. Outlook also offers it, and it can be a lifesaver. Or at least a paper-saver, because being able to see what you're about to print can keep you from wasting paper.

Once you've selected your print style, click the Print Preview button at the bottom of the Print window. You'll get a small version of the page that will be printed, as you can see in the following figure.

It's small enough that you can't see much detail, but you can click on the image to zoom in for a better look.

Print Preview shows you what will be printed without wasting paper.

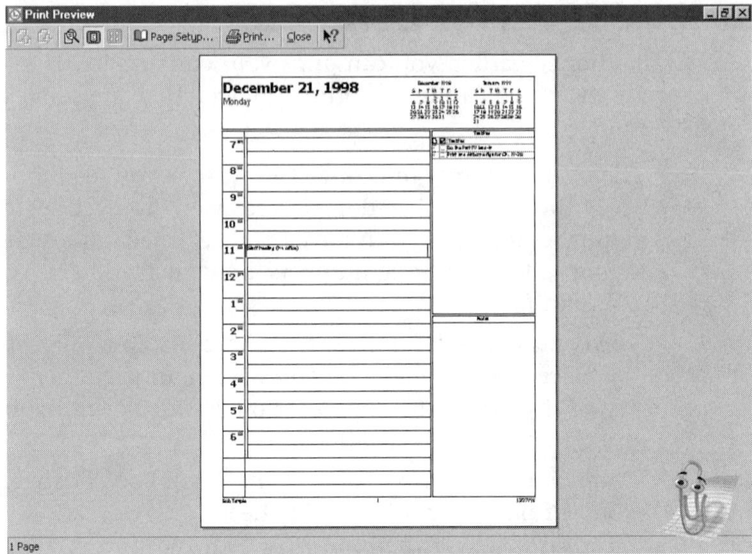

Finally, Printing

Once you've made all these choices, printing is easy. You can print directly from the Print Preview screen by clicking the Print button. Or, if you didn't open Print Preview, you can click the Print button from the Print window (where you chose your print style).

If you want to print your item(s) without selecting a style or seeing a Print Preview, you can print anytime in Outlook by clicking the little Print button on the toolbar. It looks like a printer, conveniently enough.

If you have more than one item selected, they will all print when you click the Print button.

Finding Your Files and Folders

So you've got all your contacts and appointments entered into Outlook. You've got a task list going, and you're using Outlook to send and receive email. Yep, Outlook has become a pretty integral part of your life.

What would you do if you lost it all? Chances are, you wouldn't be very happy.

Well, this section will help you prevent that from happening. You'll learn how to back up your files, and how to keep Outlook running smoothly by archiving files that aren't being used.

But before you can do any of that, you need to know where Outlook stores your files and folders so you can manipulate them as you see fit. Believe it or not, all of your personal files and folders, everything you've entered into Outlook, is stored in a single file.

The best way to find this file is to open Outlook Today by clicking on its icon in the Outlook Shortcuts bar. From the File menu, select Folder and then Properties for Personal Folders. In the window that appears, click the Advanced button. The Personal Folders dialog box appears, as you see in the following figure.

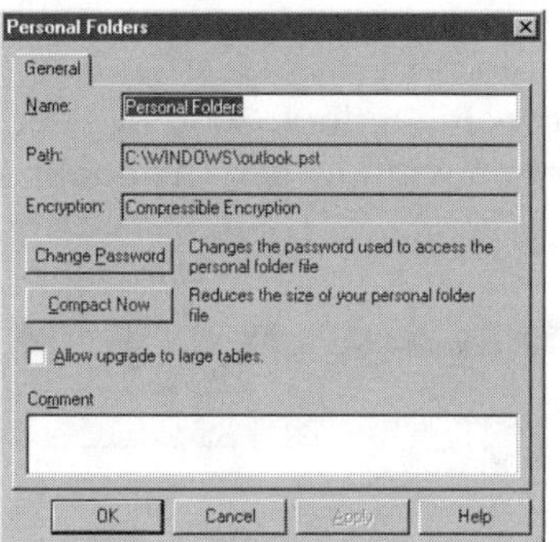

The file named in the Path field is your Outlook file.

The Path box contains the complete directions to your Outlook file, plus the name of the file. As you can see from the preceding figure, the name of my Outlook file is `outlook.pst`. It's located on my C: drive, in the Windows directory. If your path is too long to be viewed in the Path box, click inside it once and you can move your cursor right and left to see the full path.

Make sure to write this information down in a safe place so you'll know where it is when you need it.

Also, if Outlook is beginning to run a little slowly or you have deleted a lot of files lately, you may want to click the Compact Now button to reduce the size of the file. Doing so reorganizes the file so that it consumes less space and operates more efficiently.

Archive It!

If you have a filing cabinet, you know that every now and then you have to go through it and clean it out. When I go through mine, I usually find a lot of things I can throw away. But I also find a lot of stuff that should be kept around just in case I need it in the future. I pull out those items and put them in boxes that I store in our storage space. That way, I can easily find them if I ever need them again, but they don't get in the way of my daily use of my filing cabinet.

That's what an archive system is all about, and archiving in Outlook isn't much different. If you have a lot of information entered into Outlook and you don't archive any of it, Outlook's performance may slow down somewhat. If you put some of this information away—not deleting it, but archiving it—Outlook will run faster while still giving you access to the old stuff.

You can delay the need for this by being vigilant in deleting files and by regularly clearing out your Deleted Items folder. However, you simply won't have time to delete every appointment after you've had it, and eventually these items will pile up.

By Hand

You can manually archive files and folders in Outlook 2000 by selecting Archive from the File menu in any module of Outlook. A window like the one in the following figure will appear.

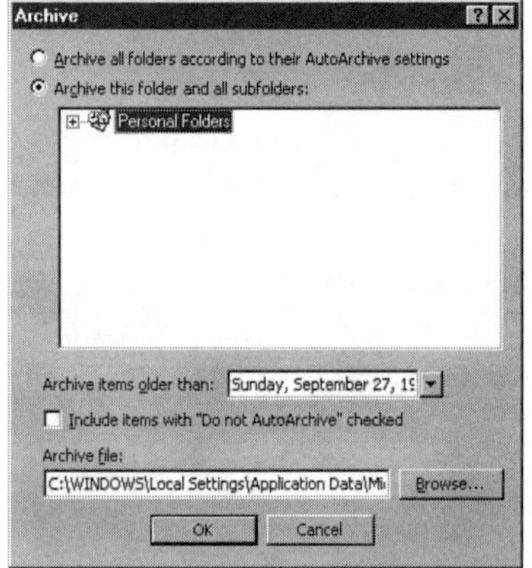

Set manual archive settings in this window.

At the top of the window, you can tell Outlook to use the AutoArchive settings to archive all Outlook folders. The AutoArchive feature is discussed in the next section of this chapter.

You can make the same settings for all of your Outlook folders by highlighting Personal Folders in the list and choosing to archive this folder and all of its subfolders.

In the date field, select the date before which all items will be archived. Below, you can set the file into which items will be archived.

When you click the OK button, all Outlook items from before the date you specified will be archived. This includes emails, appointments, tasks, and more. You will still be able to recall these items later—they are just being removed from your active file. The archived information is saved elsewhere on your hard drive. In addition, your Contacts folder will not be archived.

Using AutoArchive

Generally, it's easier and more efficient to use Outlook's AutoArchive function to decide when items should be put away. You set the schedule for archiving beforehand, and Outlook merely carries out your directions.

To do this, open the Tools menu and click Options. On the Other tab, click the AutoArchive button to bring up a dialog box like the one in the following figure.

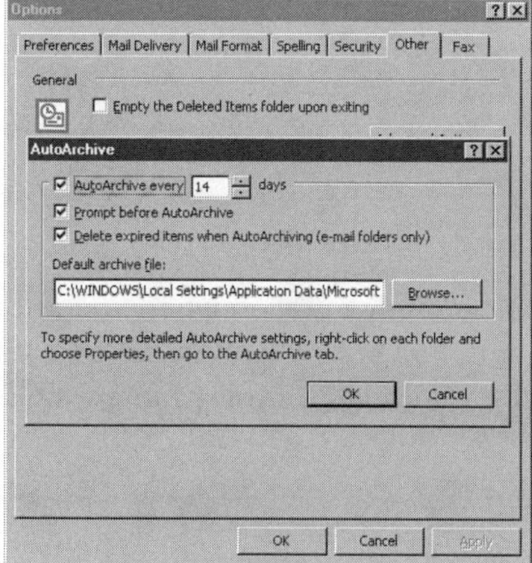

Make AutoArchive selections here.

Here you can make Outlook-wide settings for AutoArchive. You can set the number of days between AutoArchive sessions, whether you want to be prompted first, and more. Again, you can see the name of the file into which the archives will be placed.

As you can see from the bottom of the window, however, you can make different settings for different Outlook folders. To do this, right-click on the folder icon in the Outlook Shortcuts bar and then select Properties. You can then use the AutoArchive tab to make individual folder-archiving decisions.

Exporting Outlook Files

When you export a file, it makes a copy of the file but leaves the original in its place. Exporting doesn't shrink your original or remove any items from it. This is useful for backing up Outlook, but also for updating Outlook files on a second computer.

You export files one folder at a time. You can export only your contact list, or just your calendar. For example, let's say you use Outlook at work and at home. At the end of the week, you may want to update your calendar at home with the changes you made at work during the week. That way, when you refer to your calendar at home, it contains all the needed information.

To do this, first you must open your calendar at work. From the File menu, select Import and Export. In the Import and Export Wizard, choose Export to a file.

Install on Demand

The Import/Export feature is not immediately installed when you install Outlook. This feature (and some others) are installed only when you try to access them for the first time. So don't be surprised if Outlook asks you to insert a CD into the drive to install this feature.

You'll want to select the Personal Folders file (`.pst`) because later you'll be importing this information into your home copy of Outlook.

Next, select the folder from which you want to export (the Calendar folder is preselected because you entered Import and Export while in Calendar).

Finally, you can name the file you're creating and choose how you want to handle duplicate items in the Export Personal Folders box, as shown in the following figure.

You'll also have to select where you're exporting these files—a floppy drive, a Zip drive, a SuperDisk drive, and so on.

When you get home, you can walk through the same steps using Import. Your Calendar will be updated at home to match your work copy.

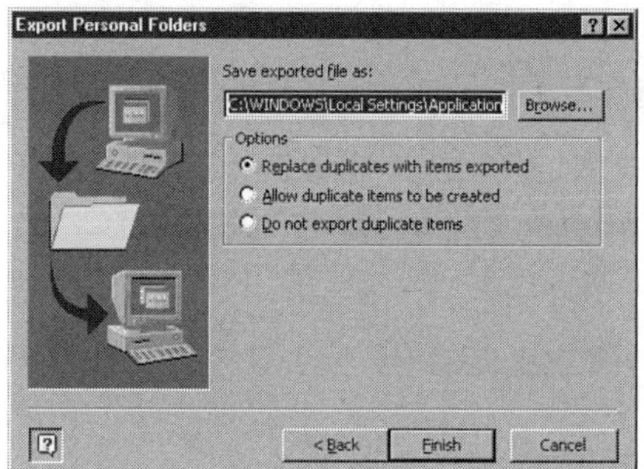

Make final choices about your export here.

Backing Up

Backing up your Outlook files and folders is extremely simple, if that's all you want to accomplish. All you have to do is go into your C: drive, find the file that contains all of your Outlook information (mine was `outlook.pst`), and copy it to a Zip disk or some other external storage device.

Find It

Depending upon your computer environment, this file might be more difficult for you to find than it was for me. If you run into trouble, use the Find feature in your Start menu in Windows and type in "outlook.pst," and your computer will locate the file for you.

However, your Outlook backup should be part of a regularly scheduled backup of your entire system, or at least of the files you've created on it. There are many different programs that can help you accomplish such a backup. Any backup device you buy (a Zip drive, a SuperDisk drive, or a tape backup drive of some sort) will come with a program or function that allows you to back up your system.

If you don't do it, you'll have no one to blame but yourself.

The Least You Need to Know

- Outlook offers two basic print styles—Memo and Table—for all of its modules, depending on the view. It also offers special print styles for Calendar and Contacts.
- You can see a preview of the item(s) you are about to print by using the Print Preview function.
- All of your Outlook items are saved in a single file. Find this file and make a backup copy of it regularly to keep your information safe.
- Archiving old Outlook items makes Outlook run more smoothly. You can archive manually or create AutoArchive settings, either for all of Outlook or for individual folders.

Chapter 22

News You Can Use

In This Chapter

- What is Outlook Express?
- Understanding newsgroups
- Using Outlook Newsreader to read newsgroups
- Setting up the newsgroup server connection
- How many newsgroups?
- Reading messages
- Participating in newsgroups
- Using Outlook's Web toolbar
- Jumping back and forth

So far, we've briefly touched on using Outlook to send and receive email through the Internet. But we haven't *really* dived into the Internet headfirst. Outlook allows you to do that in a couple of ways, but you need to have it installed as part of the Microsoft Office suite of applications (which most people do anyway). That way, you get Internet Explorer 5 and Outlook Express installed with it. Without those two programs, Outlook won't be able to handle the Internet other than through email. If that's the case and you have a full Internet connection, you have the unlimited ability to tackle the Internet.

What Do You Mean by "*Full* Internet Connection"?

A full Internet connection gives you access to all facets of the Internet, such as email, the Web, newsgroups, and so on. Remember, the Internet is more than the Web. Most people who have an Internet connection through their own modem and have Outlook configured for Internet Only are set up with their own Internet service provider (ISP) that offers these services. However, many corporations allow their employees to have email but not to surf the Web or read newsgroups.

What Is Outlook Express?

When you install Microsoft Office, you get Microsoft Internet Explorer 5. And when you get Microsoft Internet Explorer 5, you get Outlook Express.

Outlook Express is a program that rides along with Internet Explorer and provides some of the Internet services that Explorer does not—namely, email and newsgroups. Unlike Netscape Navigator, Explorer doesn't have an email program built into it. It allows you to select your own email program, and it sends Outlook Express along to give you an option.

Outlook Express's email capabilities aren't as advanced as those of the full version of Outlook. And you won't need them anyway because you're already using the full version of Outlook.

Outlook Express's main value to Outlook users is in handling newsgroups. In fact, when you access Outlook Express from Outlook, you are using Express in "news only" mode. That is, the only part of the Outlook Express program you will be using is the newsreading function. This function of Express is called the Outlook Newsreader.

What Are Newsgroups?

Participating in newsgroups, which are very close relatives to bulletin boards, is one of the oldest activities on the Internet. In fact, long before HTML technology let us share graphics and multimedia information over the World Wide Web, newsgroups were about the only fun to be found on the Internet (one man's humble opinion). While email is like passing a note to another person in class, newsgroups are like standing in front of the class and giving a speech.

Newsgroups are arranged and titled by topic, so a discussion is usually focused on the topic at hand. Newsgroups are like magazines—no matter how obscure the topic may be, somewhere there's a magazine devoted to it. The same is true for newsgroups. If you're into kite flying, Tiddlywinks, backgammon, or "Baywatch," there's probably a newsgroup for you.

But they aren't just about hobbies. (Can "Baywatch" be considered a hobby?) There are many, many serious newsgroups as well, covering everything from politics to sports to the economy to... well, you name it. There are many newsgroups devoted to Microsoft Outlook, for example.

In these newsgroups, people post messages that can be read by the entire group. Others can post their own messages or respond to existing ones. The beauty—and sometimes the main drawback—of these discussions is that they're unrestrained.

Most newsgroups are not *moderated* by any individual or corporation. When you post a message, it goes out unedited and uncensored. This can cause problems when discussions get testy and people's emotions get the best of them, but for the most part, newsgroups are places for calm discourse.

Watch Your P's and Q's

Remember, anything you post to a newsgroup can be read by anyone. You may think a particular joke is funny, and your friends might too, but there may be some who will read it and be deeply offended. Humor is generally best reserved for more private forms of communication.

Many large corporations maintain newsgroups for their own employees, and many also have people whose job it is to monitor newsgroup discussions about their products. For example, if you have a problem with a Microsoft product and you post a question about it in a newsgroup about that product, you might get a response from a Microsoft employee or, say, the author of a book about that product. You'll also get responses from regular folks like yourself who would like to help.

Using the Outlook Newsreader to Read Newsgroups

The Outlook Newsreader is designed to make reading newsgroups easy. Before you can participate in them, however, you have to find them. the Newsreader helps in that area, too.

You can open the Newsreader by opening the View menu in Outlook, selecting Go To, then choosing News. The Outlook Newsreader launches. It should appear like the figure you see below.

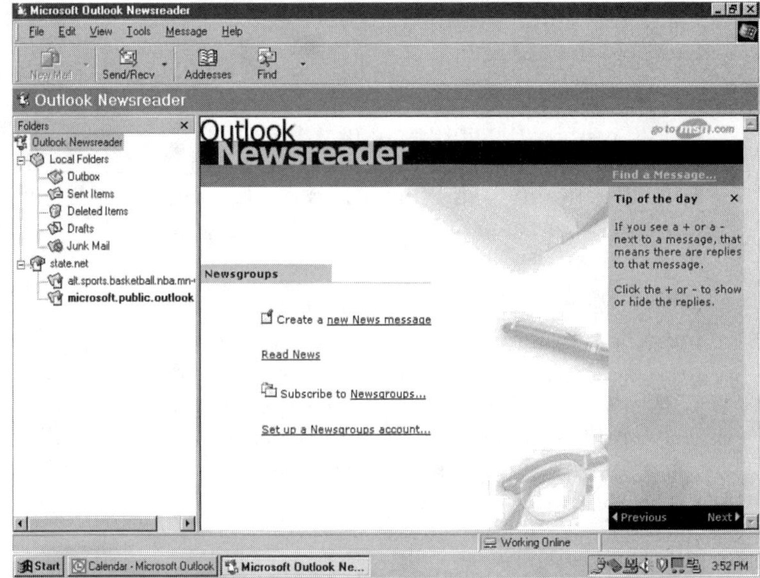

The Outlook Newsreader allows you to read newsgroups off the Internet.

Setting Up Your Newsreader

Depending on what software your ISP gave you, if any, or how they walked you through the account setup process, you may not have to do much to set up your account.

If you're a corporate user, you should be sure to get some instructions from your system administrator about setting up your newsreader before you monkey with any settings on your workstation.

In most account setup procedures, you're asked at some point to provide the server that you'll be using to read newsgroups. This is true of the Internet Account Wizard that Microsoft uses for Internet Explorer.

If you already have a newsgroup account set up, it will show up in Outlook Newsreader's folders list on the left side of the screen. If you don't, you can set one up by opening the Tools menu in Outlook Newsreader, choosing Accounts (Corporate users will select Services instead), and then clicking the Add button. This will walk you through the process, asking you to give a name, an email address people can reply to, and the address of your news server.

Want to Learn More?

There are tons of newsgroups related to Microsoft and its products. In fact, you can add the Microsoft News Server (`msnews.microsoft.com`) for discussions on Microsoft products, including Outlook.

If you want to make changes to the account at any time, you can go back into the Tools menu, select Accounts, highlight the name of the account, and click the Properties button.

Finding Newsgroups

To open your account, highlight it from the Folders list in the left side of the Outlook Newsreader window. The first time you do this, Outlook Newsreader asks if you want to download the list of available newsgroups. Depending on your news server, this can be a short list or a very long one. My ISP gives me access to more than 25,000 different newsgroups!

This only needs to be done once, and you can't read any newsgroups until you do it, so what the heck. It takes a few minutes, if the list is long. You're left with a list of newsgroups in alphabetical order, as you see in the following figure.

Your newsgroups list is downloaded the first time you access your account.

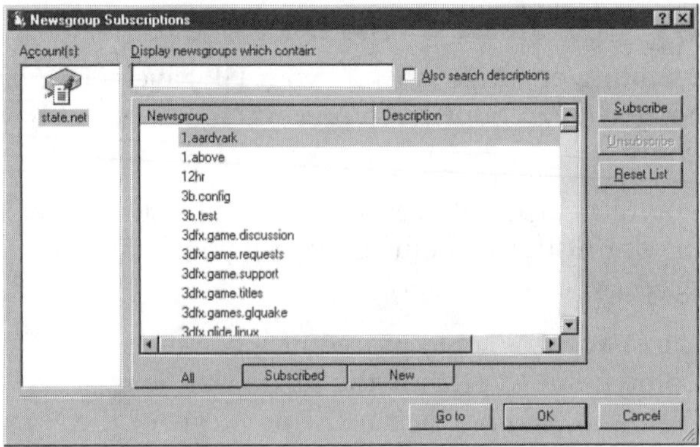

One problem—newsgroups aren't named alphabetically by the topic they cover. In fact, they have a number of different prefixes to determine their type, such as `alt` for alternative, `rec` for recreation, and so on. To find groups that meet your interests, you'll need to search that list. Outlook Newsreader makes this easy by allowing you to type in search criteria into the field called Display newsgroups which contain. Type a search word, wait, and the list will be sorted based on that criteria.

A Subscription without the 3×5 Card

Subscribing to a newsgroup is nothing like subscribing to a magazine. There's no little card to fill out, no money to pay, and no waiting for the first issue. Subscribing to a newsgroup involves much less of a commitment.

Subscribing (and unsubscribing, for that matter) is instantaneous. When you subscribe to the newsgroups that interest you, Outlook Newsreader will automatically update them and let you know how many new messages have been posted in each newsgroup since you last checked it.

Subscribing to a newsgroup doesn't mean all the other subscribers will know anything about you—unless you post a message, that is. You can subscribe to as many newsgroups as you like and just read them without anyone knowing you're doing it.

To subscribe, highlight a newsgroup's name in the window and click the Subscribe button. You can return to the full listing of newsgroups by clicking the Reset List button or by deleting your search criteria so that the field is blank. Once you've subscribed, the name of the group appears in your Folders pane at the left.

Reading Newsgroups

To view the contents of a newsgroup, just highlight its name in the Folder list. The messages will appear in the top-right window, as shown in the following figure.

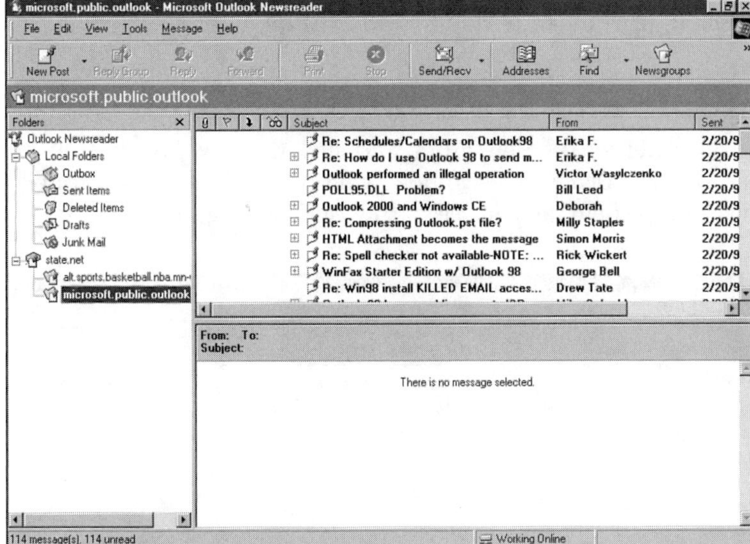

The contents of a newsgroup displayed in Outlook Newsreader.

You can sort this list by clicking one of the field headers across the top. By default, messages are listed by the date they were sent, with the newest messages at the bottom of the list.

A plus sign to the left of a message means that it has been responded to. Click the plus sign, and the responses will be listed beneath the original message.

Note that some of the messages have been responded to many times, so that they've become discussions. If you'd like to keep an eye on a particular discussion thread, click the eyeglasses icon above the subject window and then click the thread you'd like to follow. Outlook Newsreader will then keep an eye on it for you. Click the thread a second time and you'll see a red circle with a line through it next to the subject. This tells Outlook to ignore this particular thread.

To read any message, simply highlight it. The content will appear in the bottom window.

Making Your Mark

Reading newsgroups can be fun and informative. But to really get involved with them, you need to make your presence felt and contribute to the discussion.

There are two ways to post to a newsgroup. You can post a totally new message that is designed to start a discussion, or you can respond to an existing message.

Run It Up the Flagpole and See If Anyone Salutes

To post a new message, simply enter the newsgroup and click the New Post button in the Outlook Newsreader toolbar. A New Post window will open with the newsgroup's name already in the Newsgroups field, as you see in the following figure.

Making a posting to a newsgroup is a lot like writing an email.

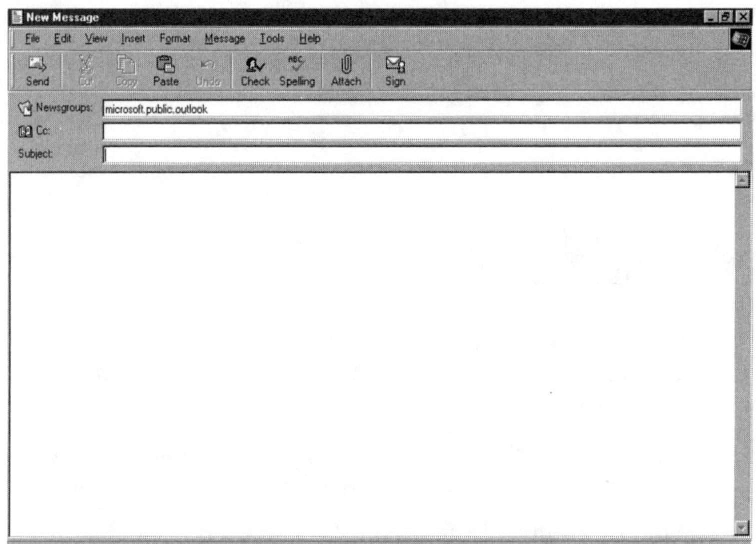

Simply type in your subject, type in the content of your message, and click the Send button. Sometimes it takes a while for your posting to show up, but it will get there. Sometimes it's almost instantaneous.

Responding in Kind

To respond to an existing message, you must highlight the message and make sure it appears in the message window. Then, click the Reply Group button.

Again, the New Post window appears with the Newsgroups field filled in. This time, the Subject field is also filled in. Type your message, click Send, and away you go.

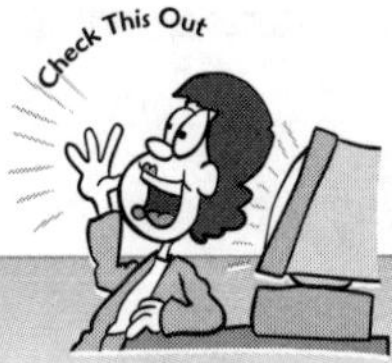

Making It Public

Remember, anything you post to a newsgroup can be viewed by everyone in that newsgroup, not just the person to whom you're responding. If you want to reply privately to a message, read the next section.

Going Private

Sometimes, you may want to respond to the individual who posted a message without the entire group seeing what you wrote.

To do this, click the Reply button. In this case, an email window opens with the person's name already in the To: field. Type in your response and send it as an email, so the rest of the group won't see it.

Working with the Web

Part of Outlook's allure is that it can commingle with other Office programs, including Internet Explorer. Outlook's links with other Office programs are covered in the next chapter.

Outlook offers a Web toolbar that you can use to quickly jump onto the Web. In other sections of this book, you have used the Standard and Advanced toolbars to accomplish the things you needed to get done.

You can display the Web toolbar as well, but you might find that your toolbar area is getting a little crowded. To show the Web toolbar, right-click anywhere on any toolbar you have open, and then choose Web. If you want to hide the Advanced toolbar, you can deselect it using the same procedure and clicking Advanced. In the following figure, all three toolbars are showing. I have displayed the Web toolbar beneath the others.

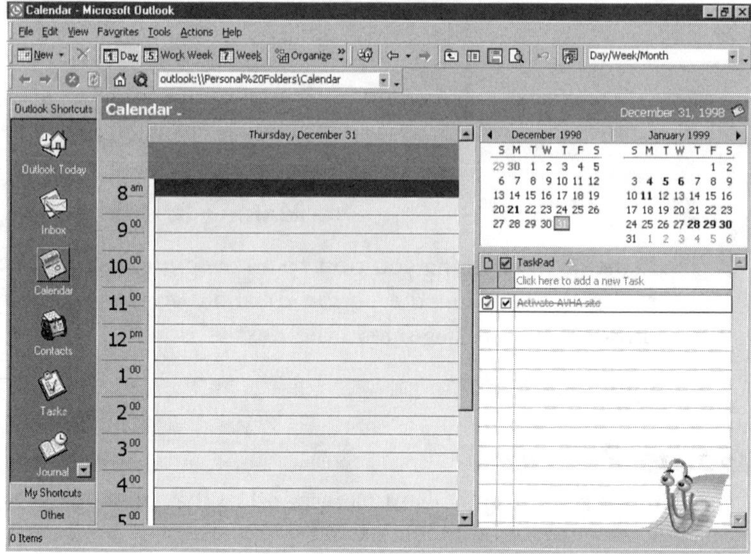

The Web toolbar is displayed beneath the others.

Site-Seeing

At the far right of the Web toolbar is an address area. It shows whatever is open on your screen at the moment. (In the figure, I was viewing my calendar, so it shows that the Calendar folder is open.) To quickly view a Web site, just type its address in this field.

What happens next is really amazing. You might think that Internet Explorer would be launched. Technically, it is, but as a built-in Web viewer within Outlook. I'd explain all the technical mumbo jumbo, but it's not necessary. All you need to know is this: Instead of having two RAM-eating programs running together, you can view Web pages right inside Outlook. They appear right in the Outlook window, as you can see in the following figure.

You can launch Internet Explorer any time you want, of course, but you don't have to do that.

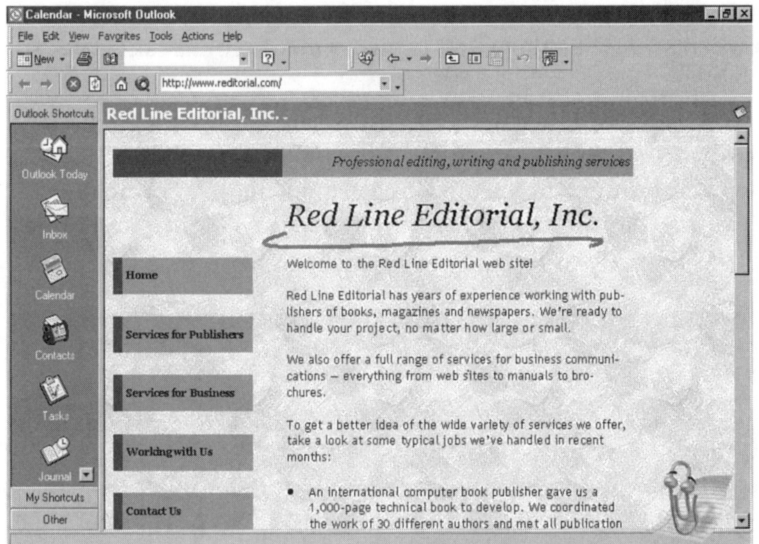

You can view Web pages without leaving Outlook.

Favorites

Outlook includes a Favorites menu, just like Internet Explorer does. In fact, any favorites you've identified in Internet Explorer (or bookmarks made in another Web browser) were imported into Outlook when you installed it. You can use this Favorites menu just like you use it in any Web browser.

To visit a site you've marked, just select its name from the Favorites menu. It will appear in the active window. You can add new favorites, too, just as you've done in Internet Explorer.

The Rest of the Web Toolbar

Working with the rest of the Web toolbar is like working within Internet Explorer. Here's a quick summary:

- *Back and Forward* The left and right arrows are the Back and Forward buttons. The Back button takes you back to the previous Web page you viewed. Once you've used the Back button, the Forward button becomes active, allowing you to move to the page you were on when you hit the Back button.
- *Stop* If a page is loading slowly and you want to move on, you can press the Stop button to interrupt the download. Then you're free to go to a different site.

- *Refresh* This button refreshes the present site. Use this when a site doesn't load properly, such as when some graphics aren't showing up. A refresh can sometimes take care of this.
- *Start Page* Takes you directly to the page you've identified in Internet Explorer as your Start Page (the page you see first when you open Internet Explorer).
- *Search the Web* Opens an Internet search page (AOL NetFind in my case) as shown in the following figure. From there, you can conduct Web searches to find sites that may interest you.

An Internet search page opens when you click the Search the Web button.

Of course, there's a lot that goes along with working on the Web. We can't cover it all in this book, but there are tons of books devoted to that topic.

Drag-and-Drop This!

A little-known feature of surfing the Web with Outlook 2000 is that you can drag a hyperlink off a Web page and drop it onto your Outlook bar. This will allow you to go to that page at a later date simply by clicking the icon in the Outlook bar.

The Least You Need to Know

- Outlook works in concert with Outlook Express to handle newsgroups (through Outlook Newsreader) and with Internet Explorer to handle the World Wide Web.
- Outlook Newsreader is basically Outlook Express functioning in "news only" mode. It allows you to read newsgroups within Outlook.
- Newsgroups are among the oldest aspects of the Internet. There are thousands of them, arranged by topic, so you're almost certain to find one that covers your area(s) of interest.
- You must subscribe to a newsgroup before you can read it. Subscribing involves a click of a button, and it doesn't obligate you to anything or release any information about you. You don't become a member of a group when you subscribe.
- You can post your own messages to a newsgroup, and you can respond to a message either with a public reply to the newsgroup or a private email.
- Outlook allows you to view Web pages without opening Internet Explorer. Using the Web toolbar, you can type in the Web address. Or, you can select one from your Favorites menu.
- The Web toolbar acts just like Internet Explorer's toolbar.

Chapter 23

Making Outlook Part of the Family

In This Chapter

- Why Outlook is part of Office 2000
- Creating a new Office document in Outlook
- Bringing Office files into Outlook
- Making shortcuts to Office files
- Importing and exporting Office files
- Linking and embedding and other naughty stuff

Whew!

We're finally here. The last chapter of this book. It's time to wrap it all up and bring it all together and any other end-of-the-road clichés you might be able to recall.

You've spent the first 22 chapters of this book learning about Outlook's modules and their many features. We even discussed how those modules can work with each other to help make you a more productive person. In the preceding chapter, we looked outside Outlook and talked about how it works with Outlook Express for newsgroups and Internet Explorer for Web surfing.

Now it's time to look even farther outside of Outlook and talk about its relationship with its brothers and sisters in the Microsoft Office suite of applications. We'll talk about how to bring Outlook data into other Office applications, and vice versa. We'll talk about how to make your access to your already-created documents easier by using Outlook.

Why Is Outlook in the Office Suite?

Everything in the computer world happens at light speed compared to the rest of the real world. It seems like suites of applications have been around forever, but in real terms, it hasn't been that long.

When Microsoft first put the Office suite together, it included Word and Excel. Over time, other programs were added, mostly for marketing reasons. For example, a Small Business edition of the Office suite will be slightly different than a Professional or Premier edition of the suite.

When Microsoft adds a program to Office, they don't just throw it in the box and say, "Here you go!" No, they completely integrate it and make it part of the family.

But in the past, Outlook has been a little different than the rest of the products in the Office suite. Most of the other programs are purchased individually all the time, but Outlook has always been kind of a "nice extra" bonus in the Office suite.

Microsoft decided with Office 2000 that Outlook has been an estranged member of the family for too long, and made it fully integrated with the other applications. Now Outlook sits at the dinner table with the rest of the Office programs, passing the corn and mashed potatoes and… excuse me for a minute. This analogy is making me a little hungry.

Creating a New Office Document

As I've probably told you many times already, I'm a big proponent of working right out of the Outlook Today screen for most of the day. Sure, there are times when you'll need to do other things on your computer. But we've already covered how easy it is to perform most basic computer functions from Outlook Today. After all, you can send and receive email, schedule appointments, get in touch with contacts, and even surf the Web—right from Outlook Today.

What if you need to create a new spreadsheet, presentation, or letter? Well, you can do that from Outlook as well.

As you may have seen when you've opened the New menu many other times in this book, it contains an option that allows you to create a new Office document. From anywhere in Outlook, just click on the New button's drop-down menu and select Office Document. The New Office Document window opens, as you see in the following figure.

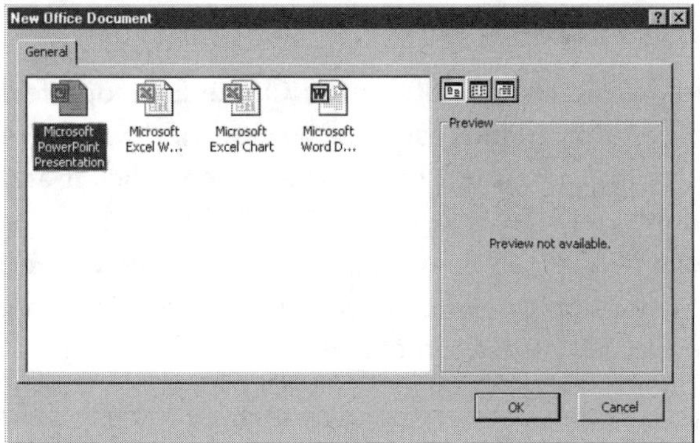

Create a new Office document from this window.

Outlook allows you to create a new word processing document in Microsoft Word, a spreadsheet or a chart in Excel, or a presentation in PowerPoint. Just highlight the type of document you would like to open and click the OK button.

Before the document opens, you're asked if you want to post it in this folder or send it to someone. In most cases, you'll select the Post option. This opens a new document that you can work in normally. However, if you want to create a document to send to someone by email, choose the Send option. An email window will open, allowing you to create a document that is part of an email. However, you can create a normal document and email it as an attachment if you want, so I recommend using the Post option.

In the preceding chapter, you saw how you can surf the Web using Internet Explorer without *really* opening Internet Explorer. That's not the case when you create an Office document. Whichever program you choose will launch and a new document window will open, minimized, on top of your Outlook window.

A Quick Send

One of the best new features within Office 2000 is the Office Envelope feature. If you're working in Word, Excel, PowerPoint, or some Access windows, there will be an envelope icon in the toolbar across the top of the screen. Click it and your document will be converted into an HTML message with all the necessary email fields (To:, Cc:, Subject) above it. You can immediately send this file, converted to HTML, to anyone you wish. They won't need to have the same application in order to view it because the file will have been converted to HTML.

Caveat This

There are a couple of problems you might encounter if you didn't install Outlook 2000 as part of Office 2000. The New Office Document option will only work if you have done so. If you're using an older version of Office or don't have it installed at all, you won't be able to do this.

What you have now is a typical Office document in whichever program you chose. You can maximize the window (or not) and work with that file just as you would if you hadn't launched it with Outlook.

From Office to Outlook

Using the drag-and-drop method, you can use Office programs to create Outlook items if you want. Although it seems silly to go out of your way to use a different program to create an Outlook item, there are times when it might be useful.

Most notably, this comes in handy when you've already created an Office document and it would be quicker to bring it into Outlook. For example, you can make a Word document into a calendar entry, if you want.

Back in Chapter 18, "Putting Calendar to Work," I told you that you can drag and drop an email on a calendar item, for example. Doing so opens a new item for the calendar, with certain fields filled in and the text of the email in the notes area. The same is pretty much true of bringing Office documents into Outlook.

From Document to Item

Let's say you have a Word document on your computer that you need to update on Monday morning. That sounds like a task to me. You could open a new Task window and enter all of the information yourself, or you could let Outlook help you.

To do the latter, use the Other Shortcuts bar to navigate to the file on your C: drive. Once you see the file in the window at the right, open the Outlook Shortcuts bar so you can see all the Outlook icons. Your screen should look like the one in the following figure.

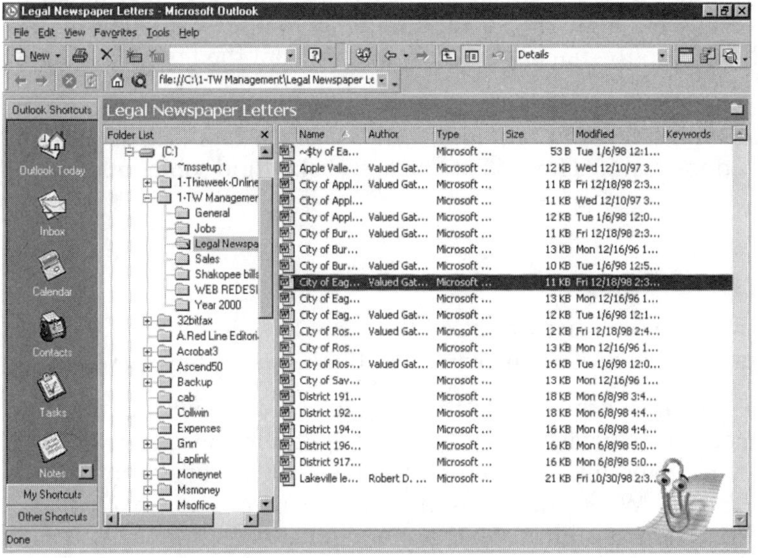

Drag the file onto the appropriate icon.

As you can see, the file is highlighted and all the Outlook icons are on the Outlook bar at the left. Now drag that file and drop it on the Tasks icon, and a New Task window will open. But as you can see in the following figure, there are some advantages.

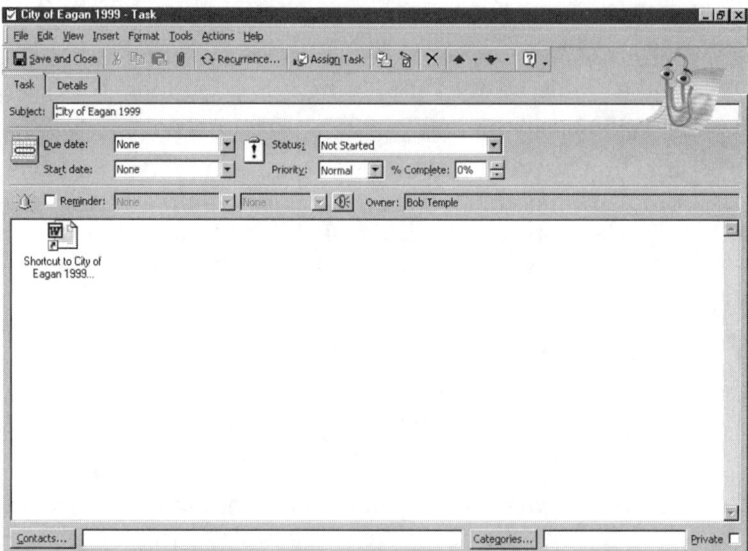

The Task window contains file information.

The filename is in the subject field, but more importantly, a shortcut to the file is in the notes area. Once you've finished entering this task it will appear in your task list, just like any other task. When you need to open it Monday to update it, you can double-click on the shortcut to the file and open it directly from the task. Now that's a time-saver.

But it doesn't just work with tasks. You can do it with any of the modules in Outlook. This is one of those Outlook features for which you'll probably find some unique uses.

A Shortcut to Your Office

A lot of us have certain Office files that we use all the time. They just keep getting updated. Why not create a shortcut to a file within Outlook? It's terribly easy.

Again, you need to open your C: drive within the Outlook window by using the Other Shortcut bar. Once you've navigated to the file, drag it into the Outlook Shortcut bar in which you would like it to appear. You'll see a black insert line within the folder as you drag the file. When the line is in the spot where you want to drop it, release the file. It will appear as an icon on the shortcut bar you chose, as you can see in the following figure.

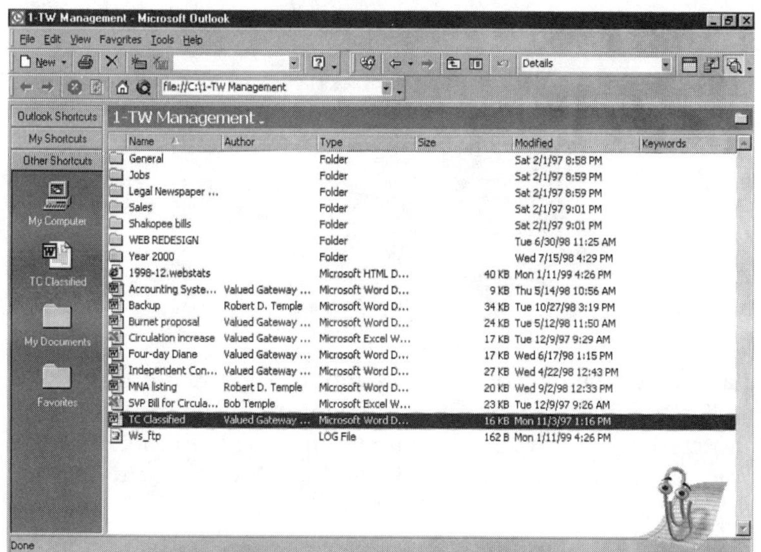

Put an often-used file into a shortcut bar for easy access.

The next time you need the file, just single-click the icon and it will launch the program and open the file for you.

Import/Export

You just learned how to bring an Office document into Outlook. When you did so, however, that document retained its original attributes. That is, it was still an Office document.

In the example, you had an icon for the file you needed to update in the notes area of the task, but it was still a Word document. It was merely embedded in an Outlook item.

What if you import data from an Office application into an Outlook folder or export Outlook data into an Office application? One of the most common uses for this is probably Contacts information.

Back in Chapter 14, "Keeping in Contact," we covered importing contacts from an outside database. Many people also export Outlook contacts information into, say, an Excel spreadsheet (or Access database).

Let's take another look at how to perform these functions. From the File menu, select Import and Export. In the window that appears, select Import from another program or file, and then click Next. Then select the program from which you're importing the file, as you can see in the following figure.

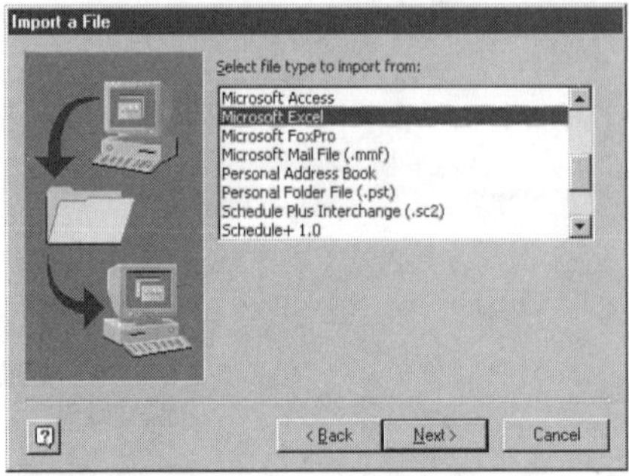

Import a file using the Import and Export function.

Next, you're asked to navigate to the file you'd like to import. Finally, select the folder into which you'd like to import the file. It's then converted into the type of Outlook item you've chosen. However, if the file you're importing has different fields than the one you're importing into, Outlook will ask you to pick which fields to import. This is called *mapping data fields*.

Exporting starts by selecting Import and Export from the File menu, and it pretty much follows the same steps as importing, except you're going the other way.

Linking and Embedding and Other Naughty Stuff

Object linking and embedding (OLE) is used by a number of Microsoft programs to allow you to update more than one file at once. Linking means creating a connection between two programs so that when information is updated in one, it is automatically updated in the other. Embedding means using one program to create something within another program, such as using Excel to create a spreadsheet in a Word document.

A common use of OLE occurs in Office. Let's say you have an Excel worksheet included in a Word document you're using to write a report. If you link the two documents, anytime you update the worksheet in Excel, it will be updated in Word automatically.

You can do this with Outlook, too. For example, you can link an important file to an email that you send on a regular basis to clients. This will keep the file updated so that whenever you send the email, the recipient will get an up-to-date file.

You can also embed a file within an email, so that every time you send that email to your client, the updated file will remain embedded within it.

To link or embed an existing object in an email, open a new email message. With your cursor in the body of the message, open the Insert menu and select Object. Click Create from File, and then find the file you would like to link or embed. Select the Link check box if you want to link the object. If you want to embed it, leave the Link box unchecked. You can also elect to display the object as an icon by checking that box. However, OLE is supported only if the email message format is Outlook Rich Text or HTML.

No Offense, But...

This is kind of an advanced topic, and frankly, OLE is used more often between other Office programs, not with Outlook. You might find it more effective to just attach files to email.

The Least You Need to Know

- Outlook fits nicely with the Office 2000 suite, adding everyday time management and other features to the many other programs Office offers.
- You can create a new Office document from Outlook's New menu. It launches whichever program you've selected.
- You can put an Office document into an Outlook item by dragging the file onto the appropriate Outlook folder. This keeps the file in its original state and creates a shortcut to it from within the Outlook item.
- You can add shortcuts to Office files to your Outlook bar, giving you one-click access to often-used files.
- Importing an Office document transfers the document's field data into Outlook. Exporting does the reverse.
- You can link and embed objects into Outlook.

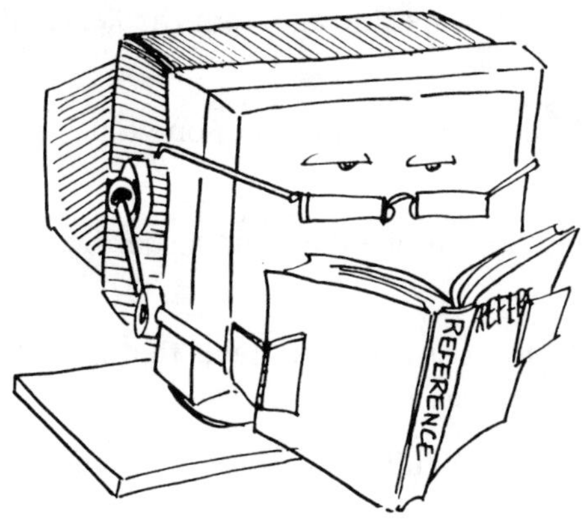

Glossary

This glossary lists terms and abbreviations you may come across while you're working with Outlook. It doesn't provide broad definitions that necessarily apply in other environments.

account Access to a network or the Internet.

address book A folder that contains the names of contacts, together with their addresses and other information.

administrator The person who controls a workgroup, local network, or service (such as Exchange Server).

America Online (AOL) An Internet service provider that also offers special services to its members.

appointment A period of time that's blocked for a specific purpose in an Outlook user's calendar.

archive A file containing Outlook items that are older than a specific age. When Outlook archives items, it moves those items from current folders to an archive folder.

attachment A file or object that is linked to, or contained in, an Outlook item. Files and objects may be attached to messages, contacts, appointments, tasks, and so on.

AutoAddress Outlook's capability to separate an address into street, city, state, postal code, and country fields.

AutoArchive Outlook's capability to move items of a specific age from the Personal Folders file into an archive file.

AutoCreate Outlook's capability to automatically convert an item of one type into an item of another type.

AutoDate Outlook's capability to convert a description of a date into a specific calendar date.

AutoJournal Outlook's capability to automatically create journal items that record activities involving specific contacts and access to Office files.

AutoName Outlook's capability to separate a person's full name into first name, middle name, and last name fields.

AutoName Check Outlook's capability to verify that names entered into the To, CC, and BCC boxes exist in an address book.

AutoPreview Outlook's capability to display the first three lines of a message without requiring the user to open the message.

AutoSave To automatically save data to a file at predetermined intervals.

balloon The message box used by the Office Assistant to display information.

banner The bar across the top of an Information viewer. The banner contains the name of the folder with the items displayed in the viewer.

blind carbon copy (BCC) A copy of a message that is sent to several people without the recipients' names appearing on the copies that other people receive. The word "carbon" comes from the carbon paper that was used to make copies on a typewriter.

browser An application that's used to find information on the World Wide Web.

calendar A component of Outlook in which users plan their activities. Outlook saves calendar items in the Calendar folder.

carbon copy (CC) A copy of an email message that's sent to more than one recipient. The CC names are included on the messages sent to all recipients. The word "carbon" comes from the carbon paper that was used to make copies on a typewriter.

Card view One of the formats in which Outlook displays or prints contact information. Resembles an index card.

category An identifier for an Outlook item. One or more categories may be assigned to each item.

CC *See* **carbon copy**.

client A computer, or software running on that computer, that accesses data or services on another computer.

contact A person or organization. Outlook maintains a list of contacts in the Contacts folder. Each item contains information about one contact.

contact list The list of contacts maintained by Outlook.

Contacts The Outlook folder that displays information about contacts. Items displayed in this Information viewer are stored in the Contacts folder.

conversation A sequence of related messages, sometimes known as a *thread*.

Corporate or Workgroup mode An Outlook installation that can use other messaging systems, in addition to the Internet, for email. *See also* **Internet Only mode**.

Date Navigator The section of the Calendar Information viewer that shows one or more complete months. You can use the Date Navigator to move rapidly to specific dates.

Deleted Items The folder that contains items that have been deleted from other Outlook folders.

dialog box A window displayed by an operating system or application that solicits a response from the user.

dial-up networking Connecting to a network by way of a dialed connection over telephone lines.

distribution list A list of people to whom a message is to be sent.

document Something created in an Office application, such as a table created in Access, text created in Word, a workbook created in Excel, or a presentation created in PowerPoint.

draft A version of a message that has been prepared to be sent but that may require revision. Outlook saves draft messages in the Drafts folder.

drafts An Outlook folder in which drafts of messages are saved.

drag-and-drop The capability to select an object and move it to another area, such as the Outlook Bar, to improve functionality.

email A message sent from one computer user to another user or users by way of a local network or the Internet.

embedded object An object included within another object. The included data consists of the object's native data and presentation data.

event An activity that occupies one or more days but does not require the user to block time.

Exchange Client The email client in Windows 95, Windows 98, and Windows NT. Provides messaging capabilities similar to those in Outlook, but does not contain scheduling capabilities. Microsoft now refers to Exchange Client as Windows Messaging.

Exchange Server An email and collaboration server that runs under Windows NT Server. The Exchange Server information service can be added to a profile so Outlook can use the facilities of Exchange Server.

Favorites A folder that contains shortcuts to items, documents, folders, and uniform resource locators (URLs).

fax An abbreviation of "facsimile." A method of transmitting text and graphics over telephone lines in digital form. Outlook can send and receive fax messages.

Fax Viewer A facility that can display outgoing fax messages.

field A space on a form that displays a specific type of information or in which a user can provide information. Outlook uses a separate field for each type of information it deals with, such as First Name, Middle Name, Last Name, Street Address, City, and so on.

Field Chooser A list of fields that can be used to add fields to a form.

field type The type of data a field can contain. Each Outlook field can contain one of the following types of data: combination, currency, date/time, duration, formula, integer, keywords, number, percent, text, and yes/no.

file The basic unit of storage on such media as disks and tape.

File Transfer Protocol (FTP) A common method of sending files from one computer to another by way of the Internet.

filter An Outlook facility used to access information that satisfies certain specified criteria. The specified criteria refer to contents of fields. Filters can be used to find items that contain certain text in text fields, certain dates (or ranges of dates) in date fields, and certain values (or ranges of values) in numeric fields.

flag An indication in a message that some follow-up activity is necessary. Messages are flagged by the flag symbol in the Flag Status column of the message list.

folder A container for information. Outlook uses a file named Personal Folders to contain several folders, one for each type of item. Each folder contains either subfolders or items of a specific type. Users can augment the initial folder structure by adding folders and a hierarchy of subfolders.

form A window used to display and collect information. Outlook provides forms for such purposes as creating and viewing messages, appointments, and contact information. Some of these forms can be modified to suit custom needs, and you can create custom forms.

forward To send a received email to someone else.

FTP *See* **File Transfer Protocol**.

group To sort items displayed in a list or timeline into sections, each of which contains items with a common characteristic. For example, a list of contacts can be grouped by category, company, or other characteristics.

HTML *See* **Hypertext Markup Language**.

hypertext Text that contains links to other information in the same document or in other documents.

Hypertext Markup Language (HTML) A language used to create hypertext documents for use on the World Wide Web.

importance In Outlook and other messaging systems, messages are marked as having high, normal, or low importance.

Inbox The Outlook Information viewer that displays messages received but not moved to another folder. Items displayed in this Information viewer are stored in the Inbox folder.

IntelliSense Office Assistant's system for offering assistance with a user's current task.

IntelliSense Menus Microsoft's "smart" menus, which are shrunk to only those choices that the user has accessed the most.

Internet A worldwide, interconnected system of computers that provides information and communication services.

Internet Explorer An Internet browser available from Microsoft.

Internet Only mode An installation of Outlook that provides only Internet capabilities. Also known as *Internet Mail Only (IMO) mode.*

Internet service provider (ISP) An organization that provides access to the Internet.

intranet An Internet-like environment accessible only within an organization.

ISP *See* **Internet service provider**.

item A unit of information in Outlook. Email messages, appointments, contacts, tasks, journal entries, and notes are all items.

Journal The Outlook facility for creating Journal items that automatically record such activities as working with Office files and sending and receiving email messages. Items displayed in this Information viewer are stored in the Journal folder.

LAN *See* **local area network**.

linked object An object included within another object. The included data consists of the object's presentation data and a reference to its native data.

local area network (LAN) A computer network limited to a small area, such as one building.

location The place where an appointment, event, or meeting is to occur.

log A record of specific types of events. For example, Outlook can create an event log that marks the completion of each CompuServe email session.

mail client A computer, or the software running on a computer, that can exchange email back and forth with a mail server. *See also* **mail server**.

mail server A computer, or the software running on a computer, that provides mail services to clients. These services include storing messages sent by clients until the recipients retrieve those messages.

mailbox The space on a mail server dedicated to storing messages for a specific user.

mailing list *See* **distribution list**.

master category list A list of categories from which a user can choose for each item.

meeting In Outlook, a period of time that's blocked by two or more users.

menu bar The row that contains menu names, immediately under the title bar. The items in each menu are displayed when you click the menu name.

message Any piece of information sent from one person to one or more others. A message usually originates and is received by a computer, but not necessarily. Email, voice mail, and fax are the principal methods of sending messages, and they may be received by other devices, such as pagers.

message status An indication of something special about a message, marked by a flag.

Microsoft Exchange *See* **Exchange Client** and **Exchange Server**.

Microsoft Fax A set of API functions that Outlook and other Windows applications can use to send and receive fax messages.

Microsoft Mail A set of API functions that Outlook and other Windows applications can use to send and receive email messages within a workgroup.

Microsoft Network A system that offers information and communication facilities to computer users. Outlook can send and receive Microsoft Network email.

Microsoft Outlook A desktop information manager that includes comprehensive messaging, scheduling, and information management facilities.

Microsoft Outlook Express An application, provided with Internet Explorer, that provides email facilities and allows access to newsgroups.

Microsoft Word A word processor that can be chosen as Outlook's email editor.

modem A device that converts digital information into analog information (sound) suitable for transmission over telephone lines, and that also converts incoming analog information into digital form.

My Computer An icon on the Windows desktop that provides access to folders on any disk on an Outlook user's computer and to disks that other network users have made available for sharing.

My Documents A folder that contains a list of documents recently created in, or modified by, an Office application running under Windows 95. *See also* **personal folders**.

Navigator An Internet browser available from Netscape.

Net folder A folder that can be shared by way of the Internet, an intranet, or another messaging system.

NetMeeting A Microsoft application that supports communications sessions between two or more Internet users. Also, a name used for that communication. During a NetMeeting, users can exchange text, sound, graphics, and video.

network A group of interconnected computers.

news server A computer on which newsgroup messages are stored. Many news servers are public access, but some are private, allowing access only to people who can provide a registered username and password.

newsgroup A collection of messages posted on a news server. People who access a newsgroup can read existing messages and post their own. All the newsgroups available on the Internet are collectively known as *Usenet*. *See also* **news server**.

note A type of Outlook item consisting of data that will be subsequently used for any other purpose.

Notes The Outlook Information viewer that displays notes. Items displayed in this Information viewer are stored in the Notes folder.

object An entity that may contain data and may have properties and methods. OLE associates presentation data and native data with objects. Outlook and other Office applications contain a hierarchical structure of objects.

object linking and embedding (OLE) The technology by which objects may be embedded into, or linked to, other objects. Outlook uses OLE to incorporate various kinds of objects into messages and other items.

Office Assistant The animated icon that may be displayed in an Outlook window to provide help with whatever task a user is attempting.

Outbox The Outlook Information viewer that displays messages that have been created but not yet sent. Items displayed in this Information viewer are stored in the Outbox folder.

Outlook bar The bar at the left side of Outlook's Information viewers that contains shortcuts to folders.

Outlook Express *See* **Microsoft Outlook Express**.

Outlook Today An Outlook window that provides a summary of information relevant to today and the next few days.

pane An area within a window that contains related information. *See also* **Preview pane**.

Personal Address Book An address book with an Outlook user's personal list of people's names and information about them. A Personal Address Book can be used to create distribution lists.

personal folders The set of folders in which Outlook stores items. Outlook creates a separate folder for each type of item. Users can add their own hierarchies of folders and subfolders and can subsequently move items from one to another.

Personal Information Manager (PIM) An application that saves and manages personal information, including a calendar, an address book, and a to-do list.

PIM *See* **Personal Information Manager**.

POP3 *See* **Post Office Protocol 3**.

post To place a message on a public folder on a server such as Exchange Server, or on a news server.

post office A facility on a network that maintains information about each user, including mailbox addresses, and manages the process of sending and receiving messages.

Post Office Protocol 3 (POP3) A messaging protocol commonly used by Internet service providers. Messages you receive are transmitted in POP3 format.

Preview pane The area within Outlook's Inbox Information viewer that contains previews of incoming messages.

private Items, such as appointments and contacts, that are only available to the person who created them.

profile A set of information that defines how a specific person uses Outlook. A profile defines the information services to be used and the passwords required to access those services. Each profile may be protected by a password.

property A characteristic of an icon, a form, or an object on a form. Properties include such characteristics as the name, the position of an object on a form, the font used by the object, and various settings.

protocol A set of rules that defines how computers communicate. A protocol may contain other protocols.

public folder A folder maintained on a server, such as Exchange Server, that can be accessed by users who have access to that server.

recall The capability to retrieve a message that has been sent. Outlook can recall messages that recipients haven't yet read.

recipient A mailbox to which a message is addressed.

recurring An appointment, event, or meeting that occurs regularly.

reminder A visual or audible warning that Outlook gives a certain time before an item is due. Outlook can provide reminders before appointments, meetings, events, and task due dates.

Rich Text Format (RTF) A method of formatting text so that documents can be transferred between various applications running on different platforms. Outlook can use RTF.

RTF *See* **Rich Text Format**.

rule A directive for how messages are to be handled by Outlook or Exchange Server. In Outlook, the Rules Wizard leads you through the process of creating rules.

search engine An application that searches the Internet to find pages and newsgroups with information matching specific criteria.

sender The person who sends a message, or the person on behalf of whom a message is sent.

sensitivity In Outlook, a sender can mark a message as having normal, personal, private, or confidential sensitivity. A message's recipient cannot change the sensitivity.

sent item A message that has been sent to a mail server. Outlook automatically moves sent items from the Outbox subfolder to the Sent Items folder.

Sent Items The Outlook folder that displays messages that have been sent.

server A computer, or the software running on that computer, that provides services to client computers.

service provider An organization that provides access to a computer-related service. For example, an Internet service provider (ISP) provides access to the Internet.

shared folder A folder on a server to which several or many users have access so they can share information.

shortcut A link to information in a folder or to an application.

signature Text that Outlook can automatically incorporate into all messages you send. Most often used to sign messages.

stationery A pattern or background that Outlook can add to the messages you send.

status bar The row at the bottom of a window that displays certain information about the rest of the window. The status bar at the bottom of Outlook's Information viewers shows the number of items in the displayed viewer.

status report Information about the progress of a task assigned to another person.

subfolder A component of a folder. In Outlook, a folder may have many subfolders. Each subfolder contains items of a specific type and may contain other subfolders.

subject A brief description of an appointment, event, meeting, or message.

subscribe To become a regular user of an online forum. When you subscribe to a newsgroup, you can easily find that newsgroup.

table Information arranged in rows and columns. In Outlook, a table displays items with one item in each row. Each column contains information in a specific field.

task An Outlook item that describes something that needs to be done. A task may have a due date and a start date. The person who creates a task can assign that task to another person. A person who receives an assigned task can accept or reject the assignment or reassign it to someone else.

Taskbar The bottom row of the Windows Desktop that displays the Start button and buttons representing the active applications.

TaskPad The pane at the bottom-left of the Calendar Information viewer that contains a list of current tasks.

Tasks The Outlook folder that displays information about tasks.

template An Outlook item that can be used as the basis for creating other items.

thread Related messages in a newsgroup. *See also* **conversation**.

timeline A view of Journal and other items plotted in relation to time.

toolbar A row of buttons, usually under the menu bar, that provide quick access to often-used facilities.

ToolTip The temporary box that appears under a toolbar button to identify that button.

user The person using Outlook or another application.

view A manner in which Outlook displays information in a folder. A user can select from several standard views and can also create custom views. Outlook uses views as formats for printing items.

Web page A group of related HTML documents that are accessible through the World Wide Web.

window An area of a display screen that provides access to an operating system or application, and that contains information relating to that system or application.

wizard A sequence of windows that helps a user through what might otherwise be a complex operation.

Word *See* **Microsoft Word**.

workgroup Two or more people using Windows 95 or Windows NT Client whose computers are connected to form a peer-to-peer network.

World Wide Web (WWW) Hypertext servers that are interconnected through the Internet and that give users access to text, graphics, video, and sound files.

WWW *See* **World Wide Web**.

Appendix A

What's New in Outlook 2000?

Many areas of Outlook have been improved since Outlook 98. Outlook 2000 offers improved performance and speed, along with new and enhanced features.

Folder Home Pages

Outlook 2000 lets you assign a default home page to any folder in your Personal Folders. This lets companies provide instructions, calendars, and other information. Individuals can associate home pages with folders, too, for quicker access to needed information.

Choice of Email Editor and Format

Outlook 2000 lets you choose whether you want to use Word as your default email editor, as well as choose between plain text, HTML, or Microsoft Outlook Rich Text Format. All three message formats are now available using either Word or Outlook as the email editor. You can choose any format for the default, as well as choose a non-default format when composing a new message.

Switch Mail Formats

You can now switch formats while editing a message.

Standard Read Receipts

Outlook now generates and tracks standard Internet message read receipts.

Personal Distribution Lists

Outlook 2000 lets you create custom distribution lists using contacts from multiple Contacts folders and the Microsoft Exchange Server Global Address List.

Contact Activity Tracking

Outlook lets you track email, tasks, appointments, journal entries, and documents related to a contact. You do this by associating contacts with specific Outlook items. For example, you can view a list of upcoming appointments and tasks for any selected contact. Contacts can also be opened from items with which they're associated.

Find a Contact

A new tool on the Standard toolbar lets you quickly find a contact. Just type the contact's name into the Find a Contact box and press Enter.

Merge Contact Information

When you're adding new contacts, Outlook tells you if the contact is a duplicate. You can automatically merge the new information with the existing contact entry, or go ahead and create a new contact.

Enhanced Mail Merge

For creating mail merge data files, you can filter the contact list and use the filtered list to begin a mail merge from Outlook.

Resource Scheduling

When you're using Exchange Server, you can define resources such as meeting rooms and equipment, which can be treated as people and can be set up to accept and decline meeting invitations automatically. Even without Exchange Server, you can do this as well. However, it would require an installation of Outlook (or a profile) defined as the *resource*.

Save as Web Page

Outlook now lets you save a personal or group calendar in HTML format for posting on the Web or sending as email.

Web Shortcuts in Outlook

With MSIE set as your default browser, you can view Web pages in the Outlook window. Choose sites from the Favorites folder, or drag shortcuts to your Outlook Bar.

Office Email

Outlook 2000 lets you create messages in any Office program, including Microsoft Word, Microsoft Excel, Microsoft Access, and Microsoft PowerPoint. Messages are sent in HTML format, so almost any recipient can read them—giving other users access to your documents even if they don't have Microsoft Office or the particular program. Outlook also lets you send email from within (almost) any Office program.

Microsoft NetMeeting

Outlook lets you use Microsoft NetMeeting to schedule real-time online video, audio, and chat conferences. Other resources include a shared whiteboard for drawing and shared documents.

NetShow Services

Outlook lets you send meeting requests/invitations to schedule NetShow Services broadcasts.

Personalized Toolbars and Menus

Outlook features optional personalized toolbars and menus that show only the commands and tools you use most frequently.

Expanded Recognition of Other Email Programs

The Outlook Startup Wizard now detects more email programs on your computer, such as Outlook Express, Eudora, and Netscape products, and configures Outlook to automatically import email messages and address book information. The Startup Wizard also detects existing Internet mail accounts and profiles and configures Outlook to use them automatically.

Appendix B

Subscribing to an Internet Account

Internet service providers (ISPs) abound, and there are almost as many ways to set up an ISP account as there are ISPs. IBM, Mindspring, CompuServe, America Online (AOL), Erols, and many others provide not only a connection to the Internet, but often their own software package (usually provided on CD) to get you up and running.

Sometimes this software is necessary—as in the case of AOL—but usually it's not. Usually it comes with other things, like outdated versions of Netscape, Microsoft Internet Explorer, and Eudora, which aren't nearly as good as what you already have on your computer. Chances are that Dial-Up Networking (DUN), which usually comes ready-to-go on most preinstalled Windows systems, is all you need to connect to the Internet. And once you're connected, your Outlook 2000 and Microsoft Internet Explorer version 5 or later should be much better tools than whatever comes on your ISP's CD.

This appendix can't begin to predict which ISP you've chosen or which combination of software they're shipping this month to connect you to the Internet. However, it *can* review the essential information and tell you how to connect to the Internet using Windows' own resources.

To use Windows DUN to connect to the Internet, you need the following, most of which should be provided by your ISP:

- A telephone line
- A modem that has been configured for your computer and is connected to a port
- A telephone number for your ISP connection
- An account name (this usually is different from your POP mail login name)

- An account password (this sometimes is different from your POP password)
- Your IP number (unless your ISP uses *dynamic* IP addressing, where your IP number is automatically assigned each time you log on)
- The IP number of your primary DNS (domain name server, if needed)
- The IP number of your secondary DNS (if available)

You'll use this information to prepare a dial-up connection to the Internet. Once you're connected, your browser, email program, and other Internet client software should function using that connection.

Note

This is the procedure for making a connection using Windows 98. Under Windows NT 4 and Windows 2000, the procedure will be different. Consult your documentation for information.

1. Choose Start, Programs, Accessories, Communications, Dial-Up Networking.
2. In the Dial-Up Networking window, open Make New Connection.
3. Type a name for the new connection (for example, "Mindspring Dialup"). In Select a Device, use the drop-down arrow to select your modem if the correct one isn't listed. The default settings usually are correct. If your connection fails, you can open the connection's properties later for troubleshooting. Click Next.
4. Enter the area code, phone number, and country code, and then click Next.
5. Click Finish to complete the basic setup.
6. The new connection object appears in the DUN folder. Right-click it and choose Properties.
7. Click the Server Types tab. Under Type of Dial-Up Server, the default PPP: Internet setting is usually correct. Change this only if you know your setting has to be different.
8. Click TCP/IP Settings. If your ISP automatically assigns IP and DNS addresses, you don't need to do anything here. Otherwise, supply the IP number and DNS addresses that were provided to you by your ISP. Click OK when you're done.

Note

Most ISPs dynamically assign IP numbers. Some ISPs automatically configure DNS numbers as well. However, faster logins usually can be obtained for those if you provide the DNS addresses in the spaces provided.

9. Remove the checks next to NetBEUI and IPS/SPX Compatible in the Server Types (if they're checked). Click OK to close the settings for your connection.

Note

In this discussion, we have not mentioned the Scripting tab. For most ISPs in the United States, you need not worry about scripts. If Windows' built-in scripts do not result in a connection, you might need to log on manually to determine whether a connection can be established by typing information yourself. If it can, then you probably need to use a script. If it can't, then some of your other settings might be wrong, or, your ISP's authentication server might not be working. In either case, you would need to call your ISP to determine the nature of the problem. If you do need a script, see Manual and Script Logon later in this appendix.

10. Back in the DUN folder, double-click the connection to open it.
11. This starts the dialing process. When the User Login dialog box appears, provide your account name or number and your password. These sometimes are different from your mail ID and password. Then click OK.
12. Windows negotiates a connection and the Connecting to message box is minimized to the Windows Task Bar—usually to the left of the clock.

To disconnect from the Internet, right-click the Connection icon on the Task Bar and choose Disconnect. To see how long you've been logged on and how much data has been transmitted and received, right-click the Connection icon and choose Status.

Manual and Script Logon

Scripting is an issue mostly for atypical ISPs that do not conform to standard logon procedures. A *script* in this case is a list of prompts and responses used to simulate the logon session so you don't have to manually connect each time you connect to the Internet.

For most ISPs, a standard internal script is used—one you never see—and no intervention by you is required. In rare cases, however, you might need to obtain a script from your ISP. You might also need to try to manually log on to your server so you can determine whether there is a problem.

Logging On Manually

1. Choose Start, Programs, Accessories, Communications, Dial-Up Networking. Right-click your connection icon to open the settings for your connection.
2. In the General tab, click Configure.
3. In the Options tab, click to check the option Bring Up Terminal Window After Dialing. Click OK to close your modem properties, then click OK to close your connection settings.
4. Double-click your connection to begin dialing. After a modem connection is negotiated, the Post Dial Terminal Screen is displayed. Click the Maximize button to fully expand the window. Proceed with manual logon. Once you are connected, you can press F7 to minimize the connection window to the system tray on the Windows Taskbar. Or, if you're connecting manually for diagnostic purposes, press F3 to cancel the connection.

Note

Once you've established a method for connecting automatically, return to the Options tab to remove the check from the Bring Up Terminal Window After Dialing option. Then you won't see the terminal window each time you connect.

It might also be that you need to use a script. If built-in scripting isn't working, manual logon can sometimes give you enough information to develop your own script. Your best bet, however, usually is to call your ISP to try to obtain a script from them. If you do have to develop your own script, Windows comes with several you can use as a starting point.

Note

When performing manual login, copy prompts and other information to the clipboard. Then, open a scratch text file with Notepad, and paste the prompt into it. This scratch file can provide useful data for creating or amending a script. To open Notepad, click Start, Programs, Accessories, Notepad.

Accessing Logon Scripts

1. Choose Start, Programs, Accessories, Communications, Dial-Up Networking. Right-click your connection icon to open the settings for your connection.
2. Click the Scripting tab. To specify a script, click Browse. Looking for files ending in .SCP, navigate to the location of script files on your system. Windows defaults to the standard location for .SCP files. If you have added scripts to your system in a different location, then navigation might be necessary to locate them. Provided scripts usually include one for logging on to CompuServe (cis.scp), a PPP menu system (pppmenu.scp), a standard SLIP non-menu system (slip.scp), and menued SLIP system (slipmenu.scp).

3. Double-click the script you want to use; this copies it into the File Name box in the scripting tab. If you anticipate needing to debug or otherwise modify the script, click to de-select Start Terminal Screen Minimized, and click to select Step Through Script. Click OK to close your connection settings. Note: Once you have a working script, restore these checks to their defaults so your connection can take place without your having to see it each time.
4. If this is a diagnostic/script development session, open Notepad (Start, Programs, Accessories, Notepad) to keep a scratch pad for any oddities you discover in your script. Double-click your connection to initiate dialup. Once you've successfully negotiated a connection, copy the entire session (Ctrl+A, Control+C) to the clipboard and paste it into Notepad to aid with script development. Consult the notes inside any existing .SCP file for additional information. Also, choose Start, Help, and type Script into the Index keyword field. The entries "Script files, Dial-Up Networking" and "Script.doc" both contain useful information.

Index

Symbols

A

B

C

F

G-H

I

J

O

P-Q

R

S

T

U-V

W-Z